Tattoo Bible

BOOK ONE

BY
SUPERIOR TATTOO

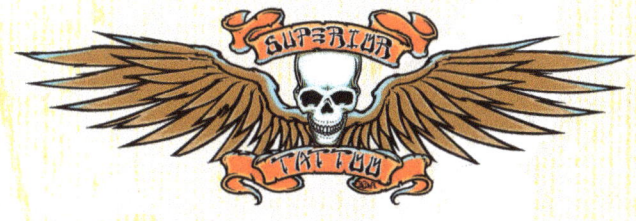

Published by:

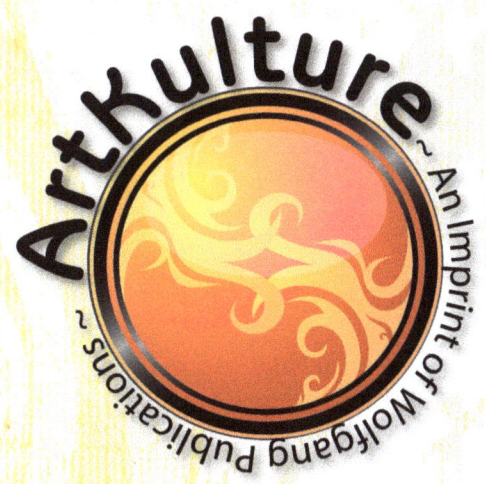

PO Box 223
Stillwater, MN 55082
www.wolfpub.com
www.artkulture.com

Legals

First published in 2009 by
ArtKulture an Imprint of Wolfgang Publications Inc.,
PO Box 223, Stillwater MN 55082

© Superior Tattoo, 2009

All rights reserved. With the exception of quoting brief passages for the purposes of review no part of this publication may be reproduced without prior written permission from the publisher.

The information in this book is true and complete to the best of our knowledge. All recommendations are made without any guarantee on the part of the author or publisher, who also disclaim any liability incurred in connection with the use of this data or specific details.

We recognize that some words, model names and designations, for example, mentioned herein are the property of the trademark holder. We use them for identification purposes only. This is not an official publication.

ISBN-13: 978-1-929133-84-0
ISBN-10: 1-929133-84-7

Printed and bound in USA

Tattoo Bible
BOOK ONE

CHAPTER ONE
    Hearts 6

CHAPTER TWO
    Dragons 18

CHAPTER THREE
    Nautical 30

CHAPTER FOUR
    Roses 42

CHAPTER FIVE
    Skulls 52

CHAPTER SIX
    Lower Back 70

CHAPTER SEVEN
    Butterflies 80

CHAPTER EIGHT
    Celestial 90

CHAPTER NINE
    Crosses 100

CHAPTER TEN
    Girls 112

CHAPTER ELEVEN
    Tribal 130

CATALOG 142

ABOUT SUPERIOR TATTOO 144

Acknowledgements

Superior Tattoo would like to thank all the skilled artists whose artwork has been selected for this amazing collection of tattoo art. Additional thanks to Karen Bachler, Crystal Simeister, Tom Kaczor, and Jim Watson at Superior Tattoo Equipment for their time spent in design selection, scanning, and artwork setup. Much time was spent sifting through the thousands of design sheets selecting quality art that we hope you will reference again and again for hundreds if not thousands of tattoos. We hope you will agree that there has never been a book packed with so much absorbing tattoo art.

Aaron Coleman
Kevin LeBlanc
Nicole McCord
Bob Sims
Nate Powers
Danny Beck
Pat Jones
Jeff Bartels
Katelyn Eileen
Jim Watson
Doni Castello
Scott Stinnet
Stoneface
Heather Alvin
Chris Bailey
Darrin Yeisley
Clint Frederici
M .Robyn Birk
Prakash
Danny Boy

William Blanchard
Christopher Borchik
Despo & Banaszak
Wish
Einstein
JDS
Edward Chambers
20 Minute Designs
Radical Ron
Michael Fitts
Doug Willis
Moth
Lisa Van Pelt
Joe Zuniga
Martin B
Tom Nickels
Johnny Pacheco
Daniel Acosta
Sage

Introduction

This book has been designed to provide imaginative ideas for the perfect tattoo, and to act as a resource of images that cannot be found anywhere else. Let us know your thoughts on future categories that you would like to see in upcoming books at sales@superiortattoo.com

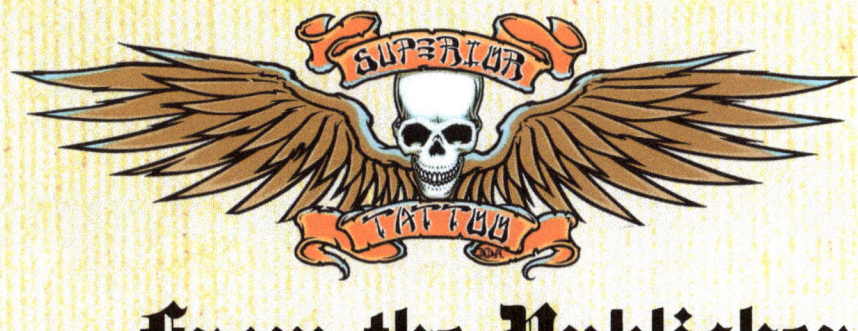

From the Publisher

At Wolfgang Publications and ArtKulture, we are accustomed to working with an individual author. So when Martin Grimm from Superior Tattoo suggested we collaborate on a book, I hesitated. Visions of "committees" filled my brain. One of those situations where too many people have a better idea for a cover design or the wording in chapter two.

I'm pleased to say that from the first communication to the final approval of the book, Martin and the entire staff at Superior Tattoo could not have been any easier to work with. Superior did most of the layout and design for the book, and when we asked them to make a modification so an image or page would better fit our format, they complied without any drama.

It turned into a team project, each member contributing good ideas and wonderful art, always respectful of the other members of the group. To sum up the experience, I can only say that we are looking forward to working with Superior on Book Two.

Timothy Remus

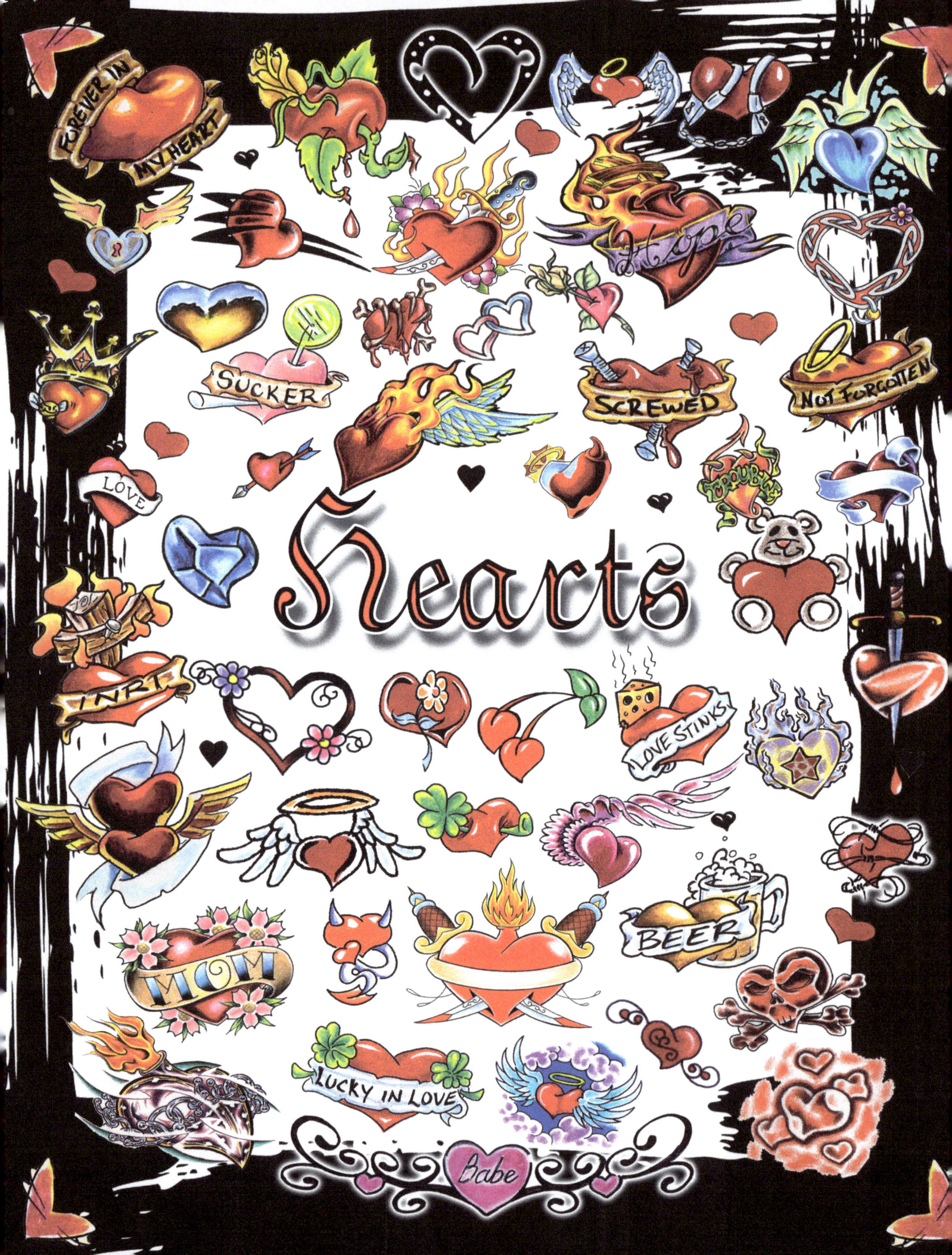

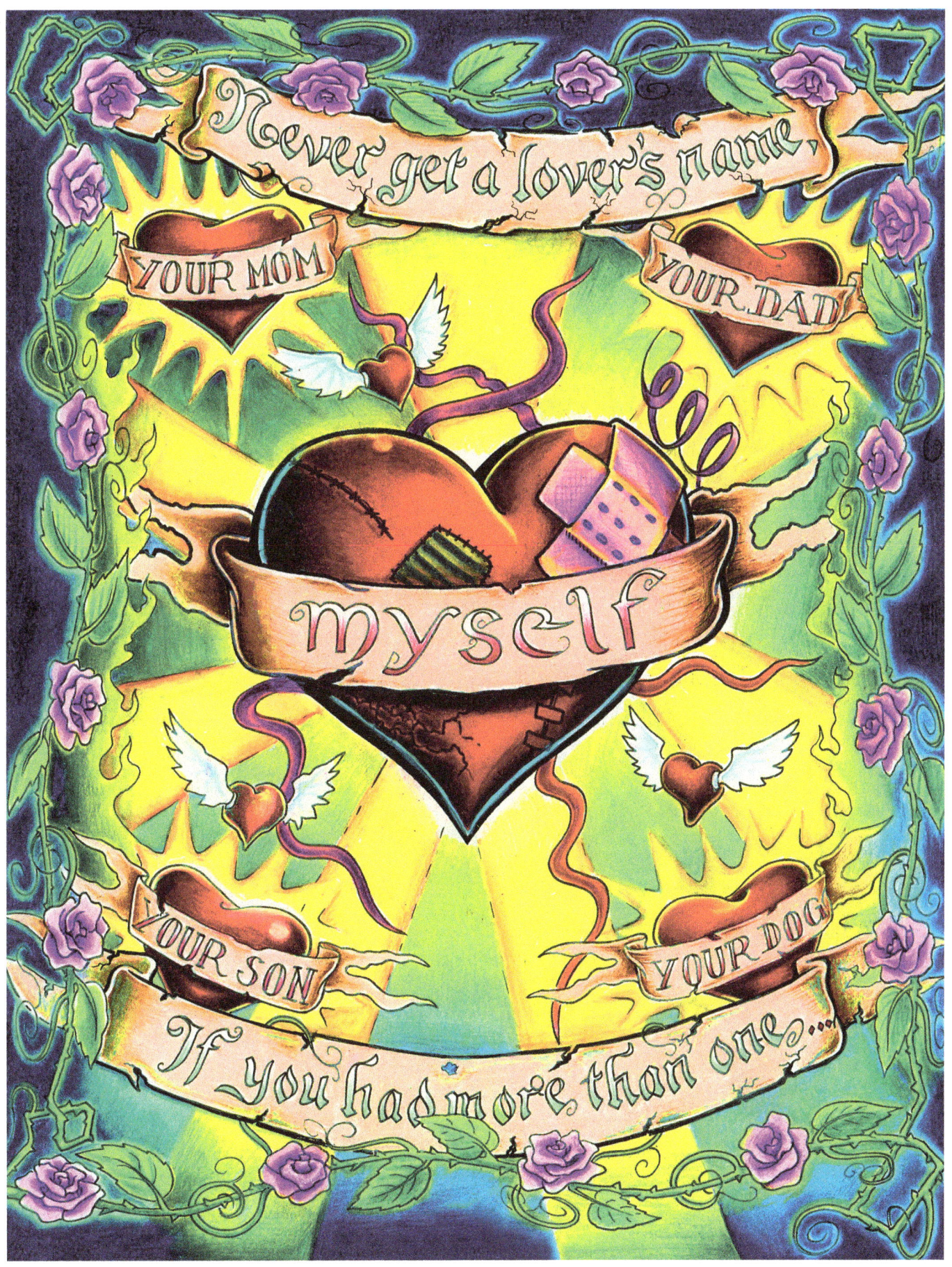

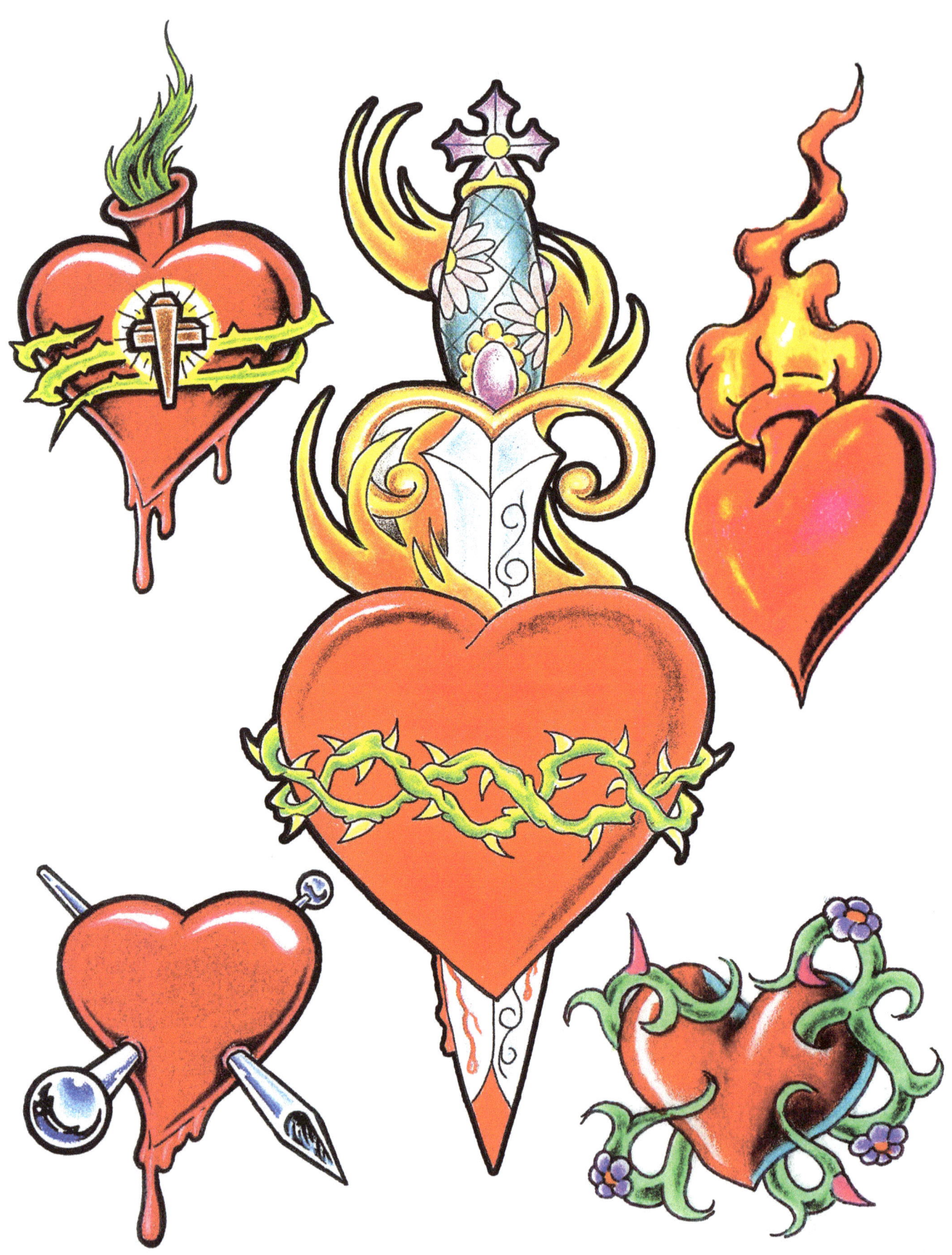

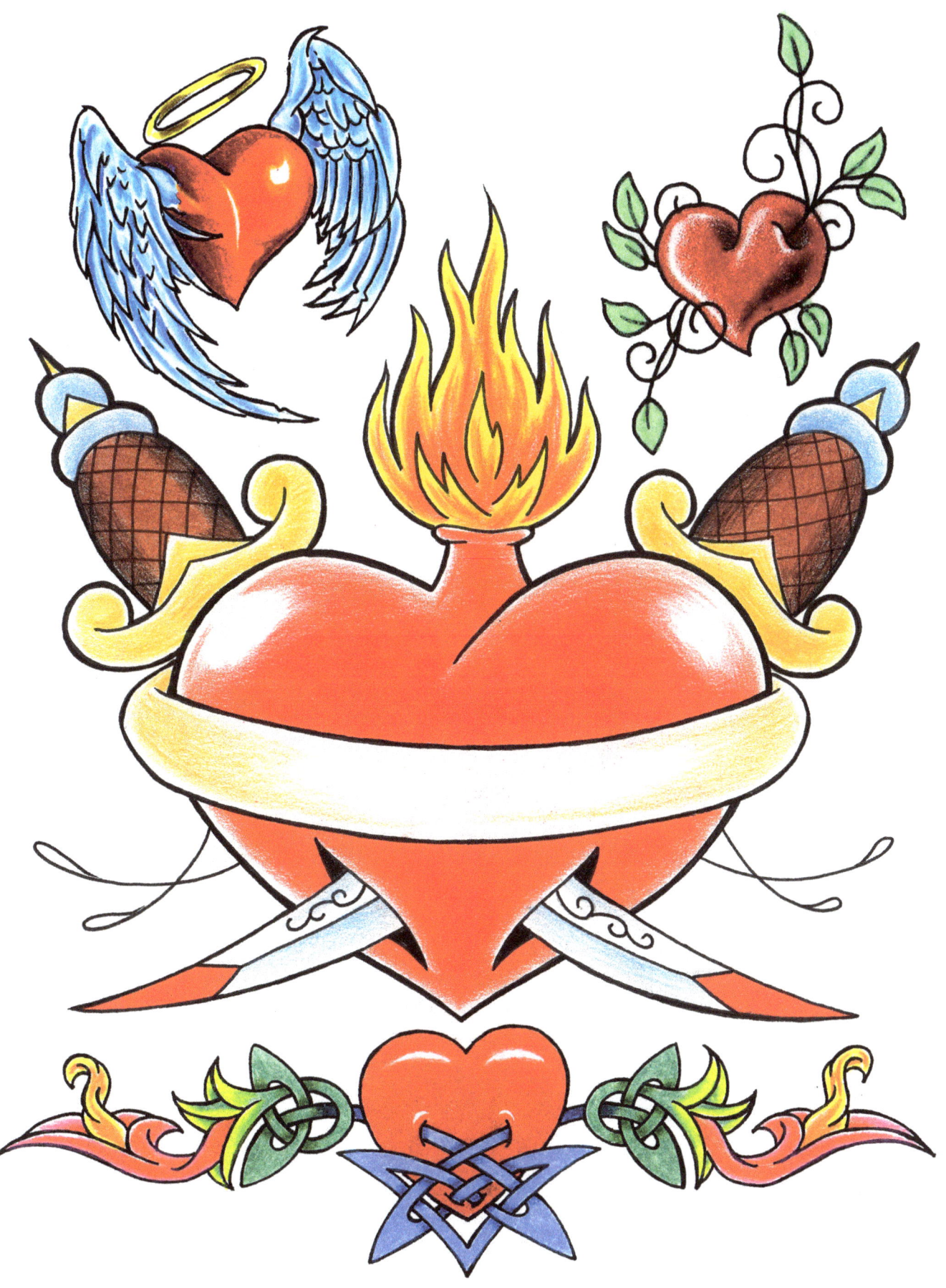

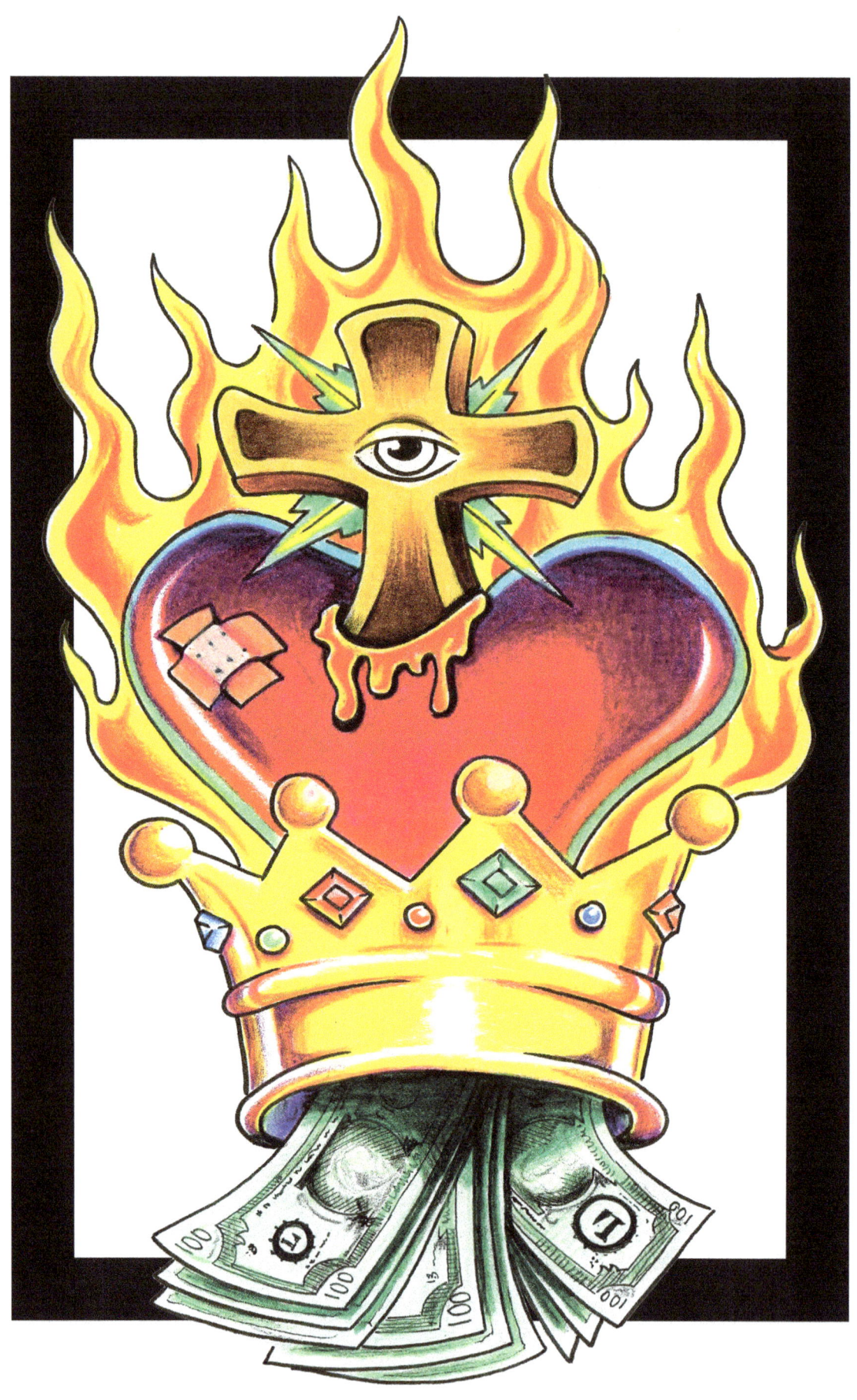

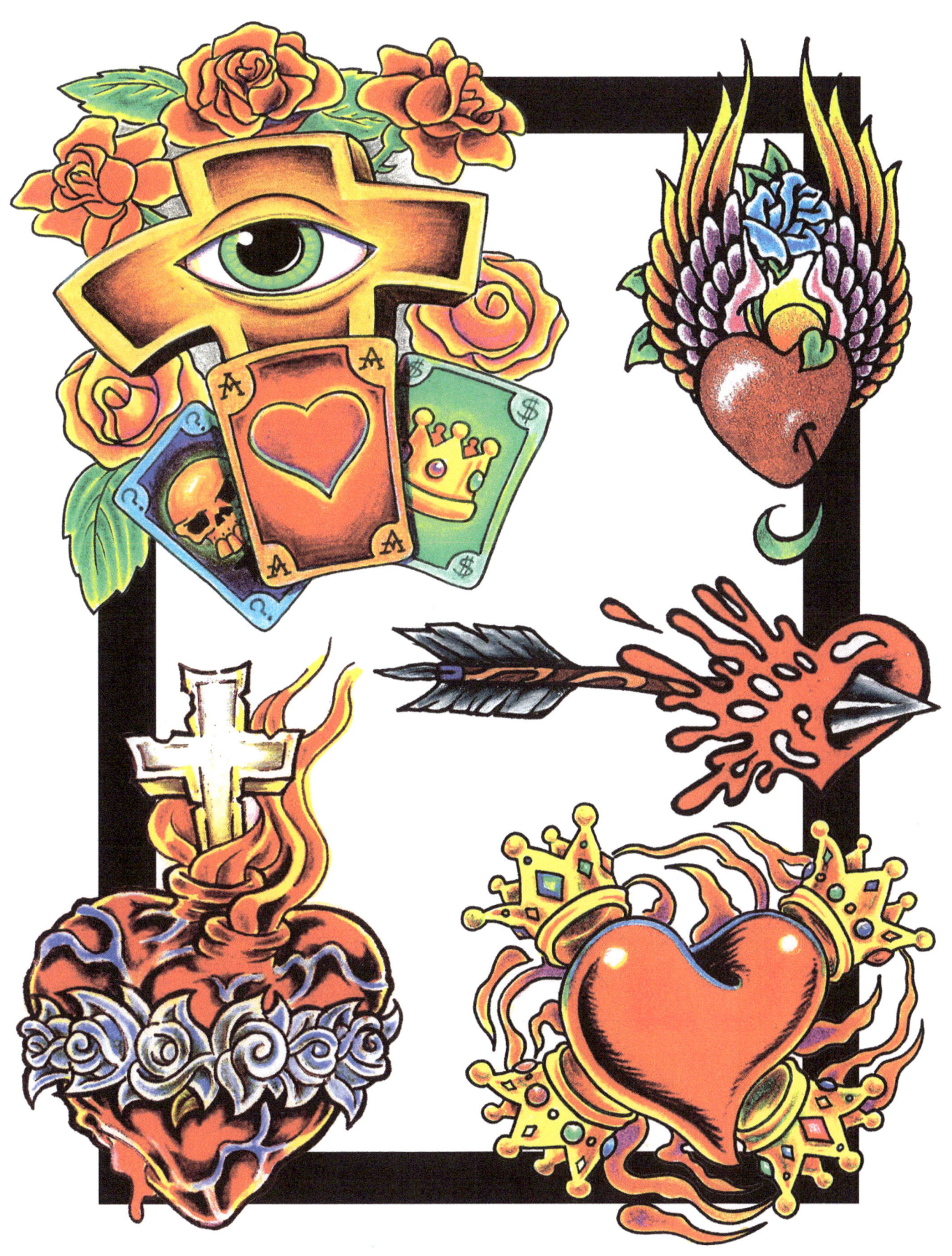

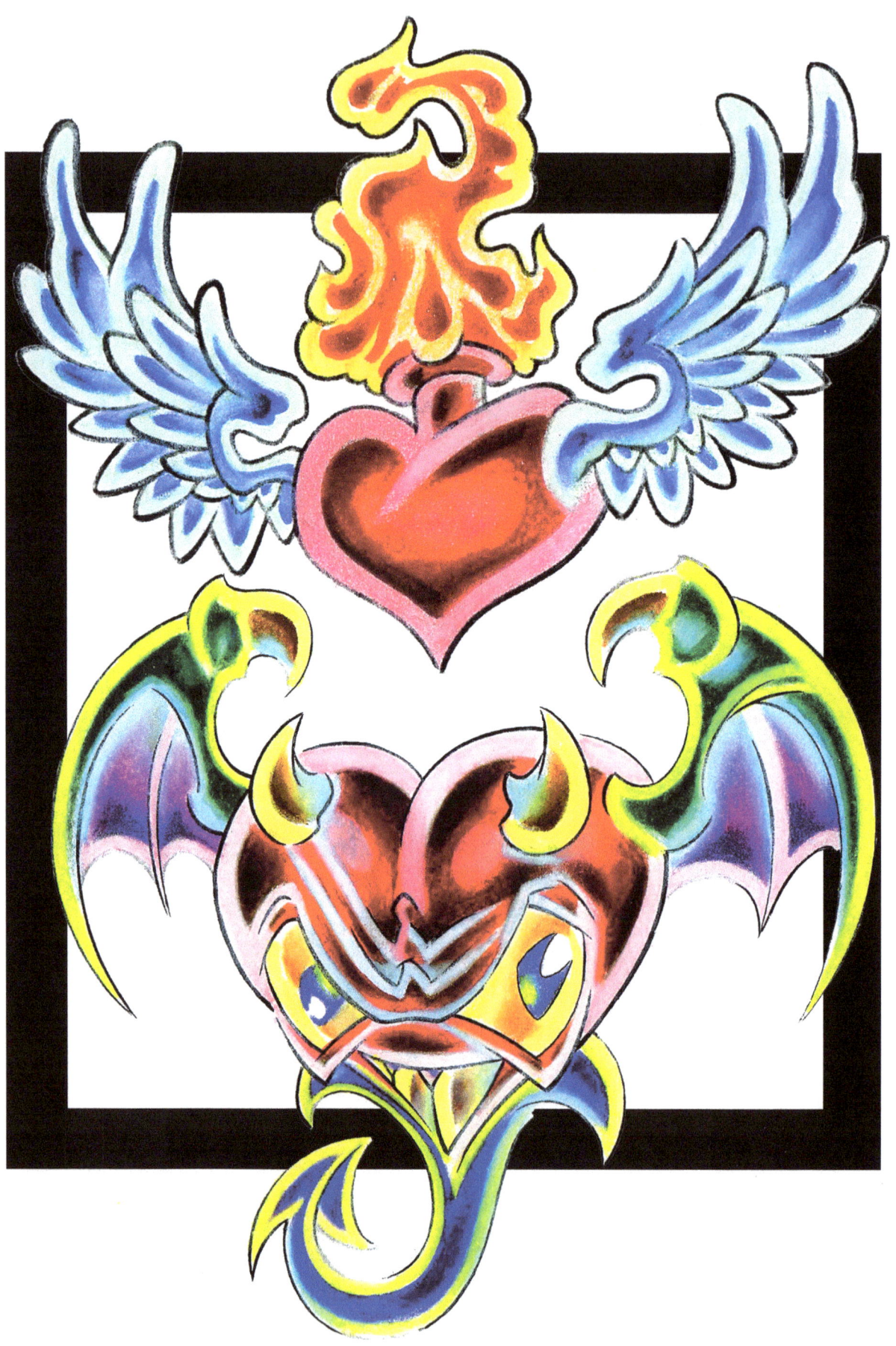

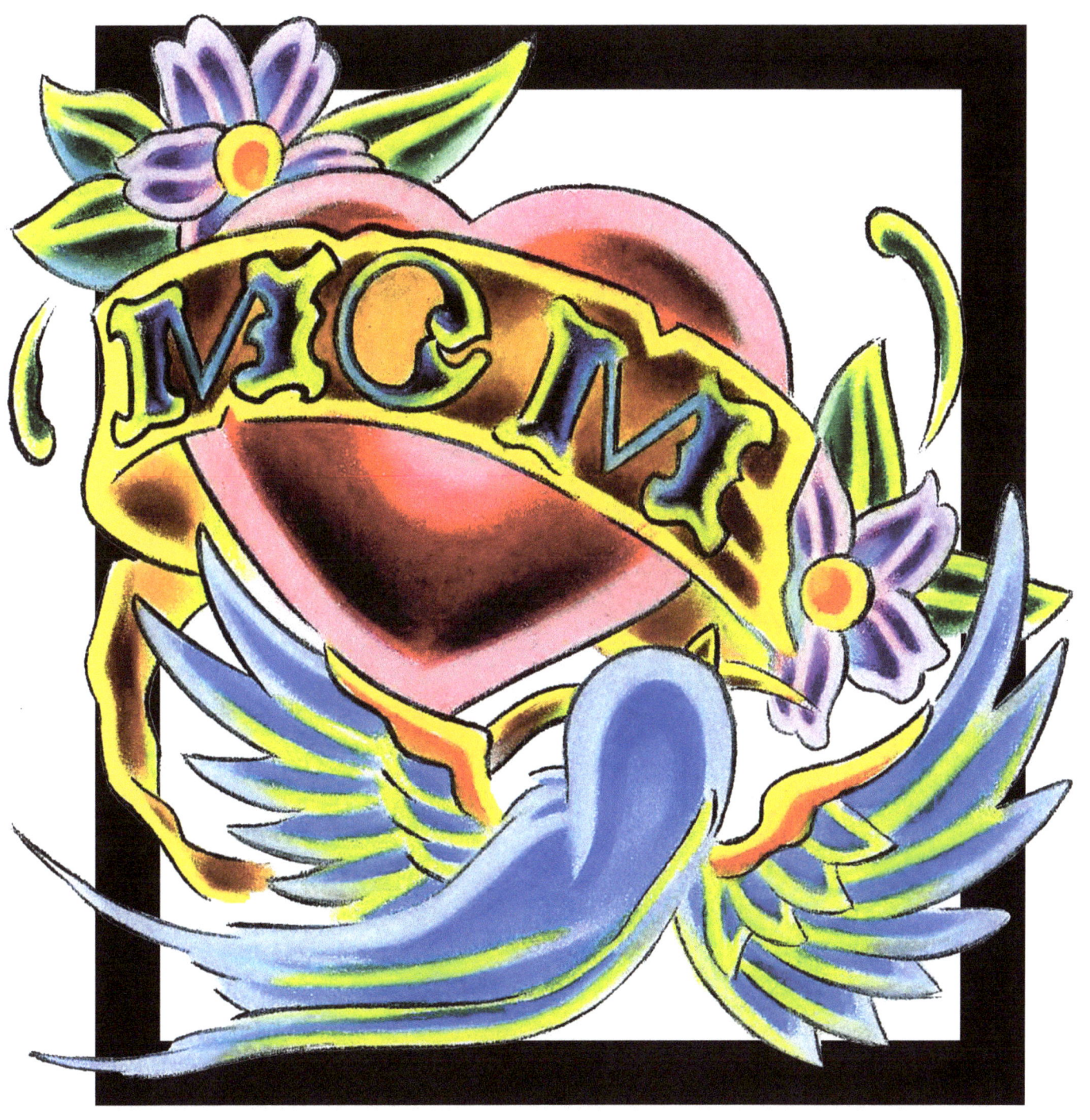

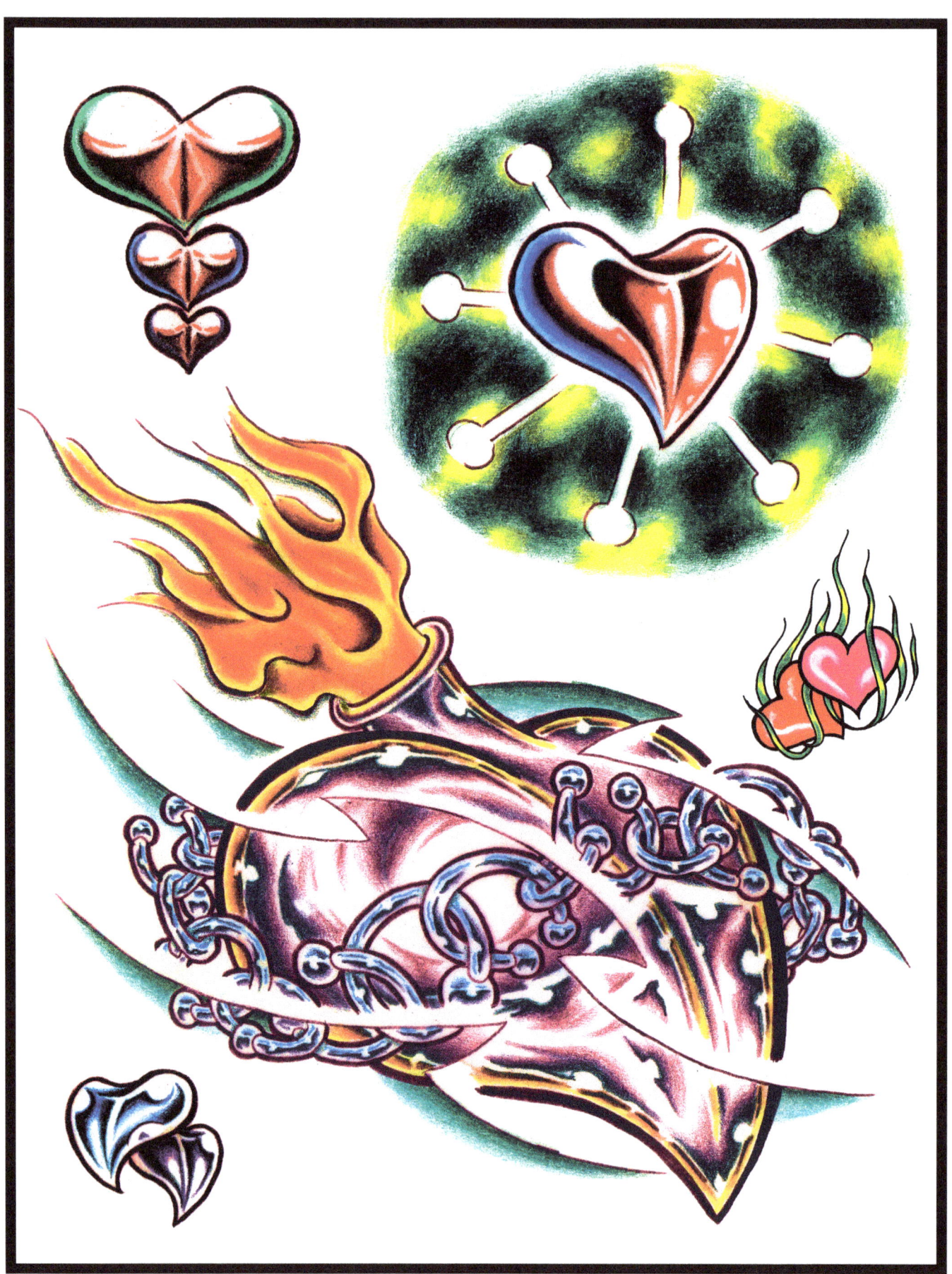

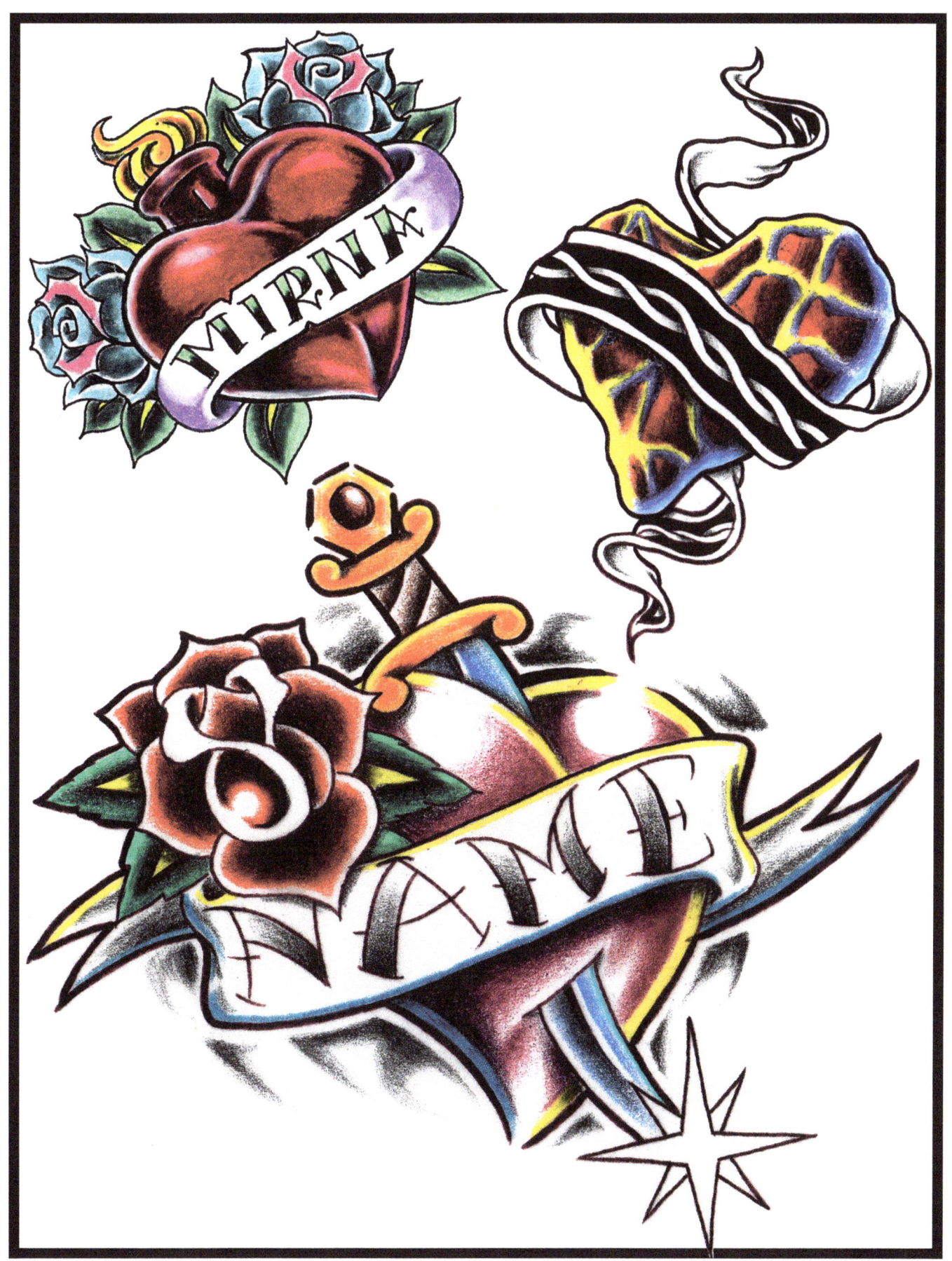

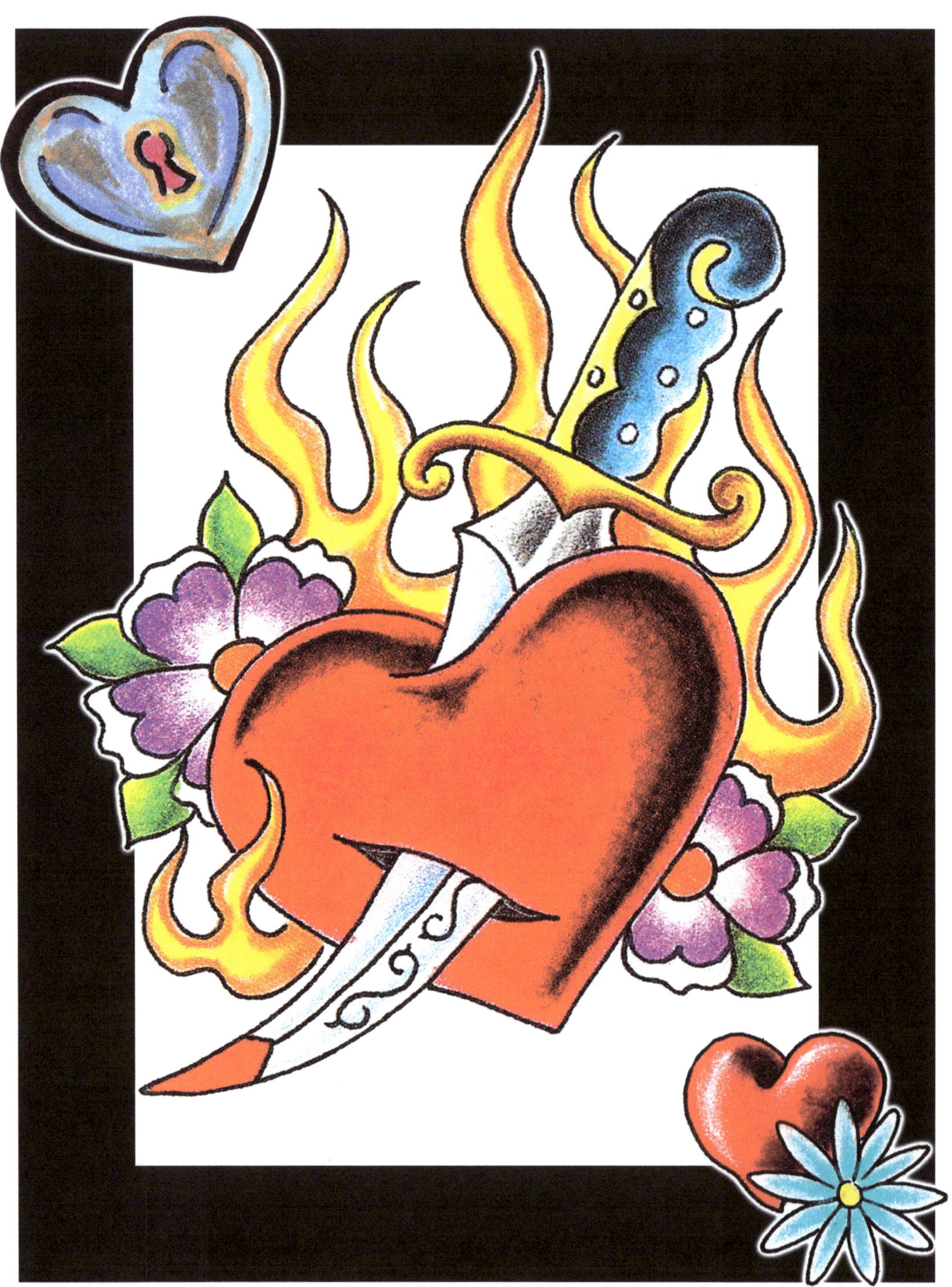

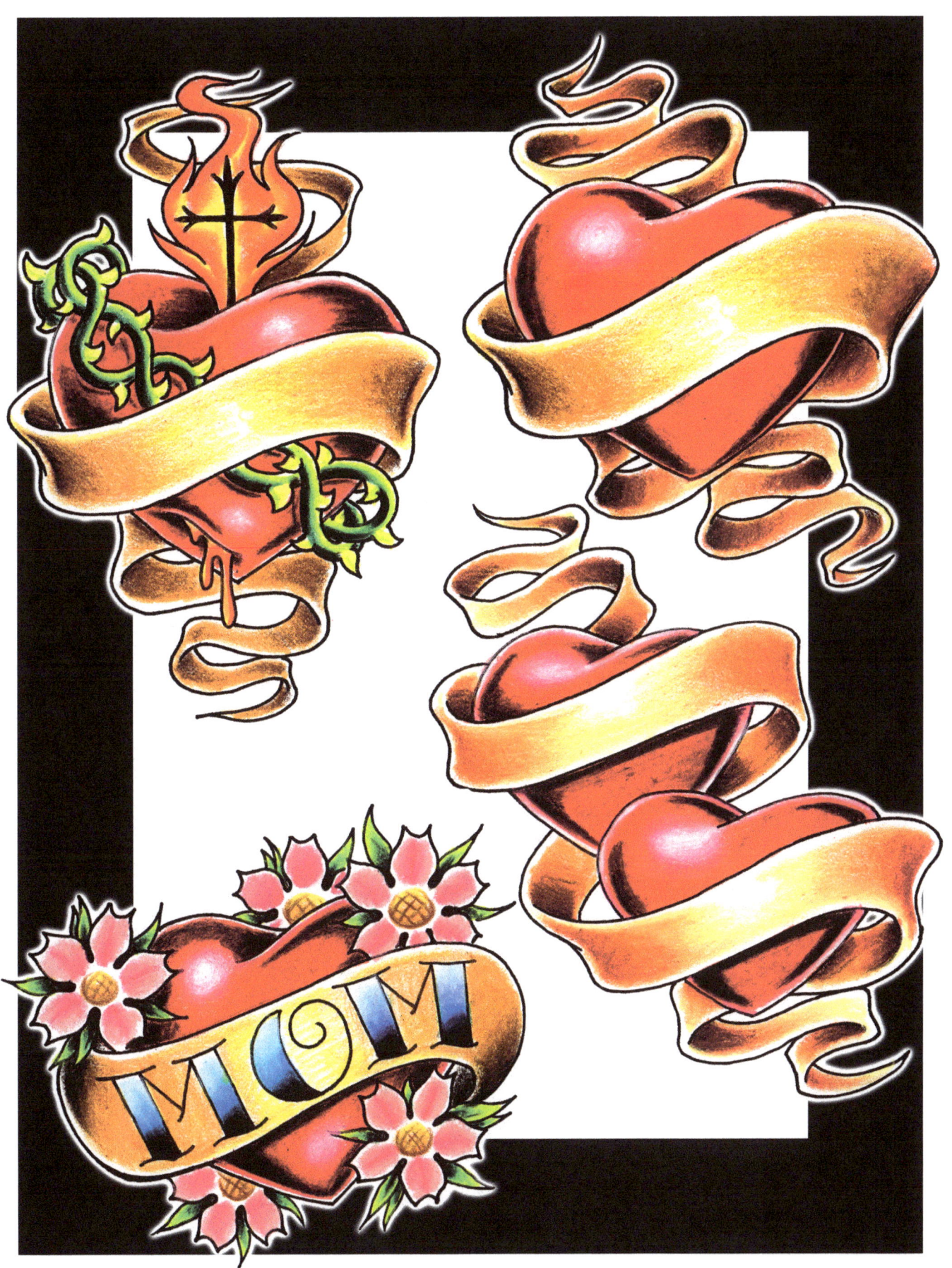

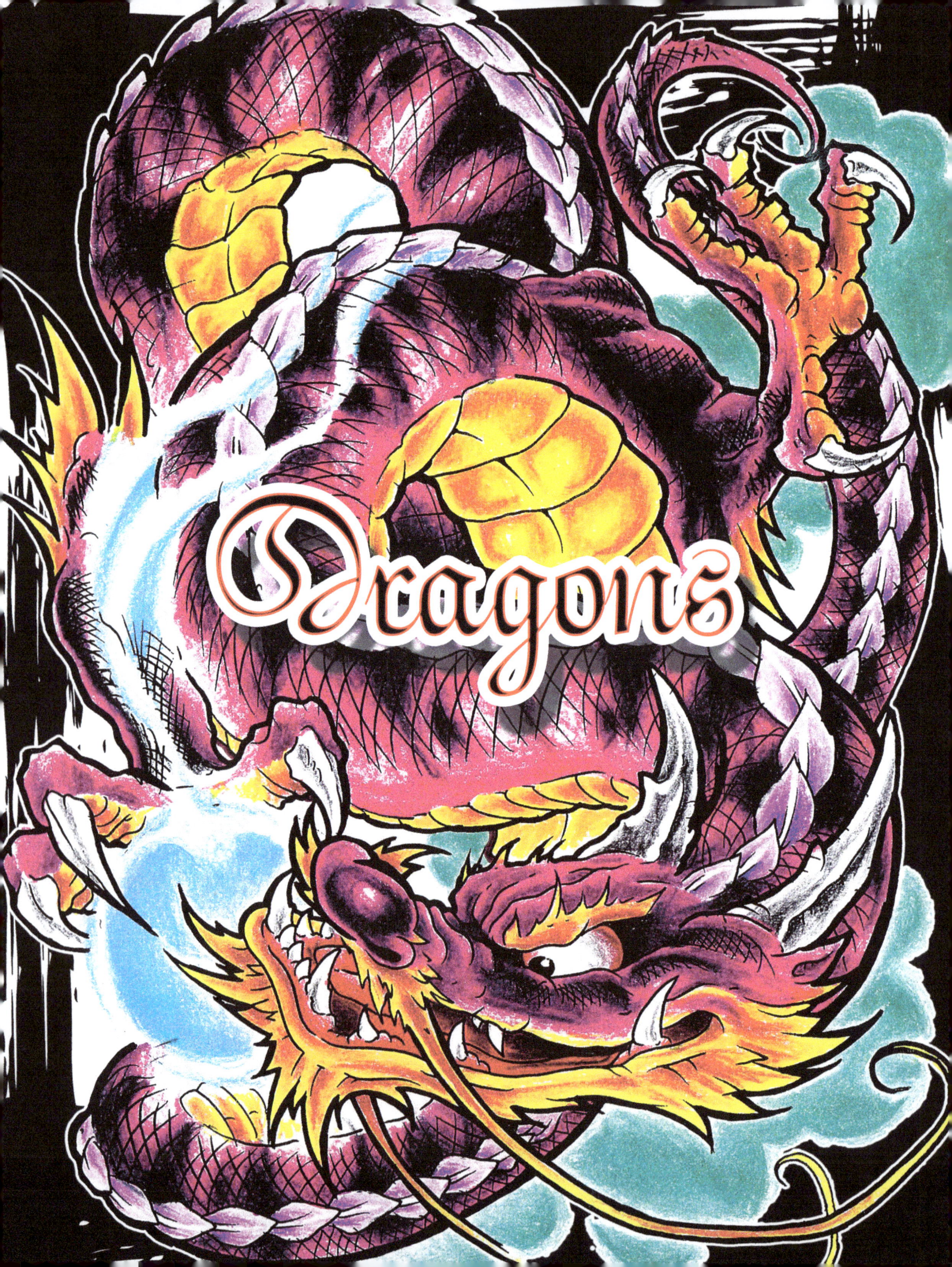

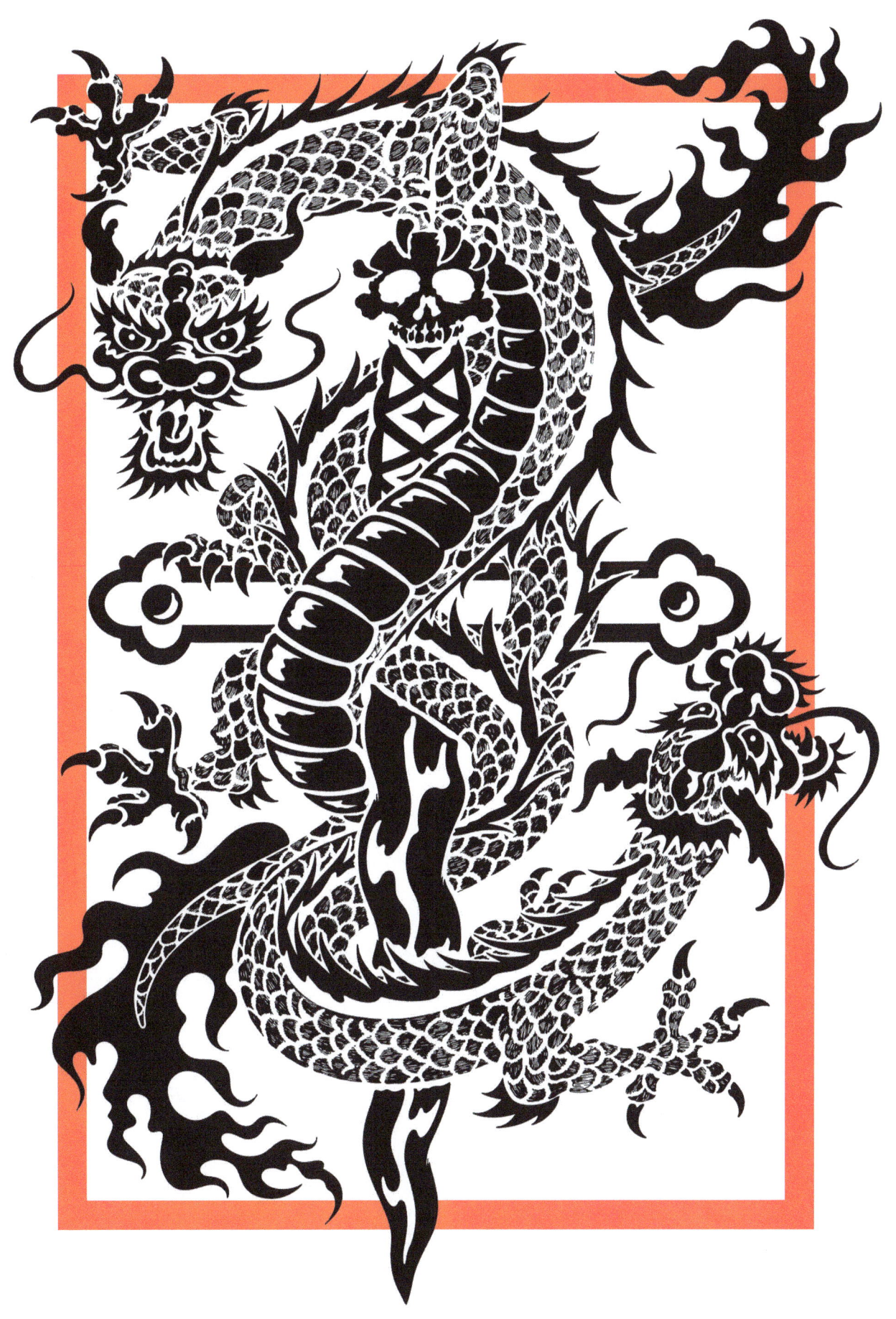

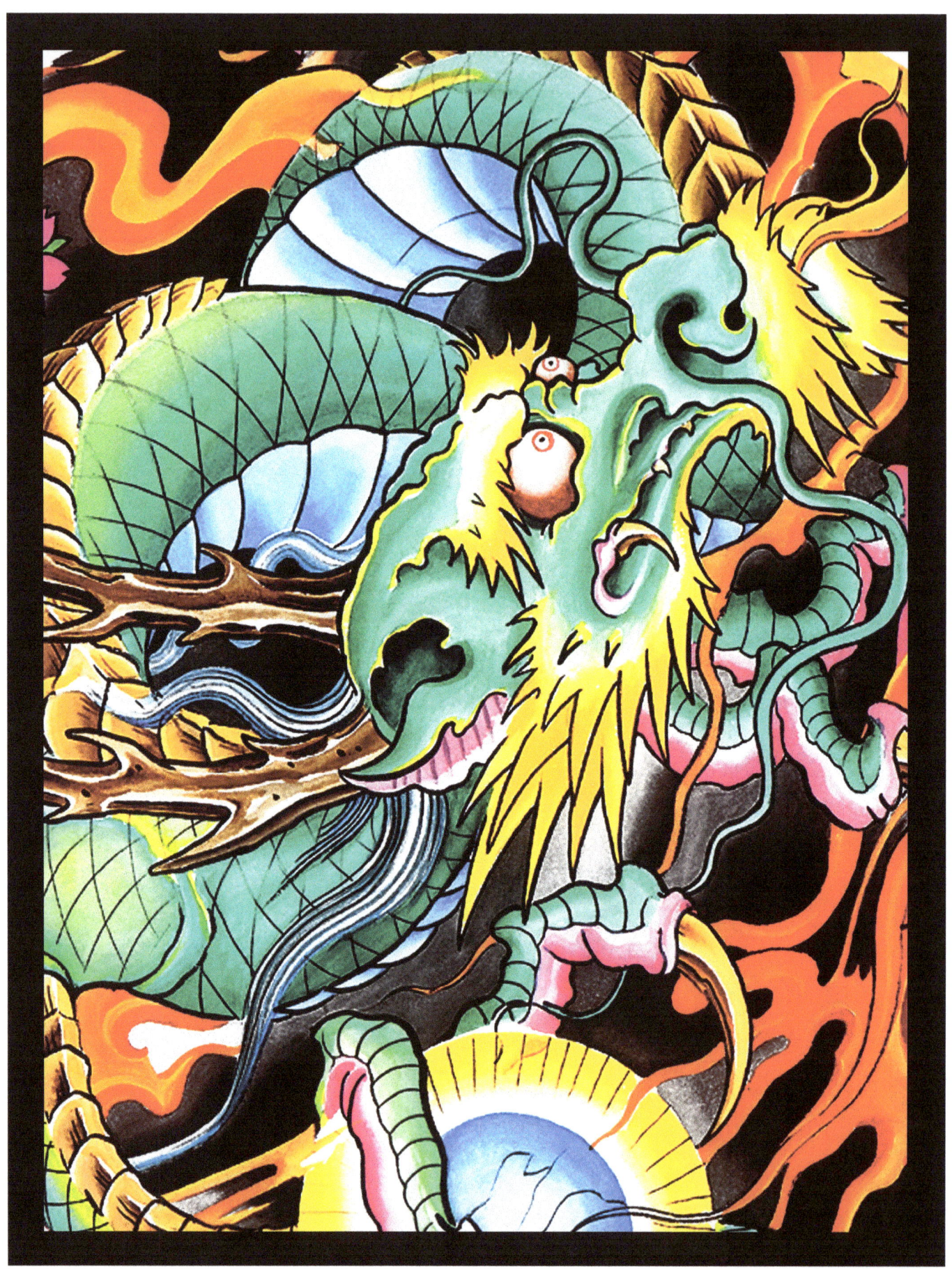

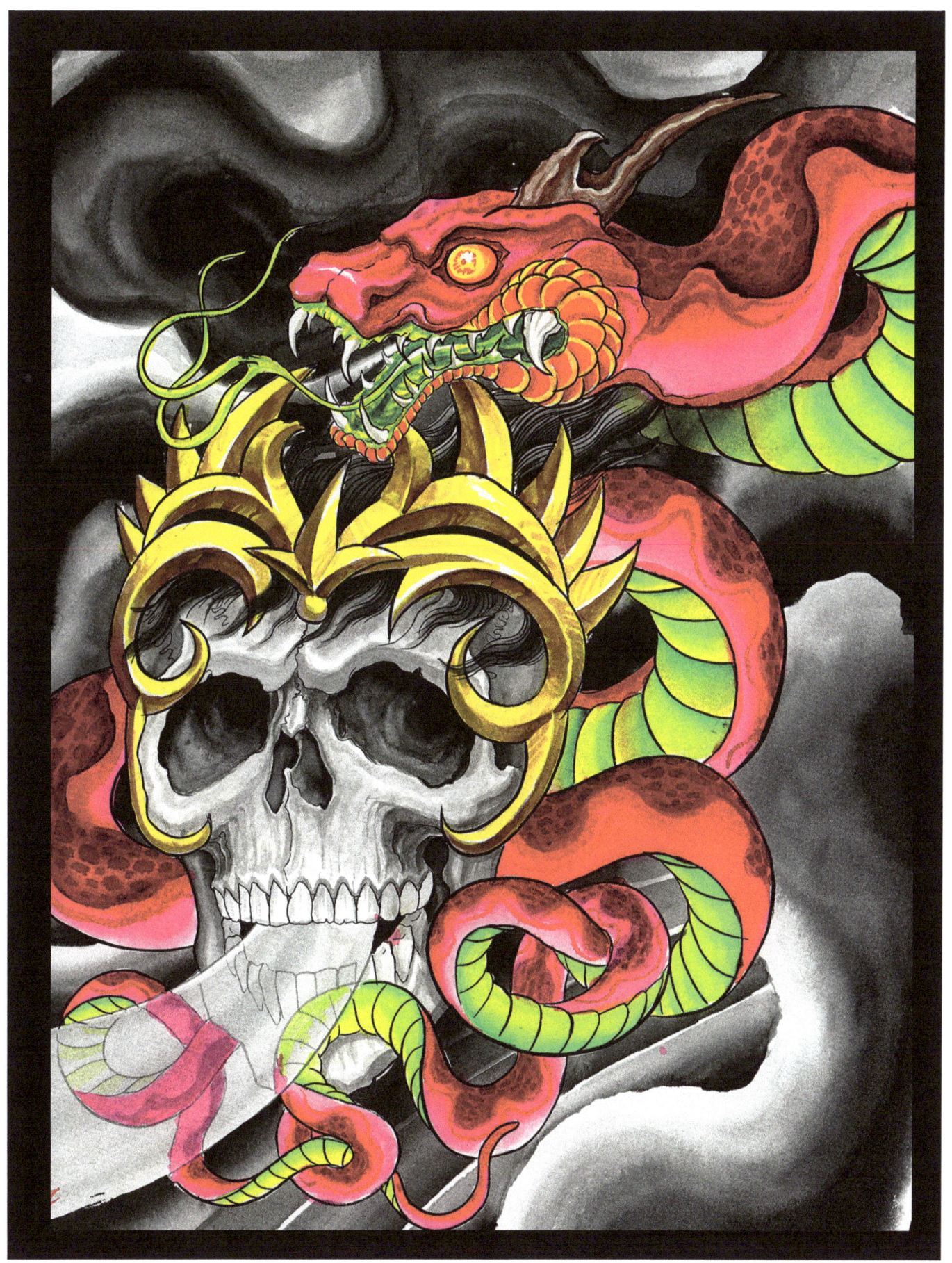

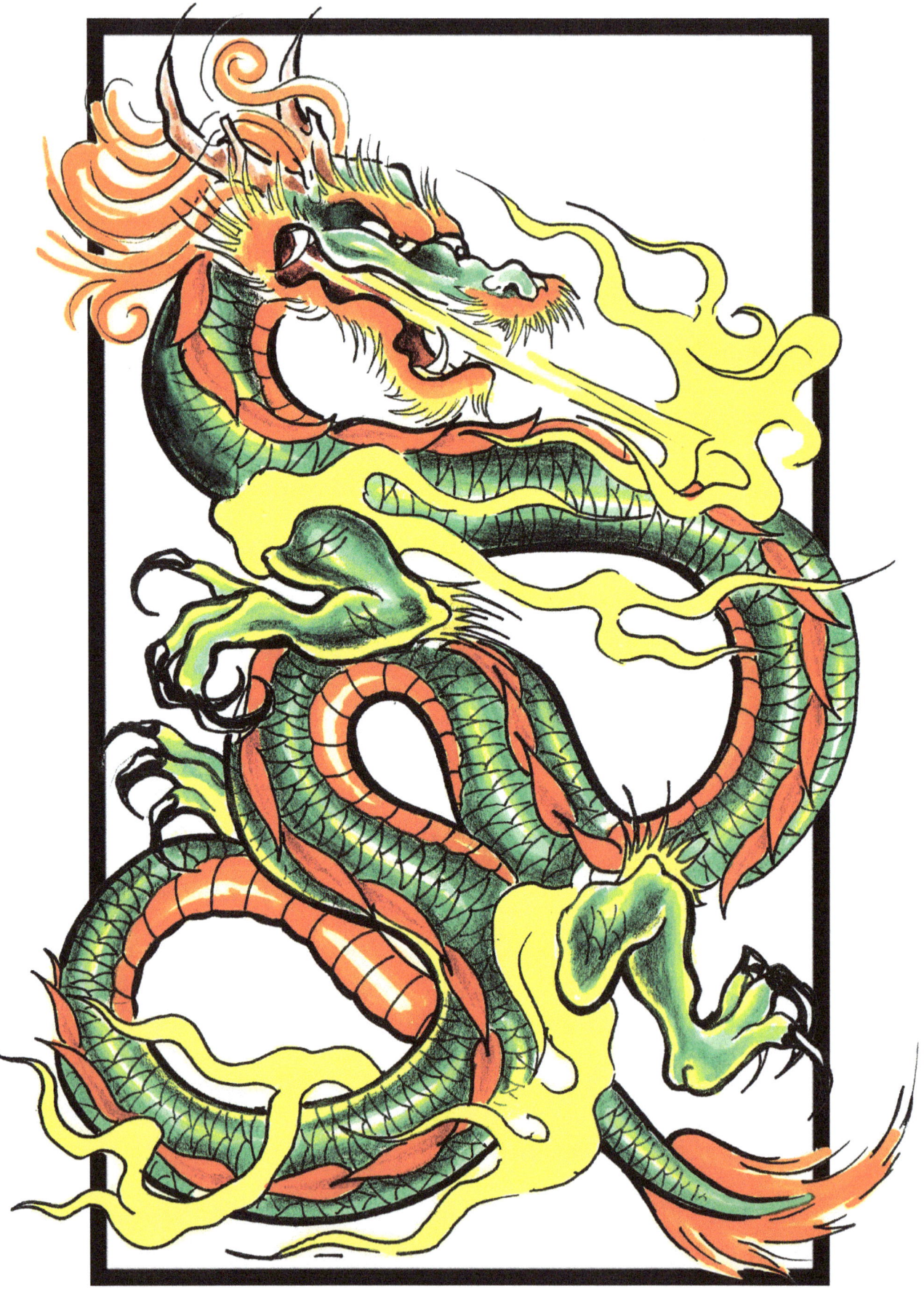

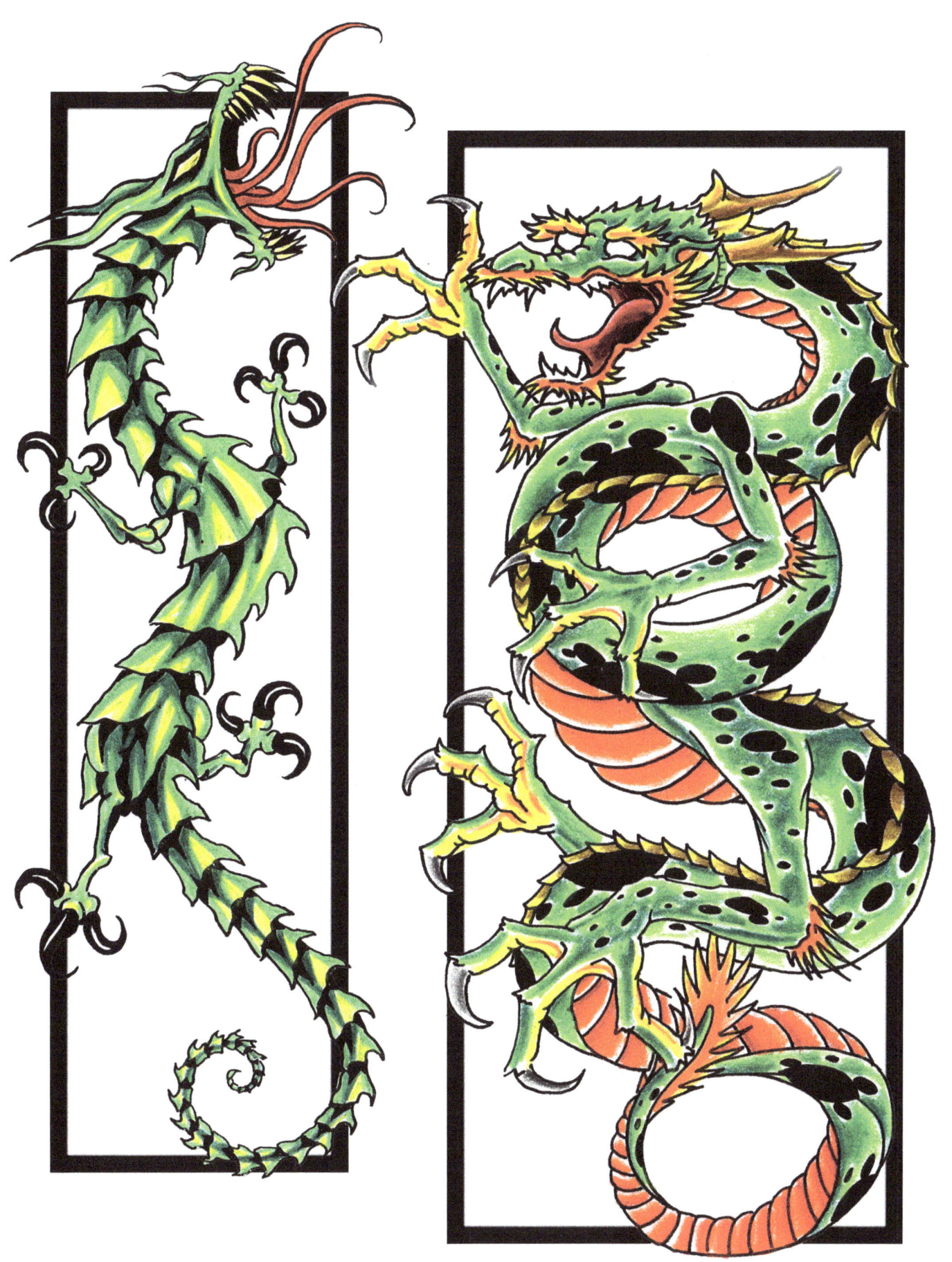

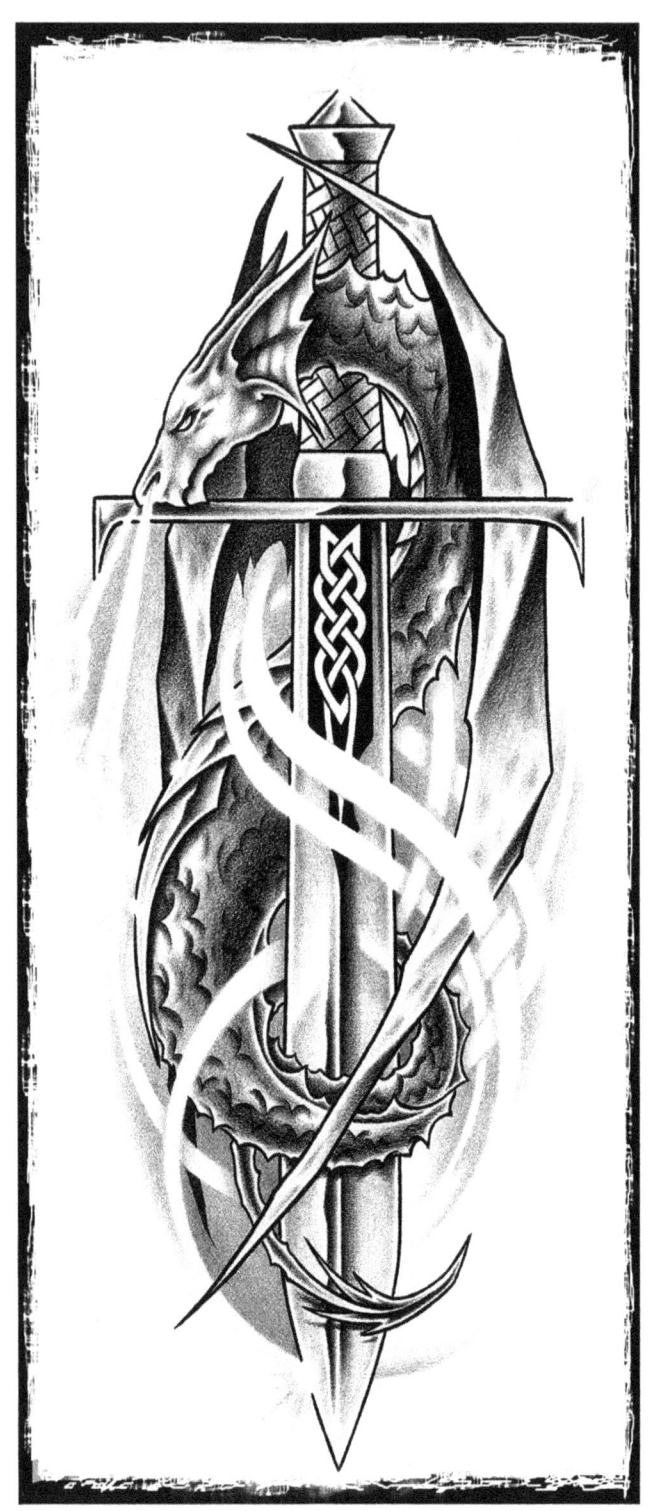
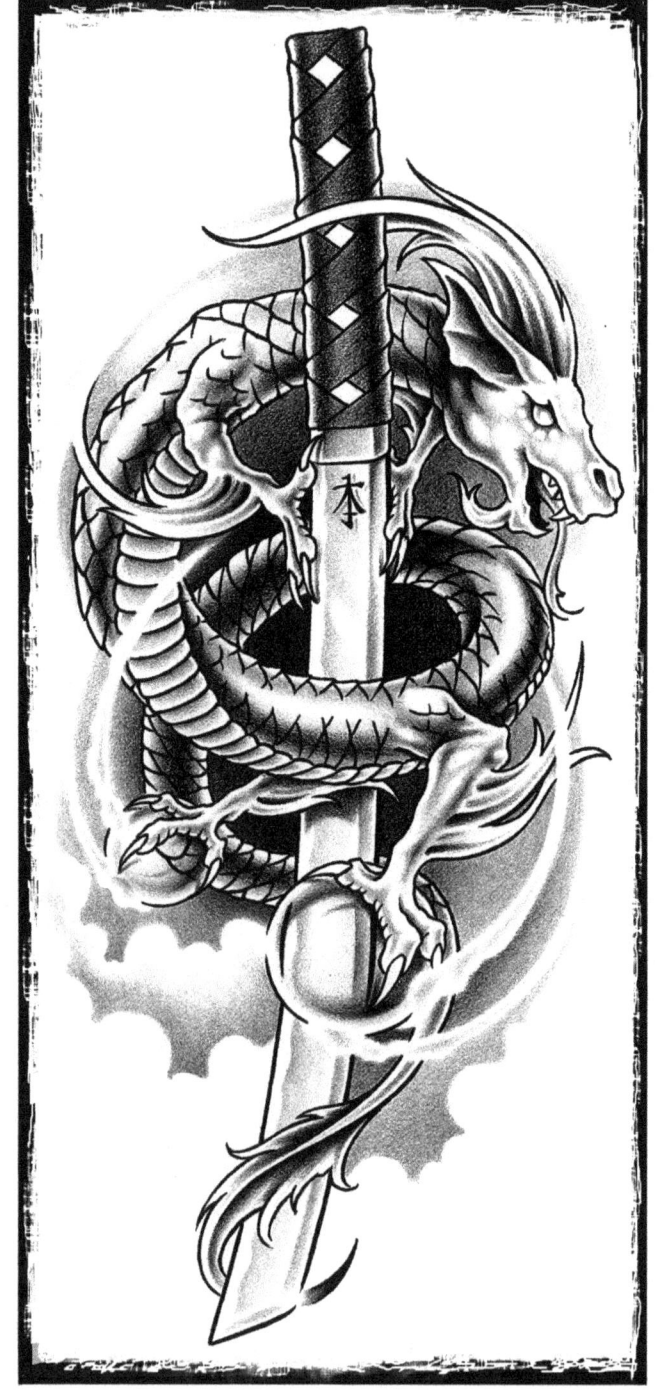

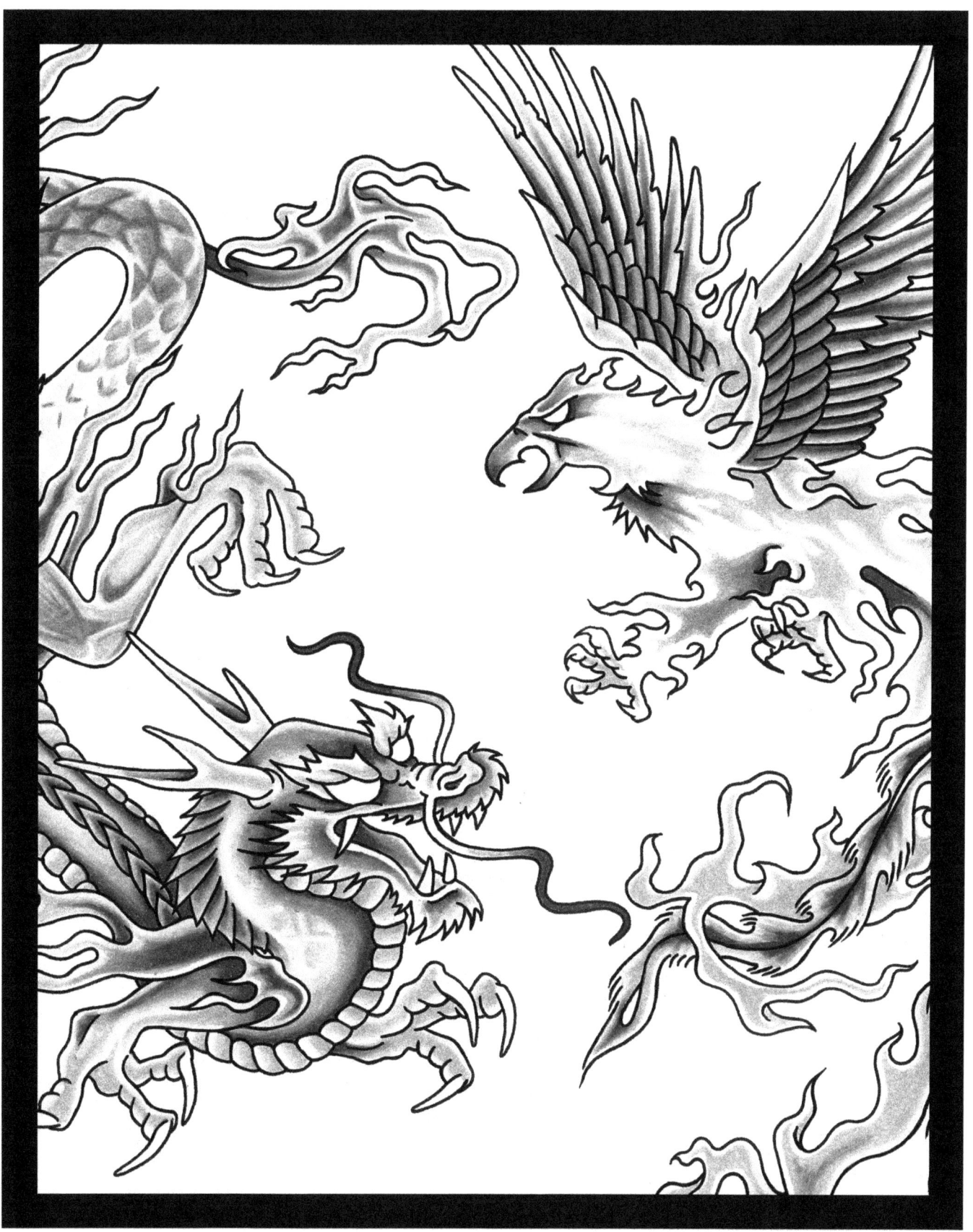

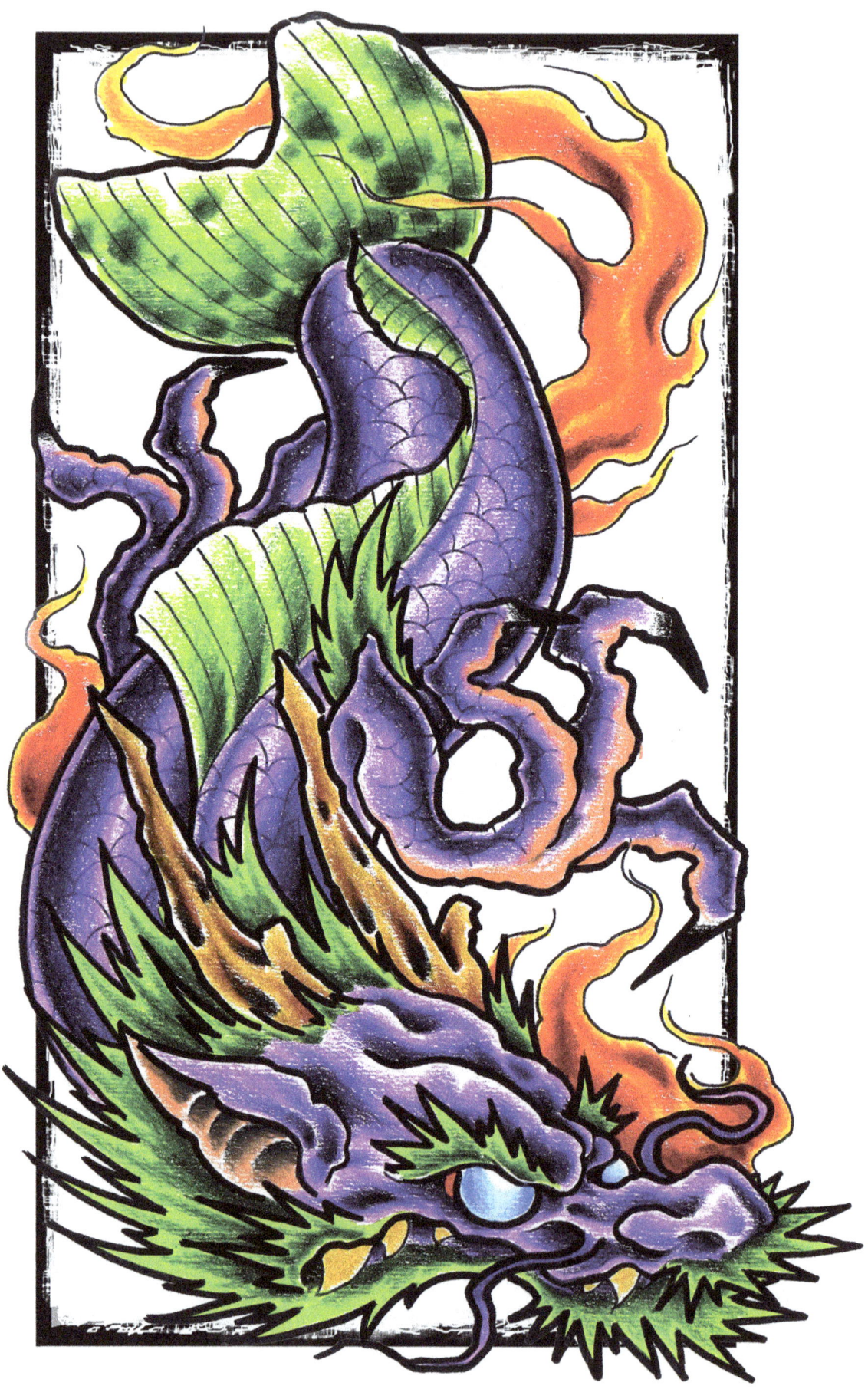

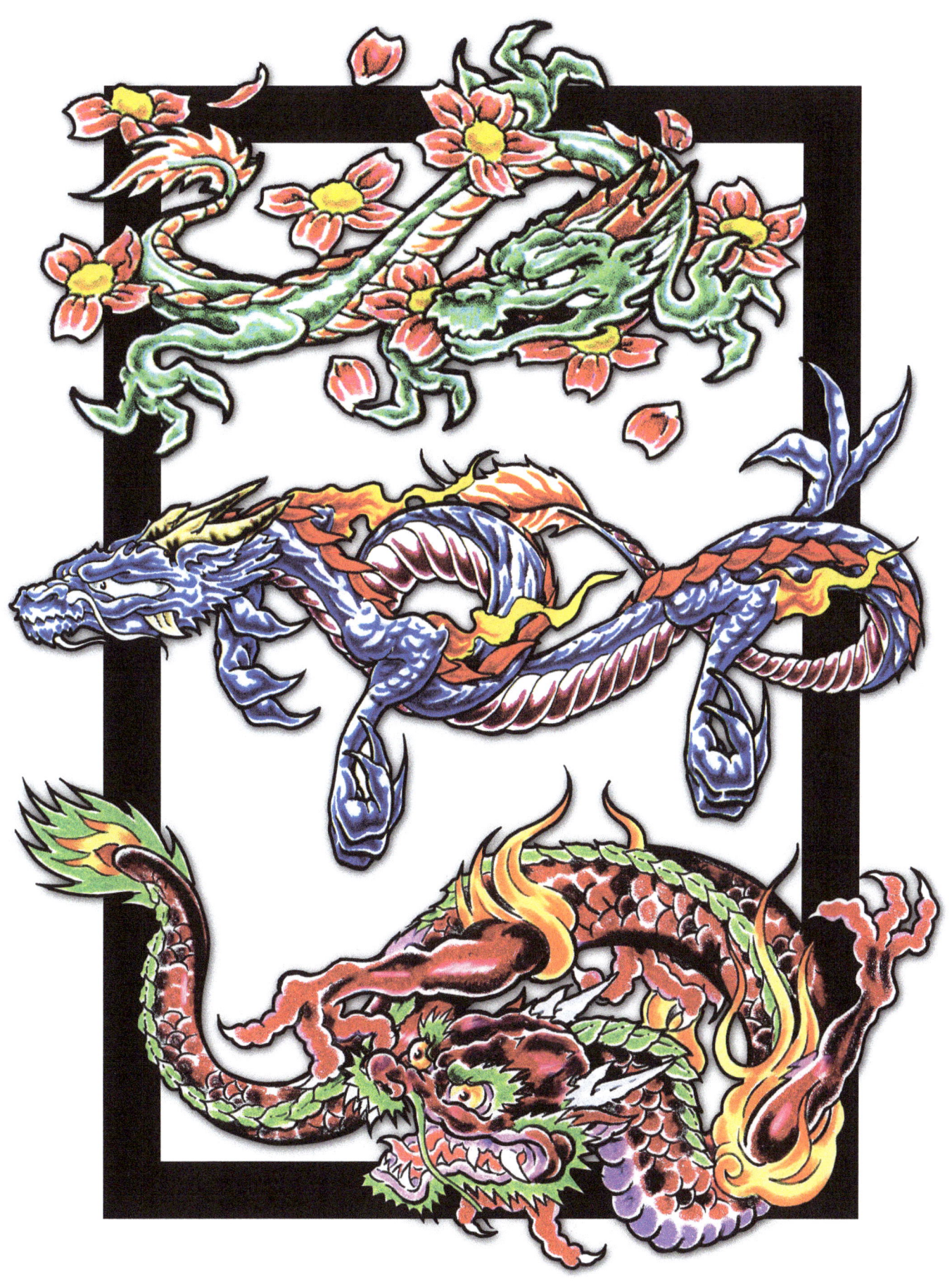

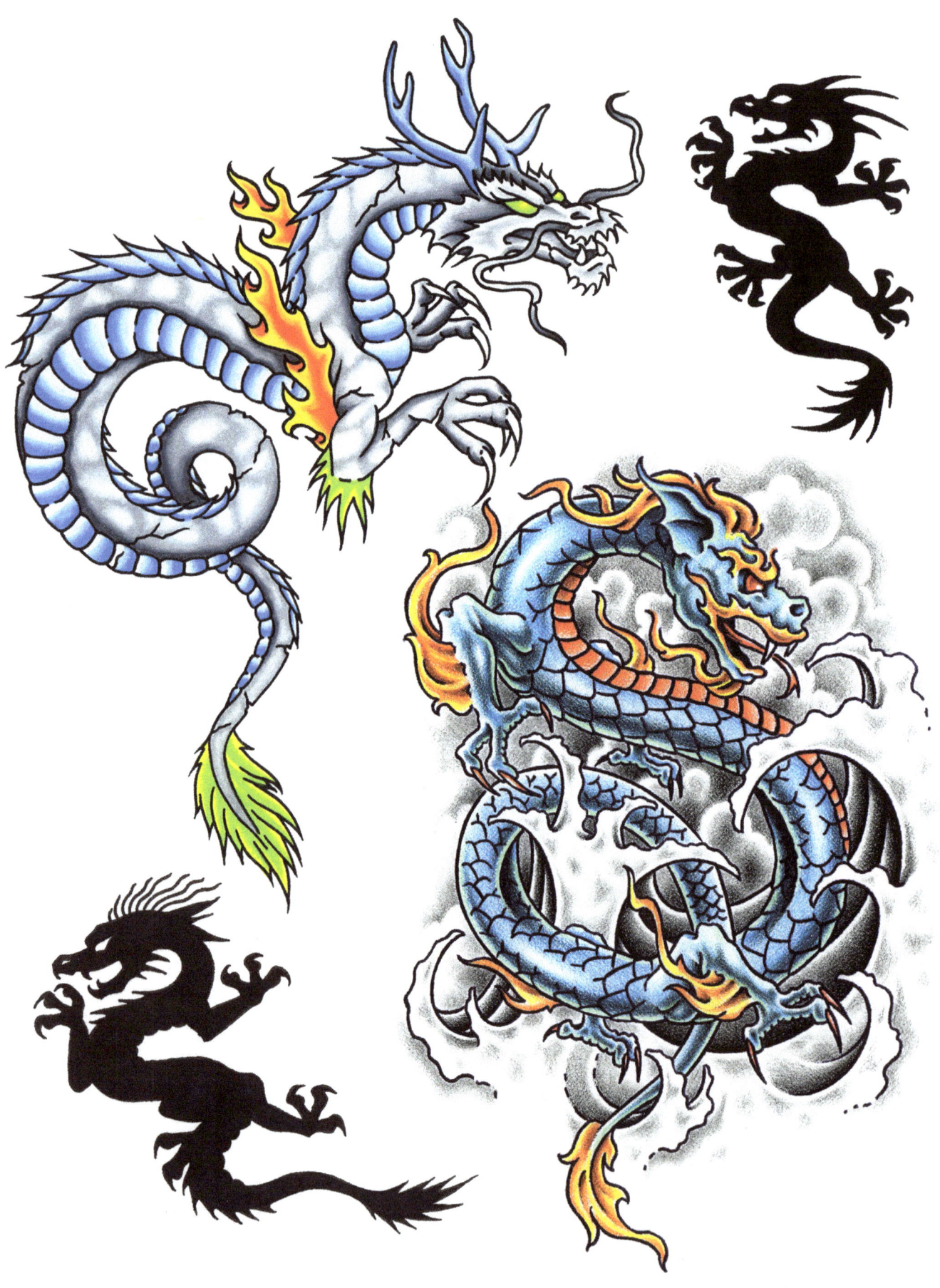

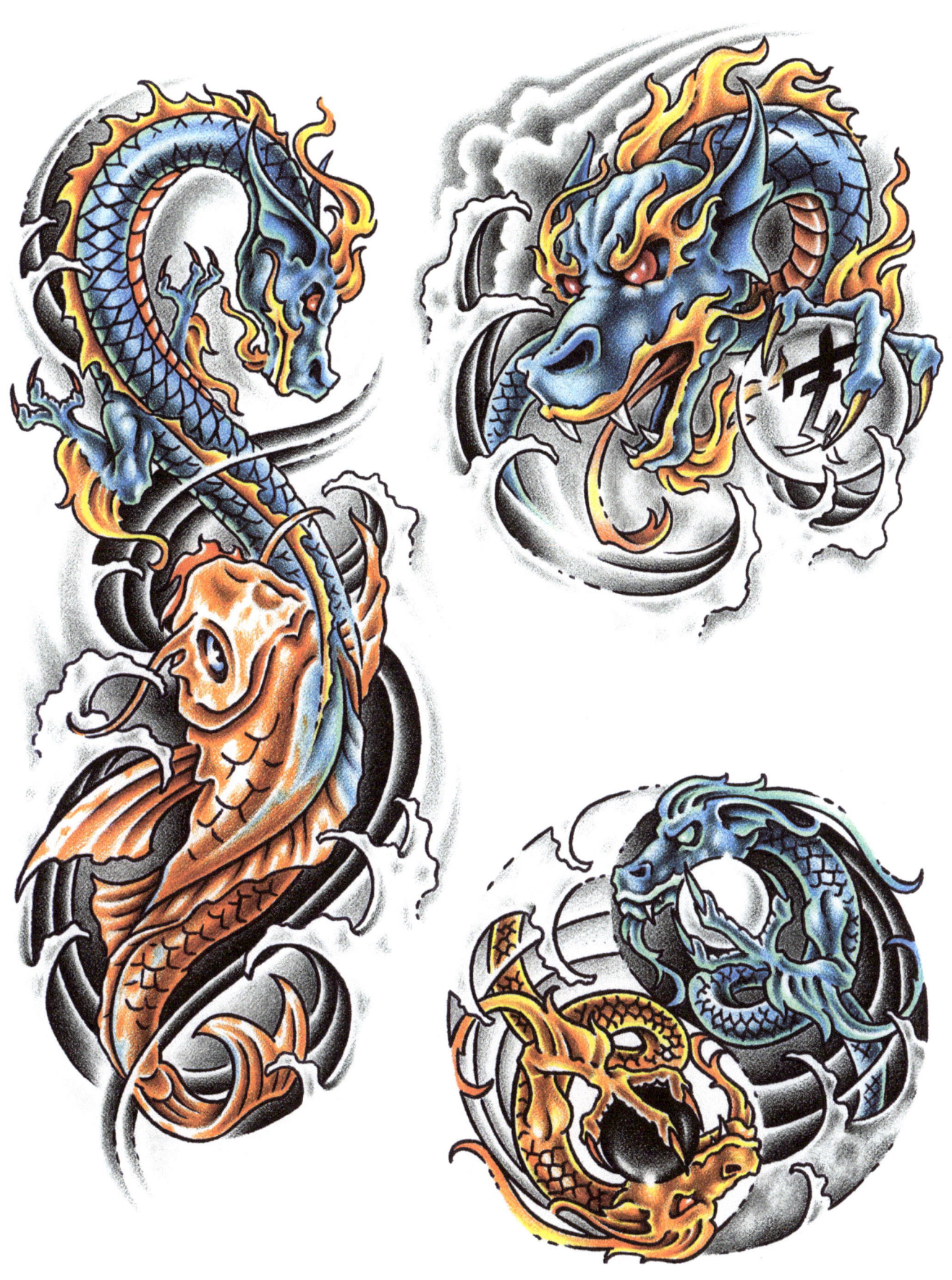

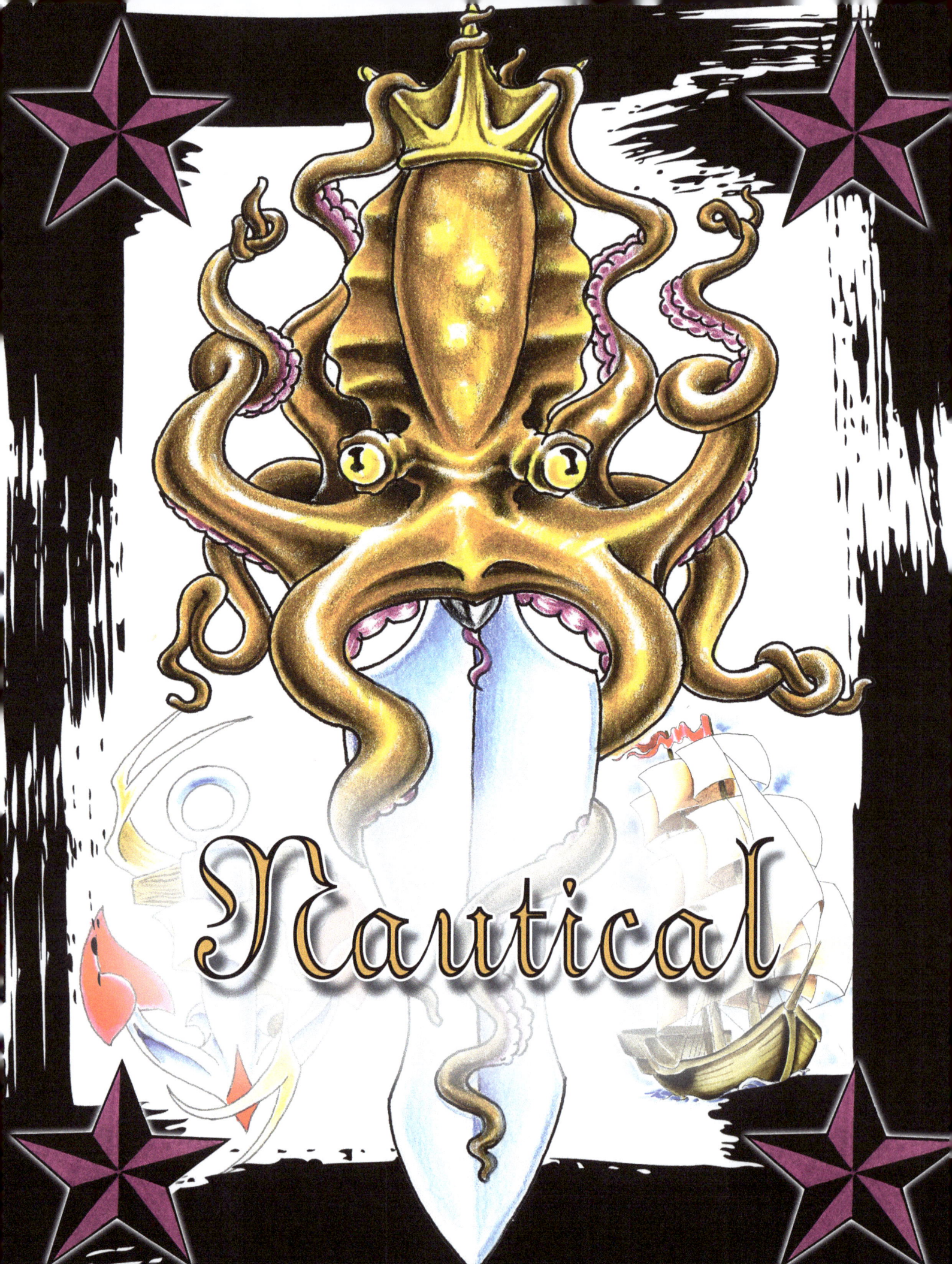

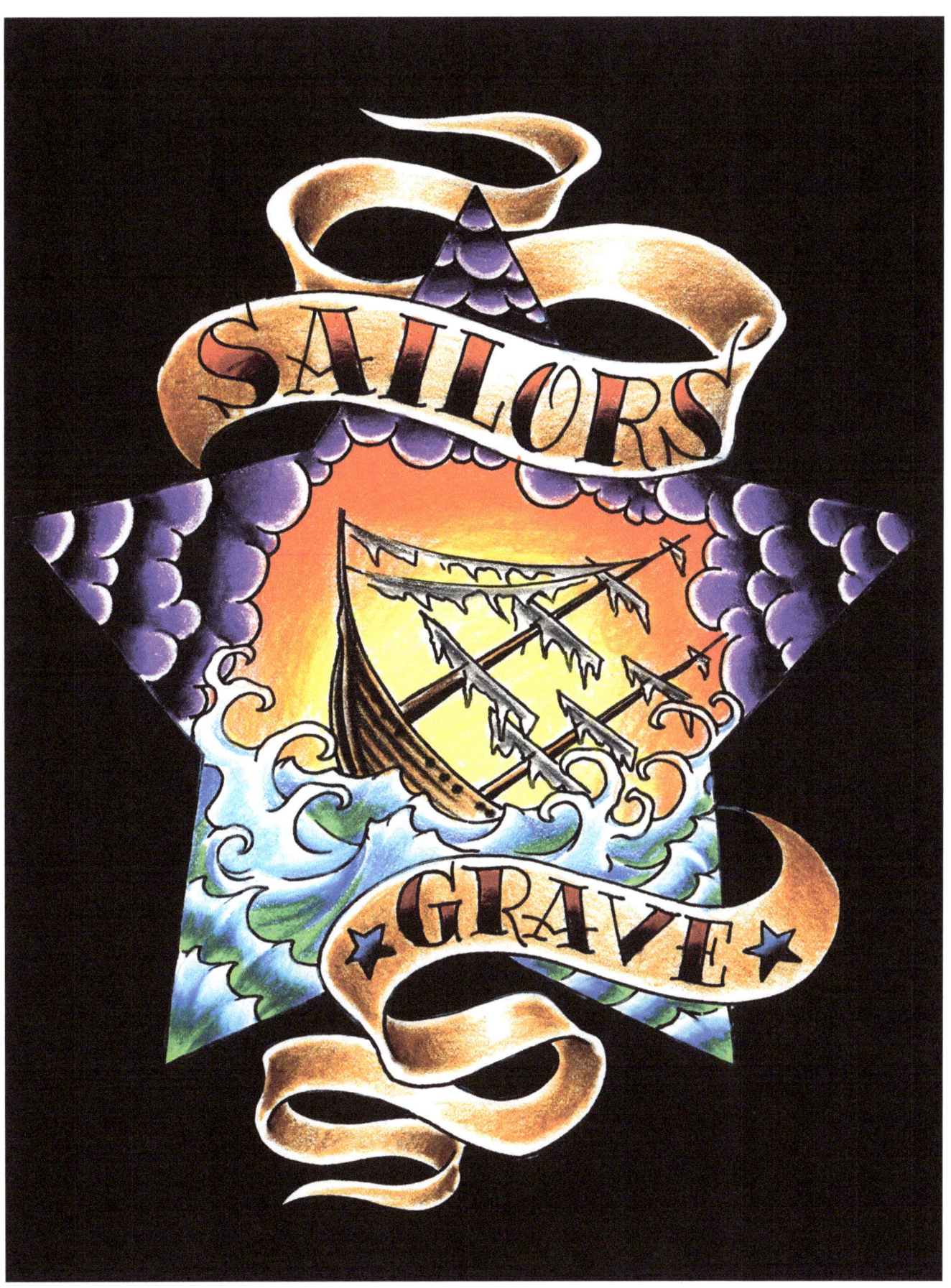

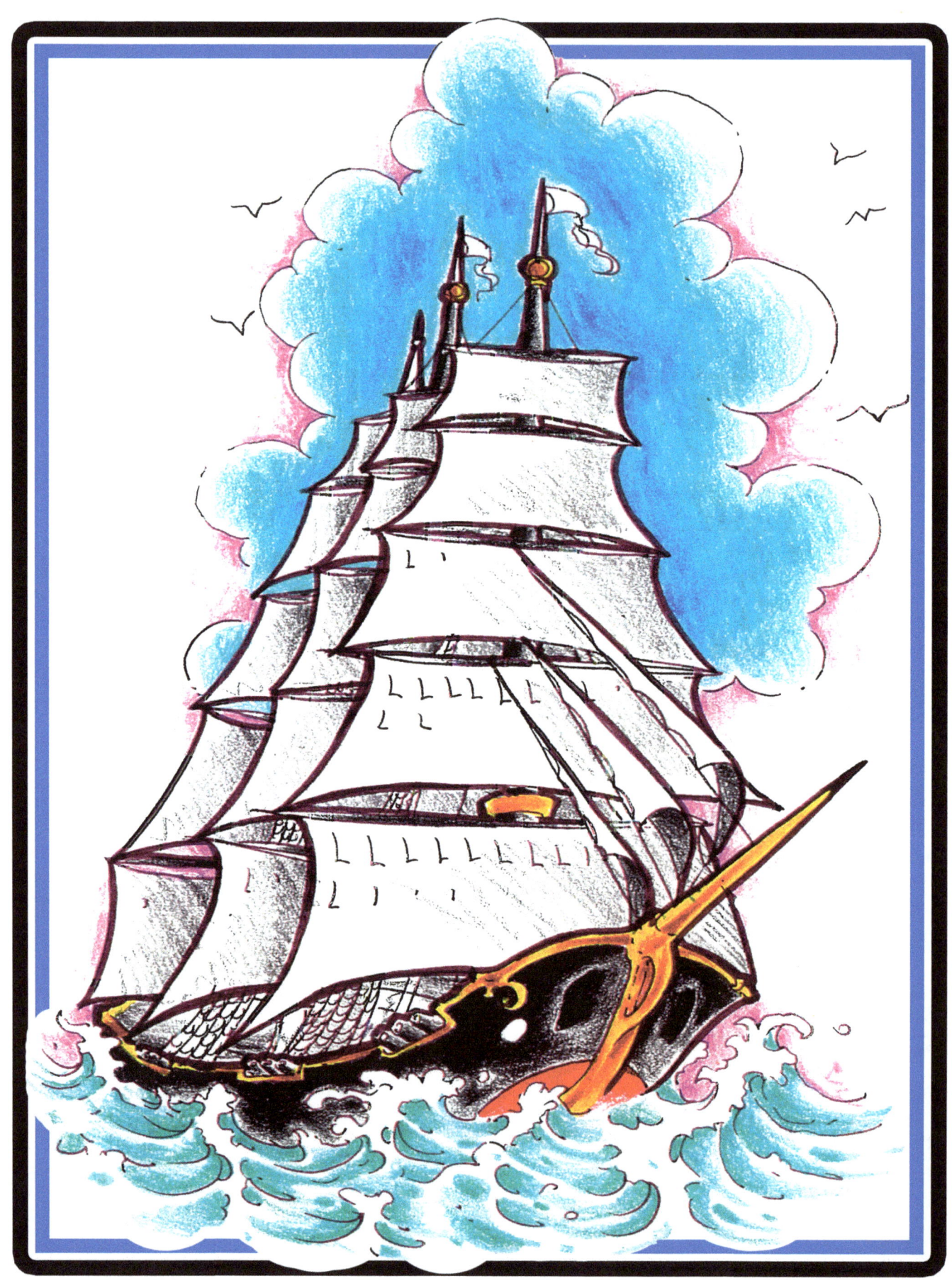

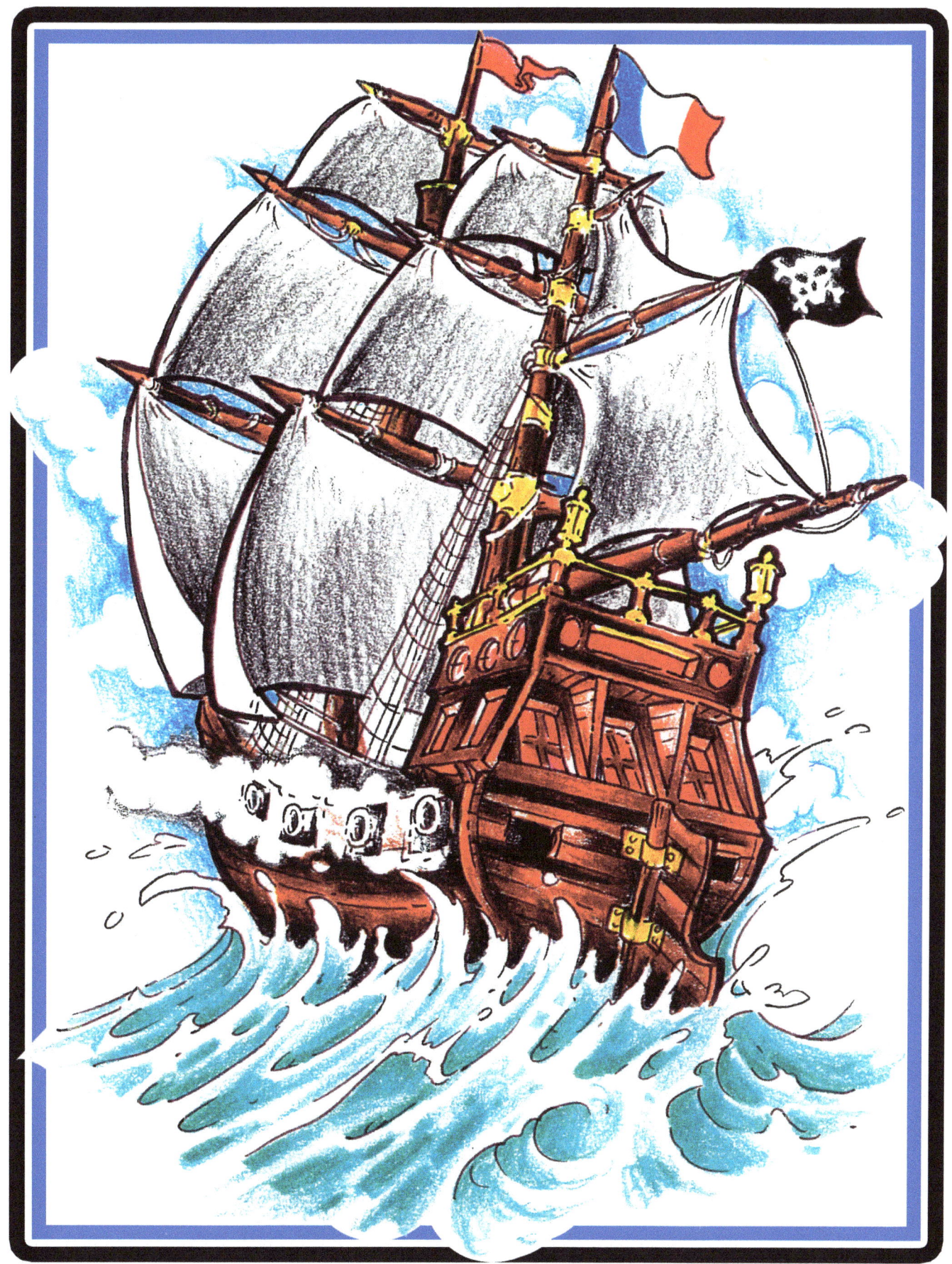

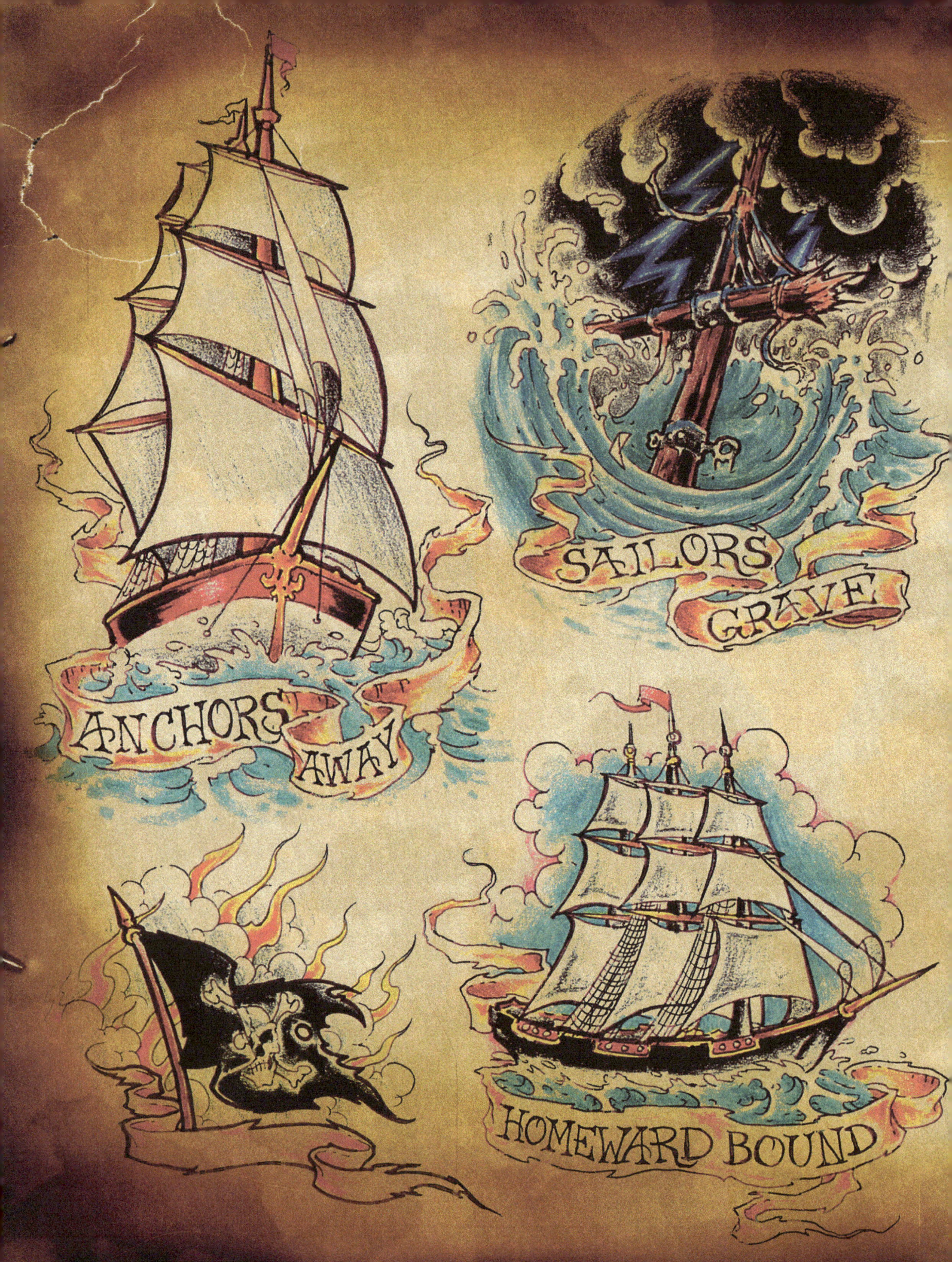

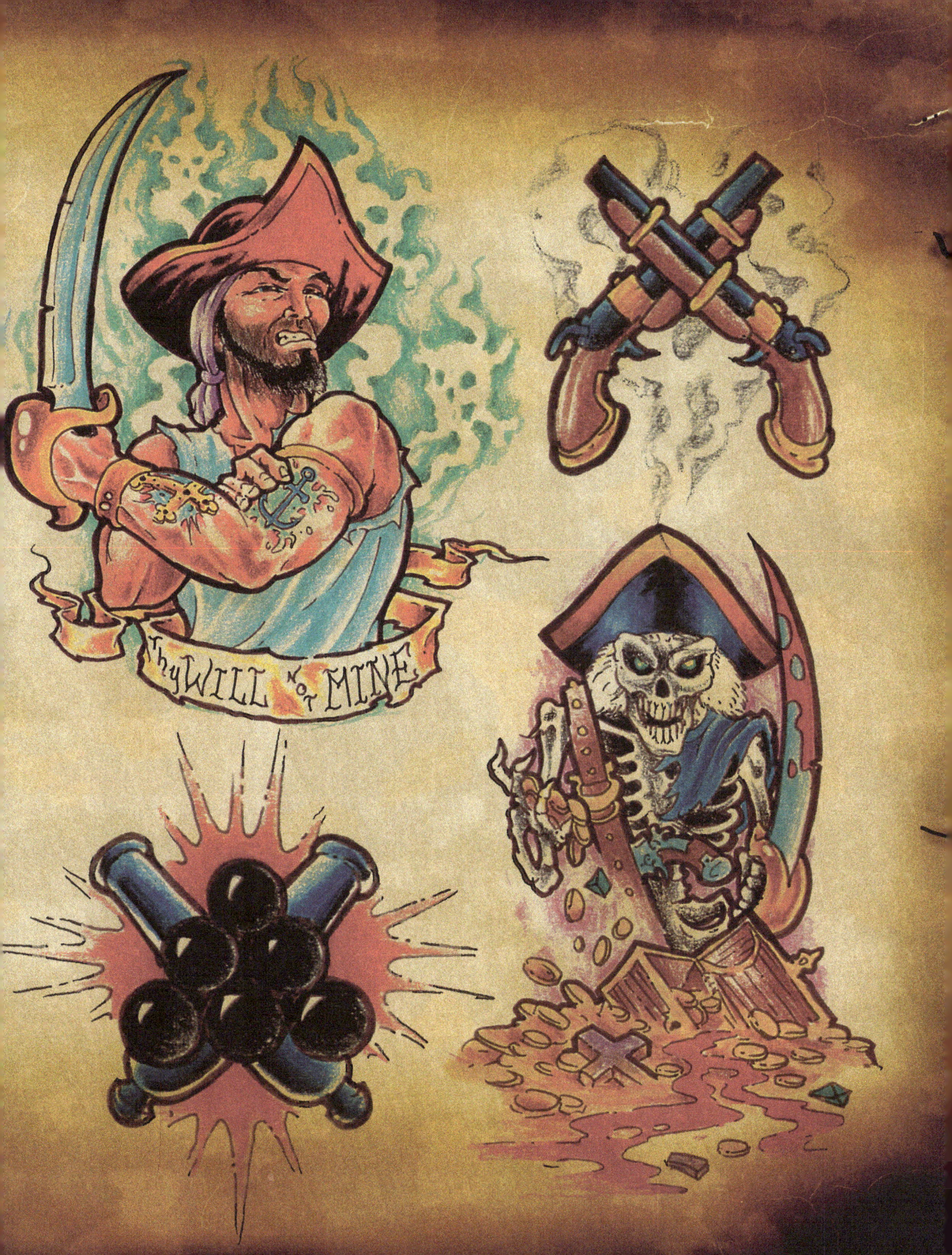

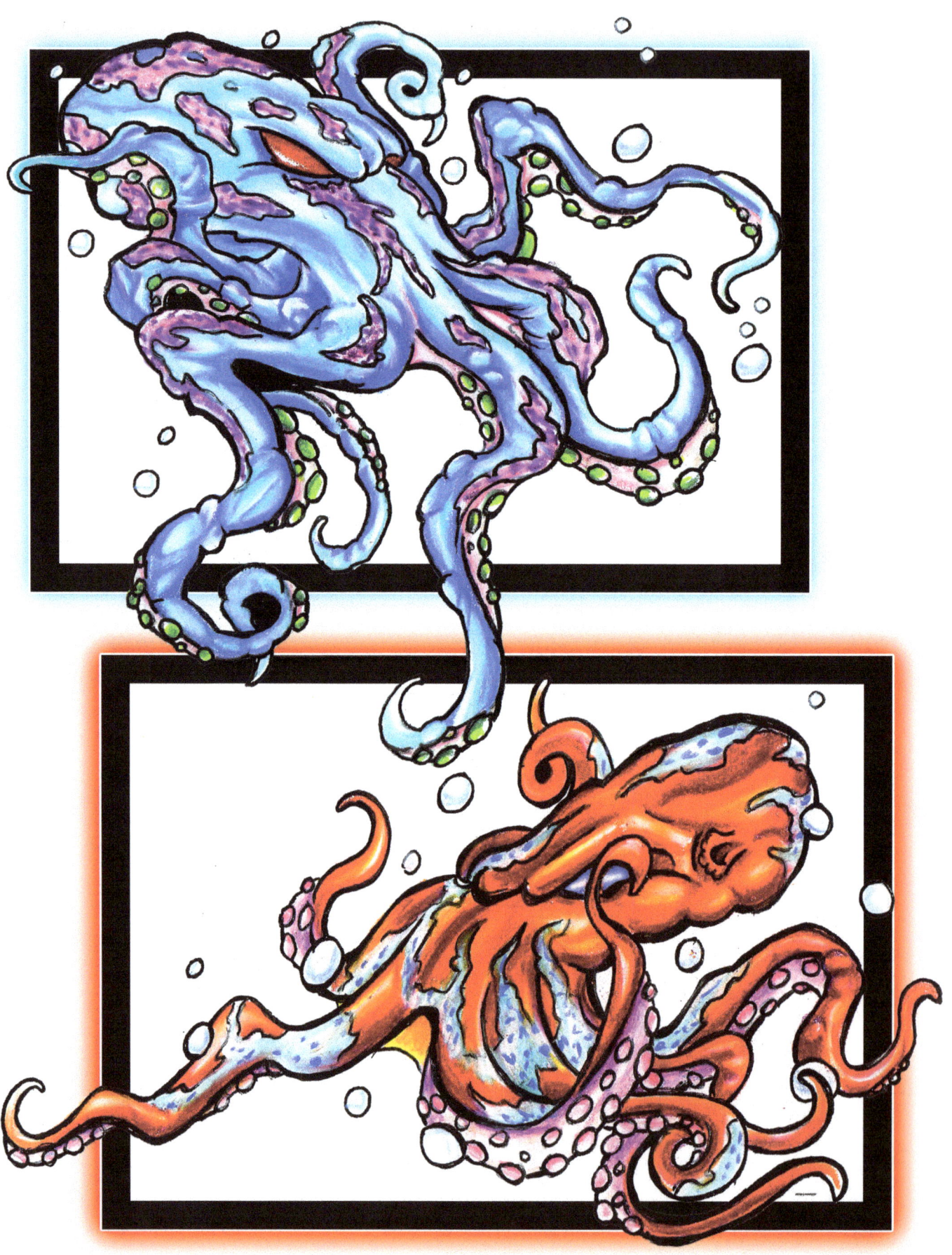

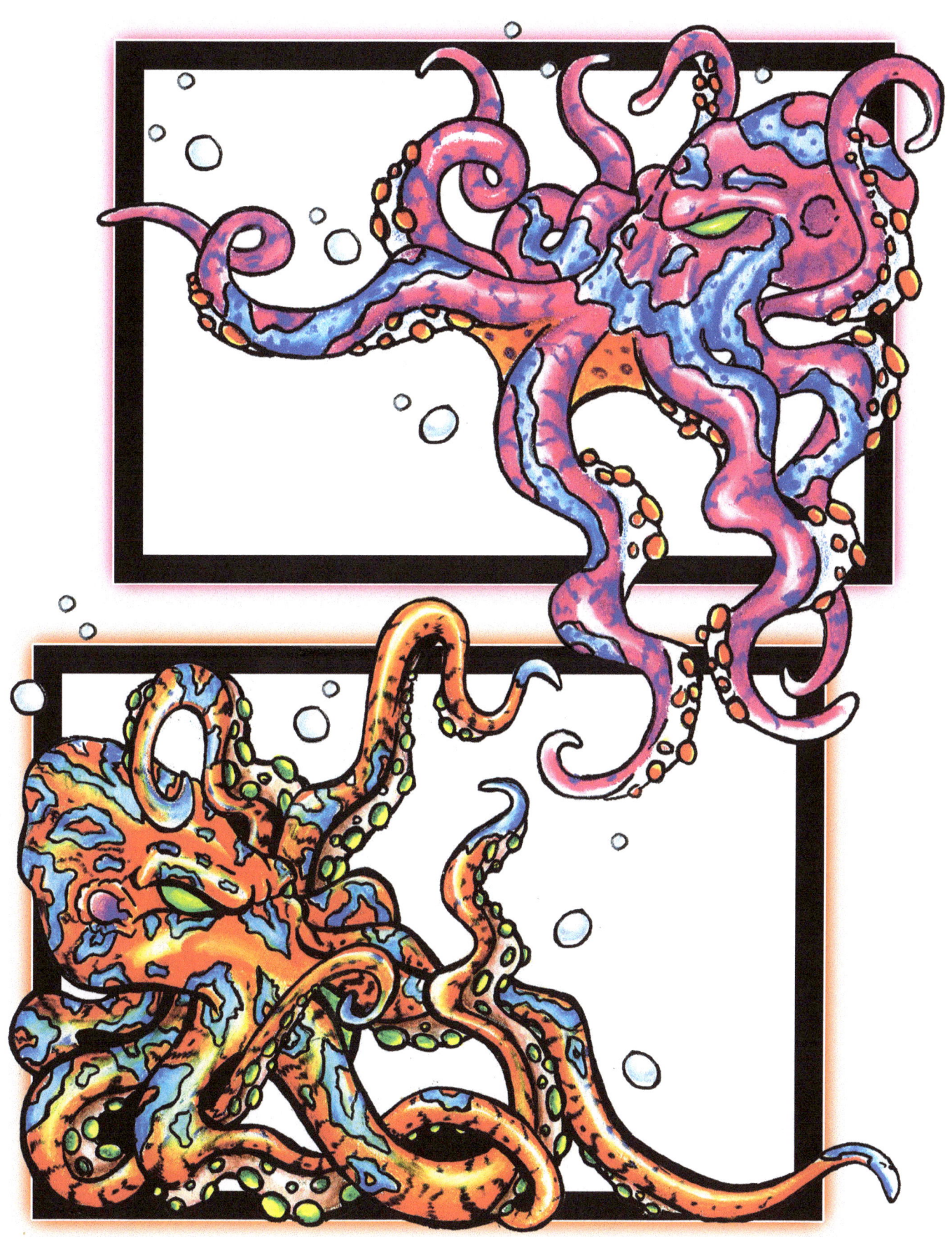

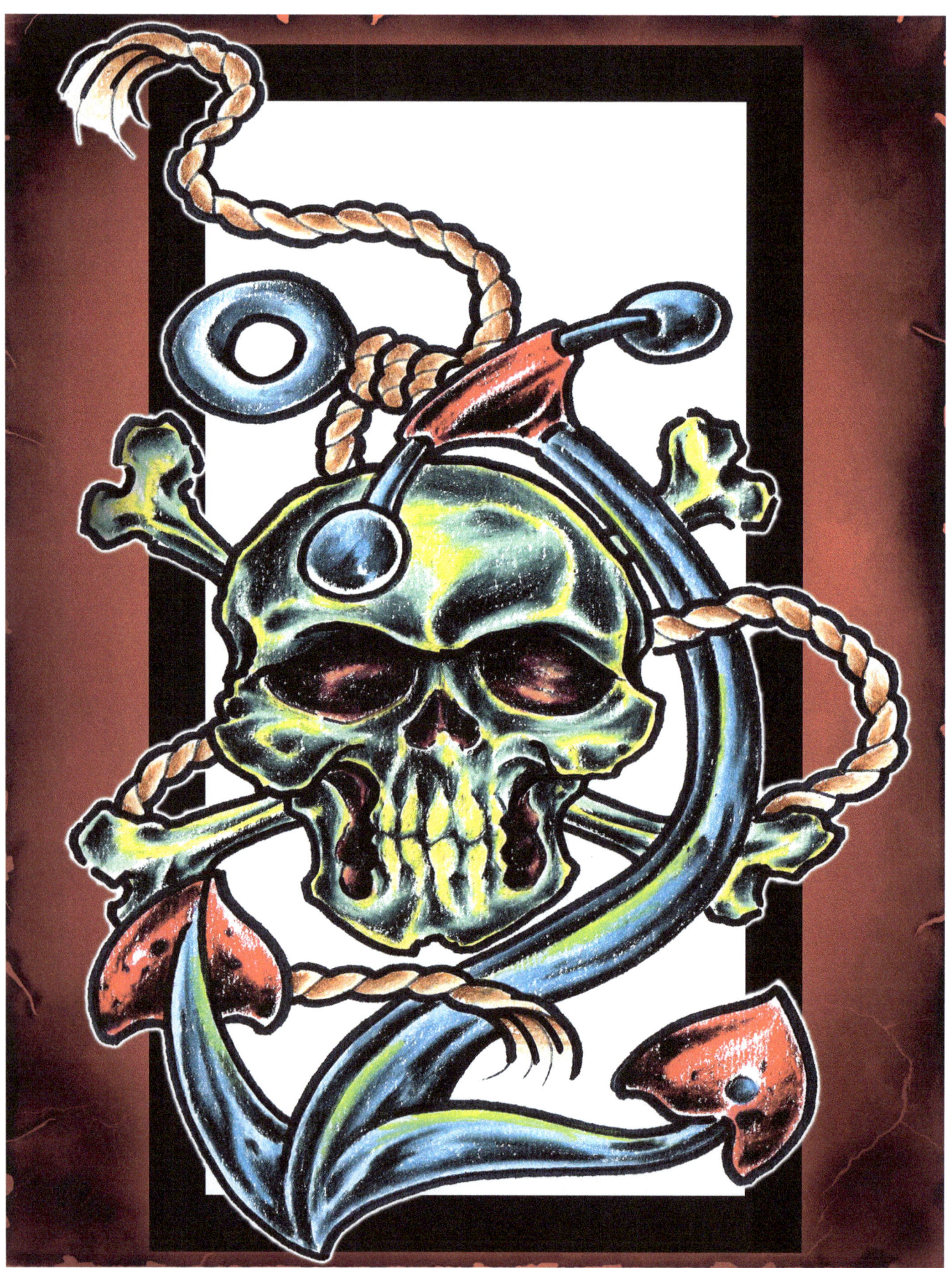

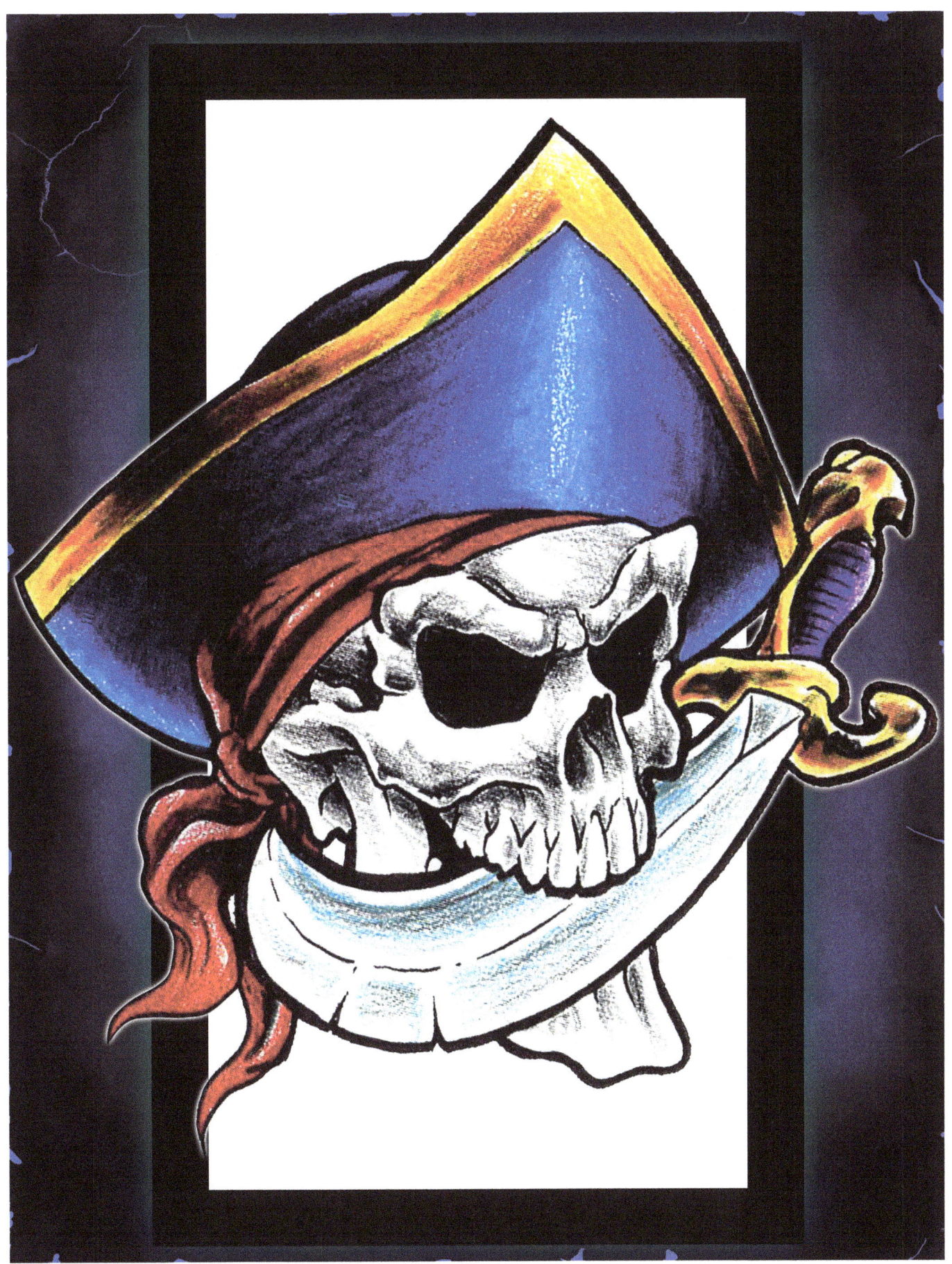

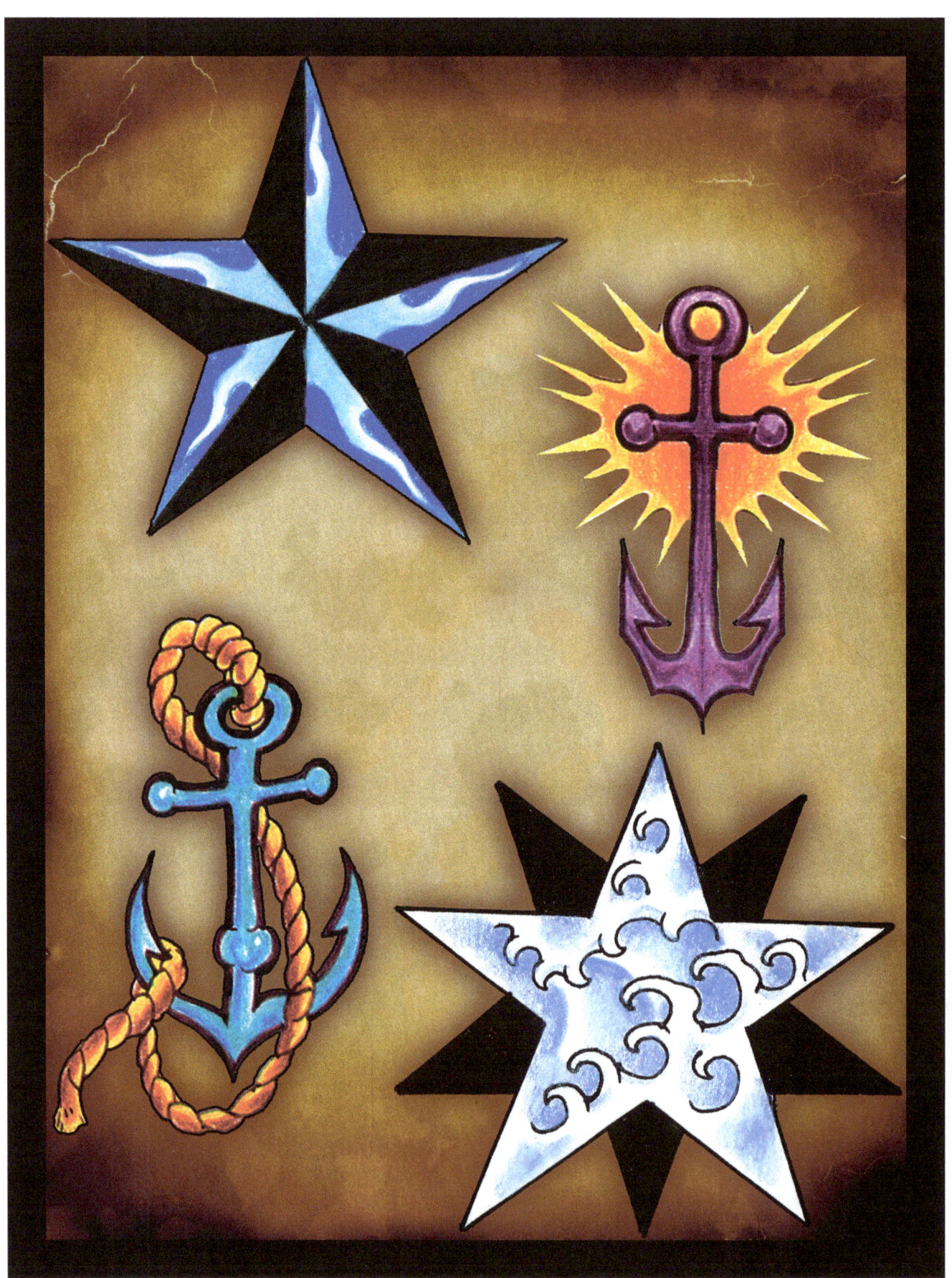

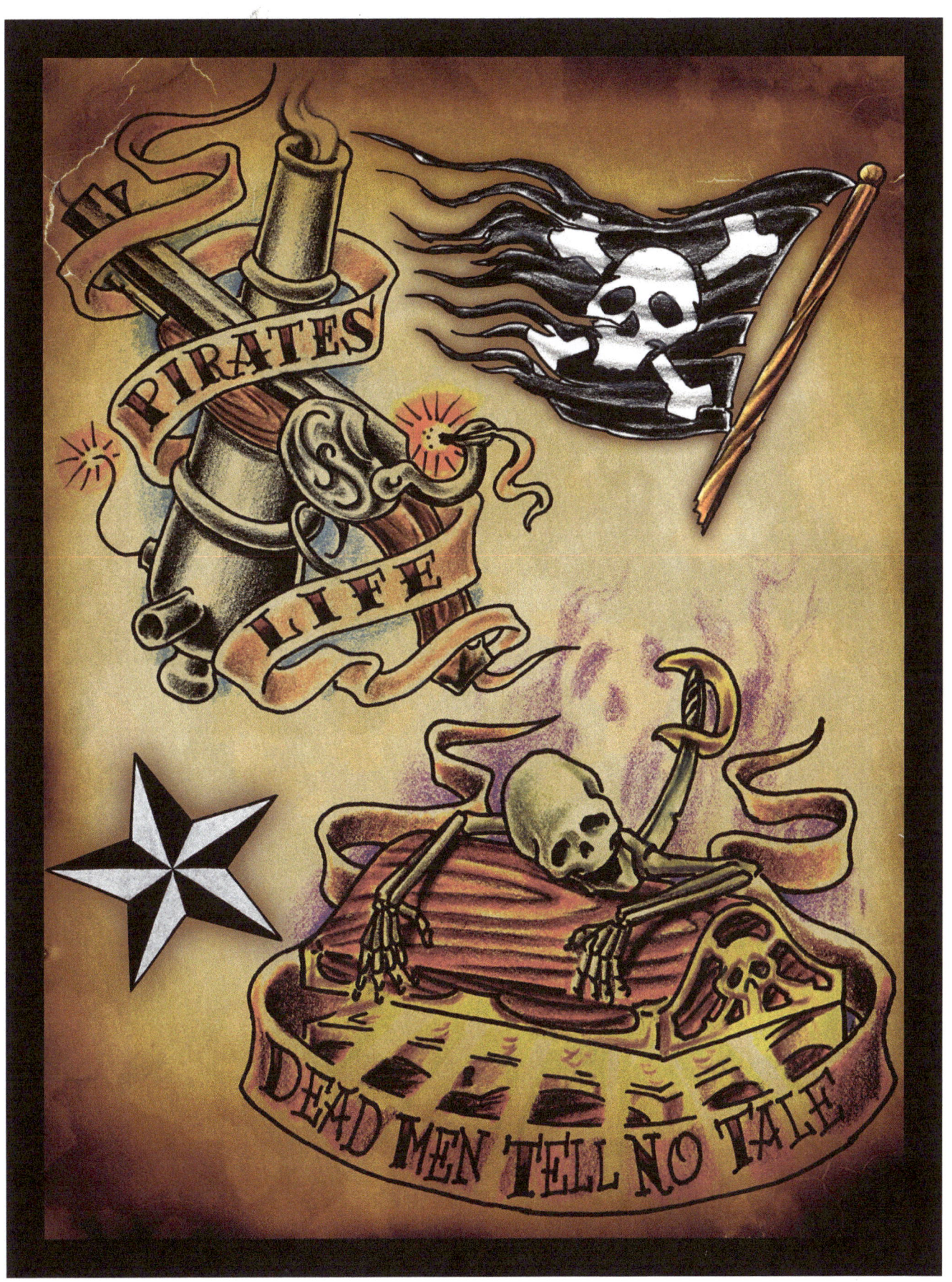

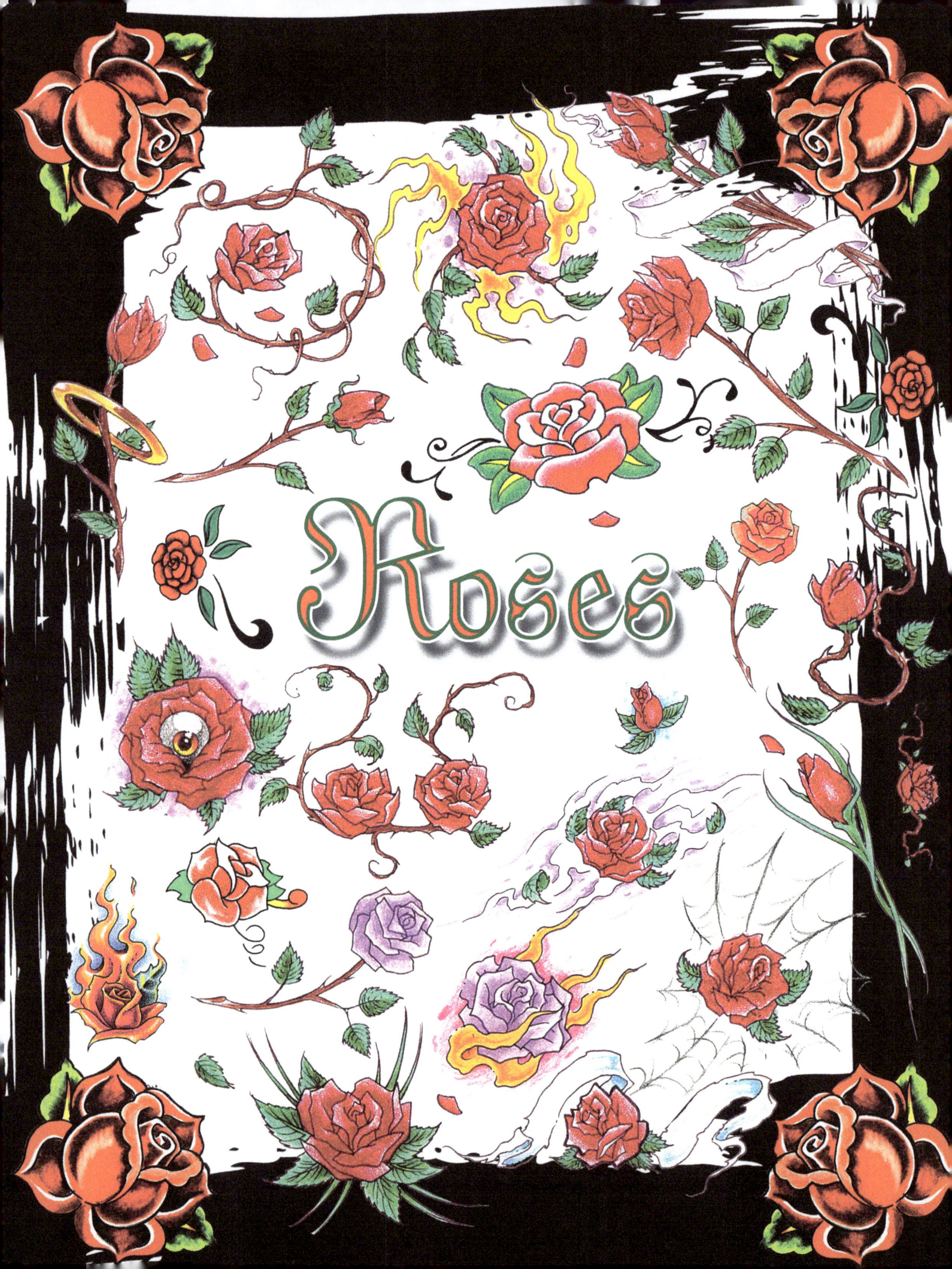

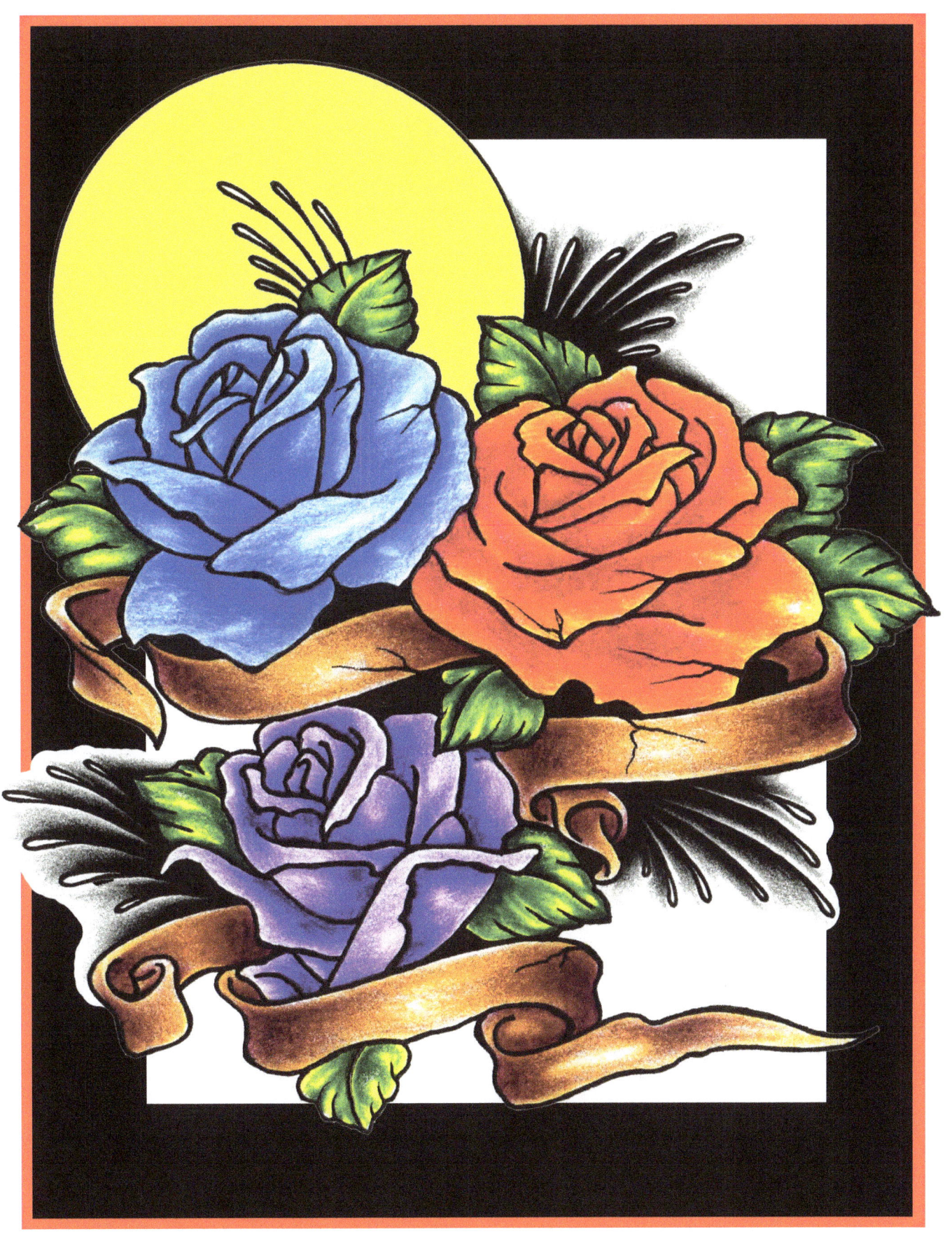

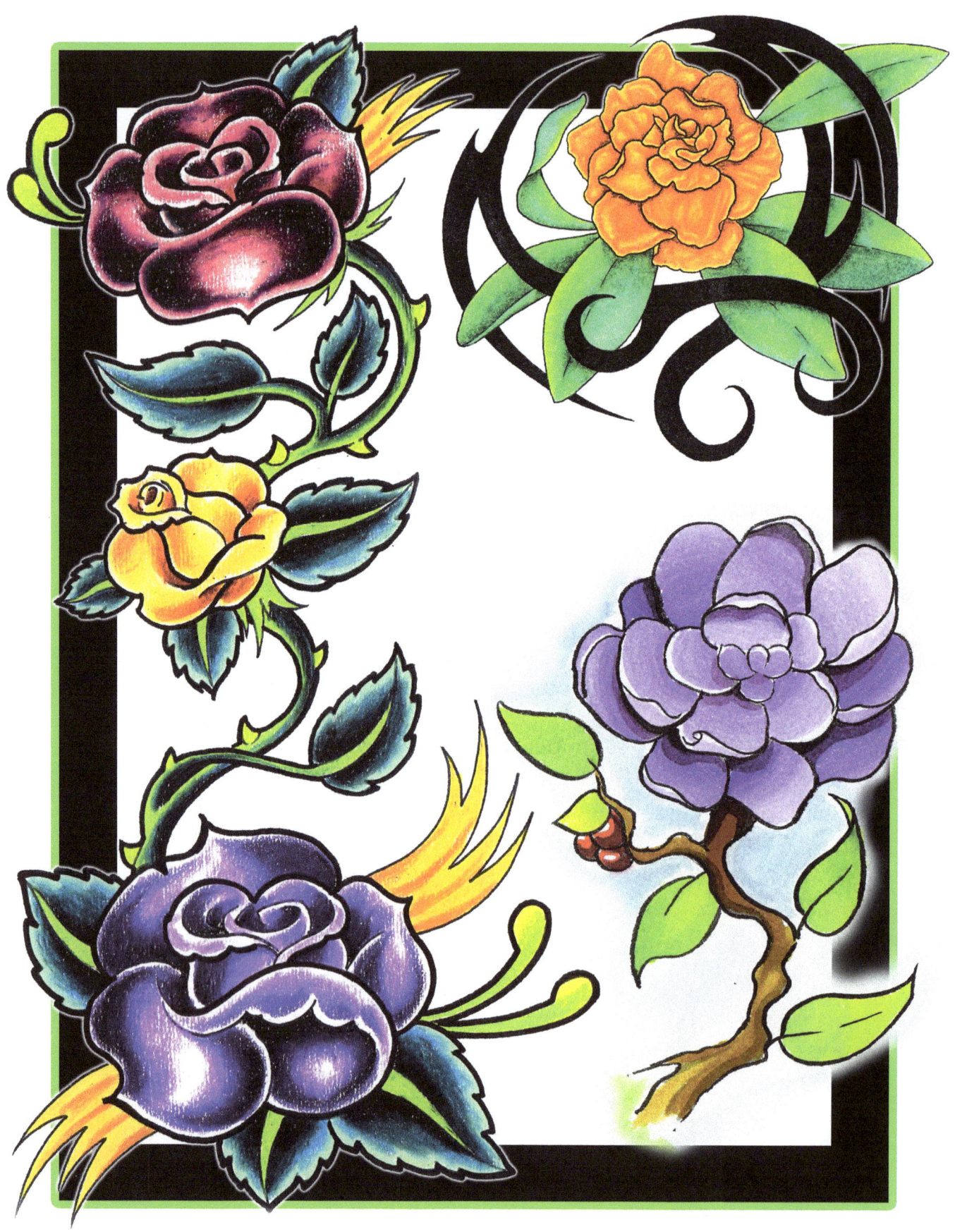

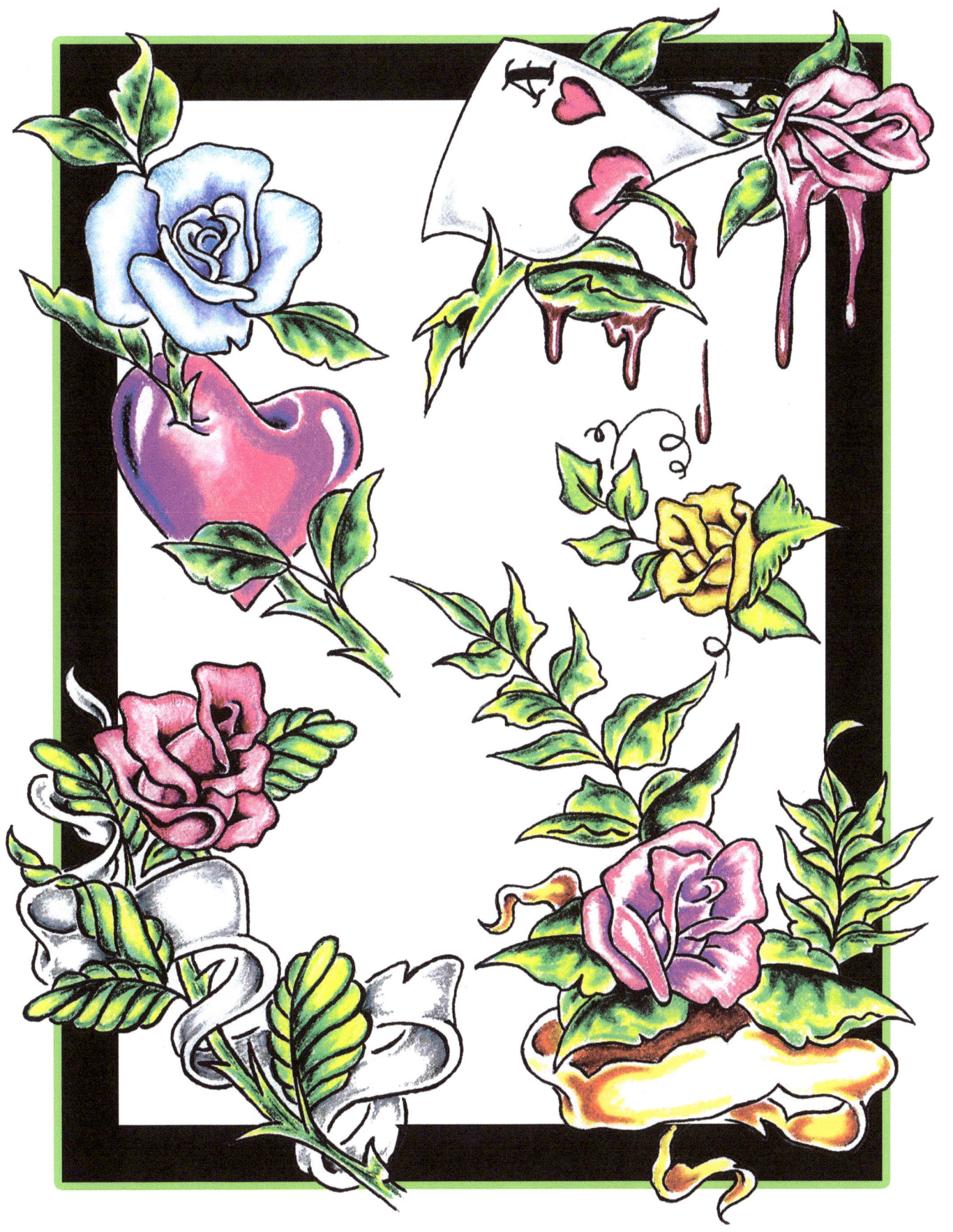

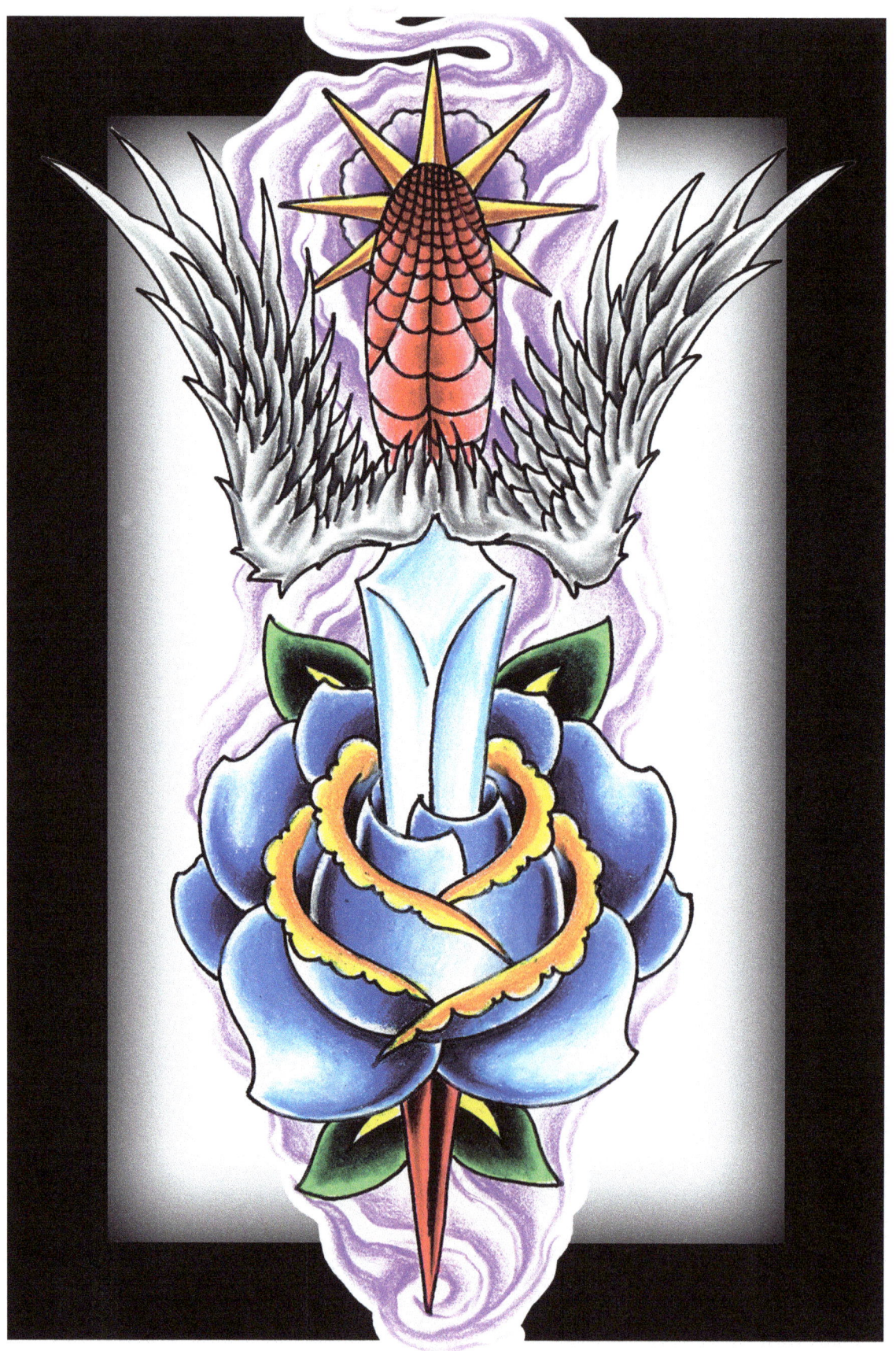

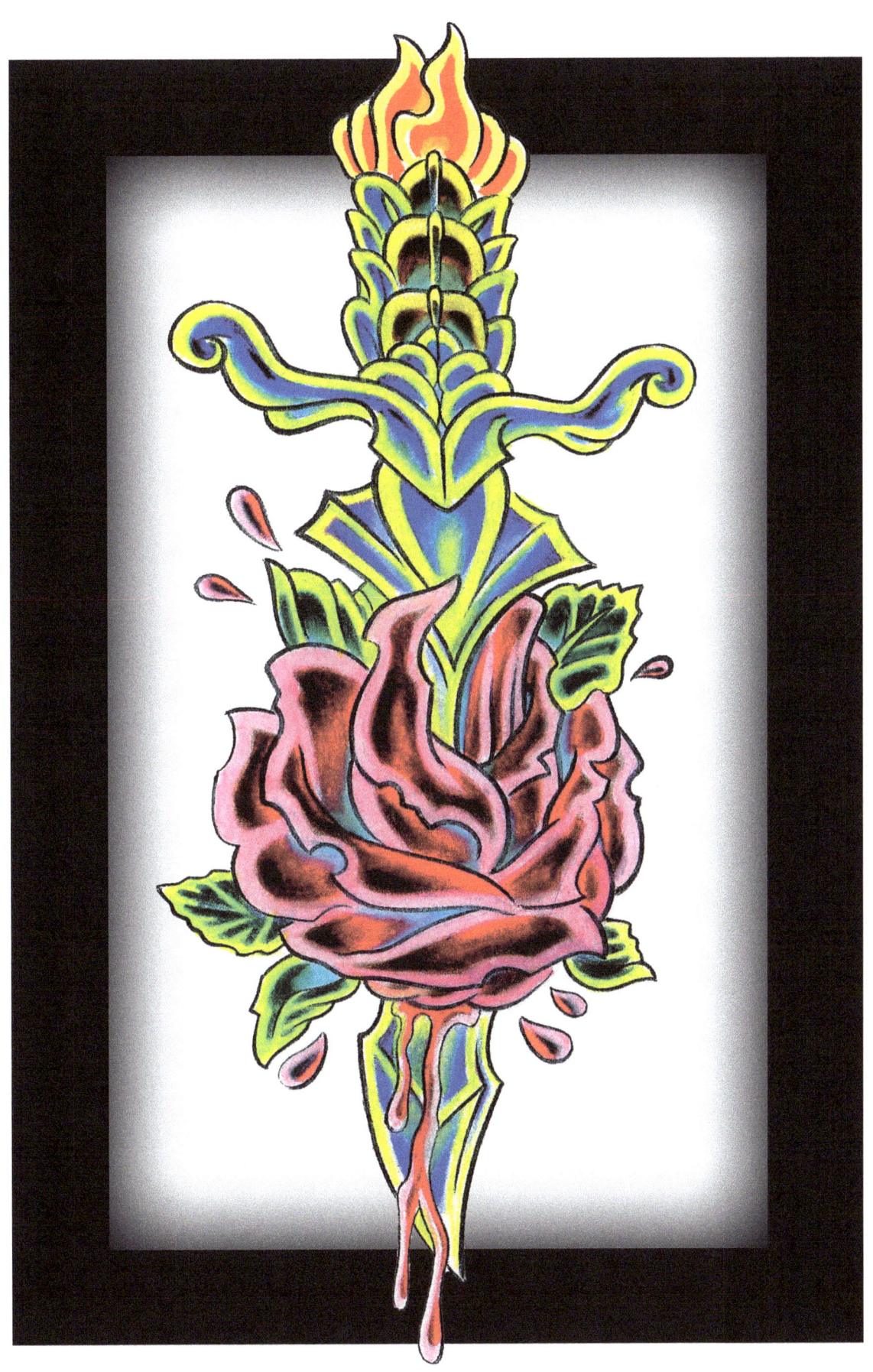

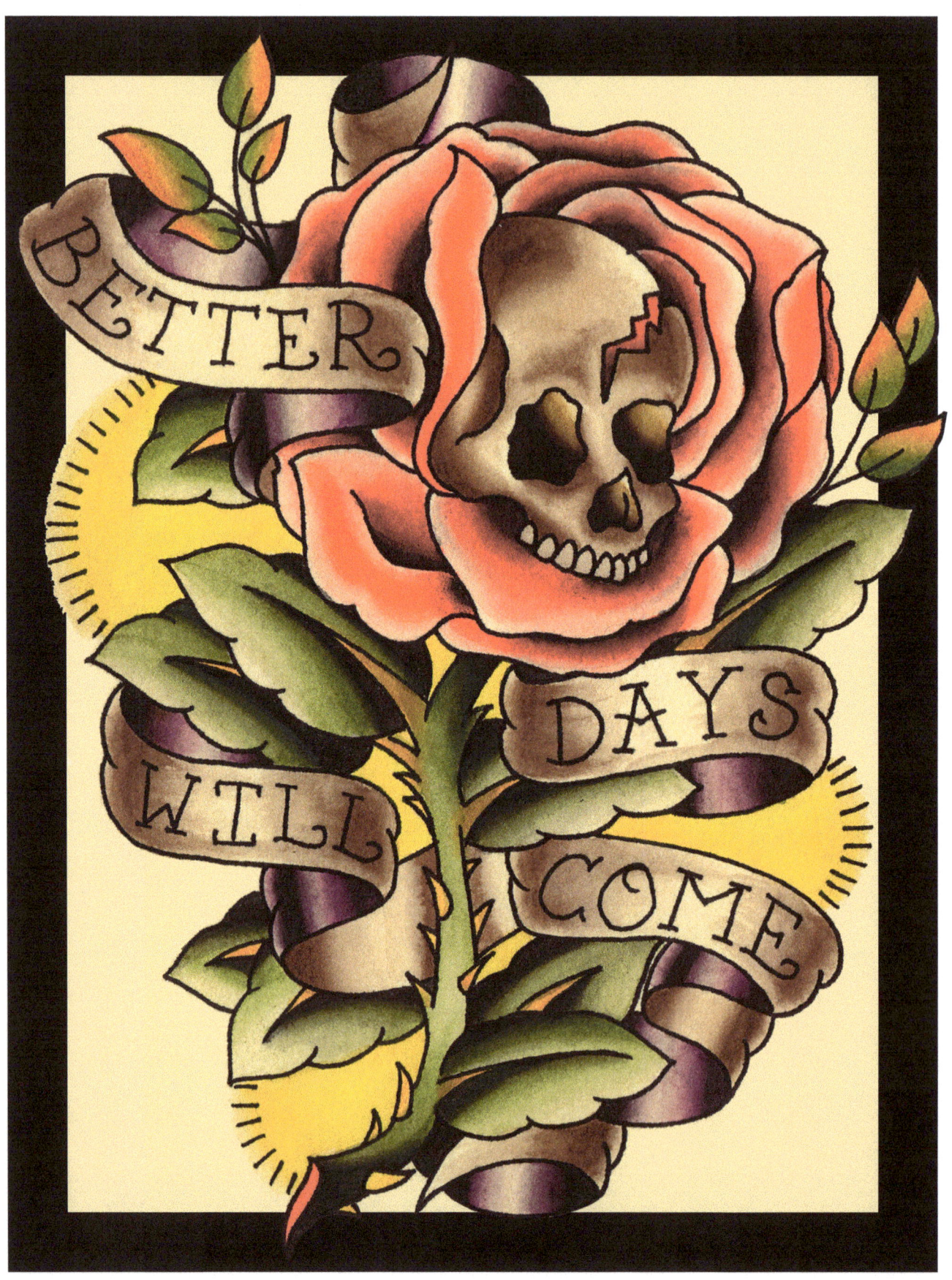

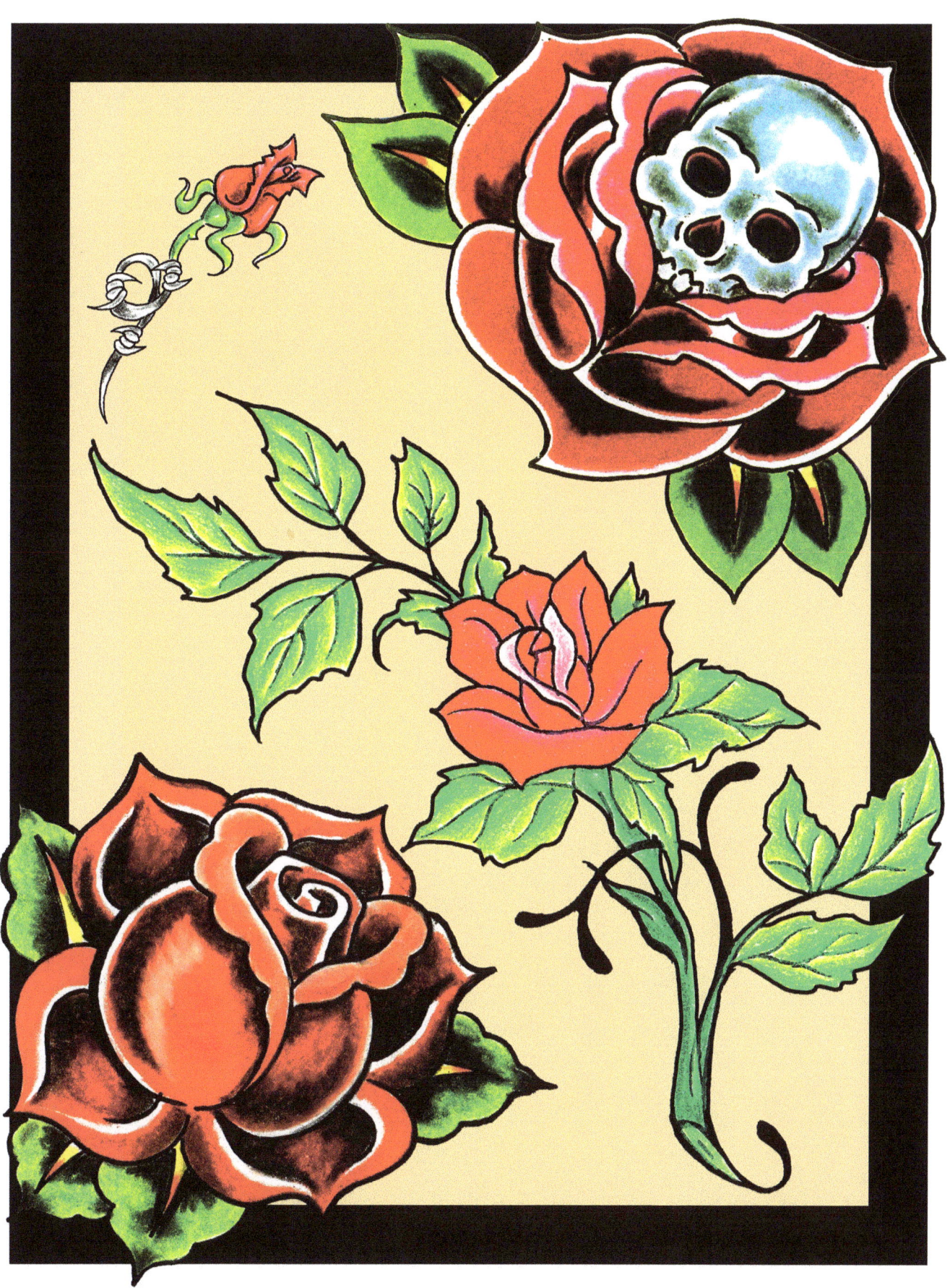

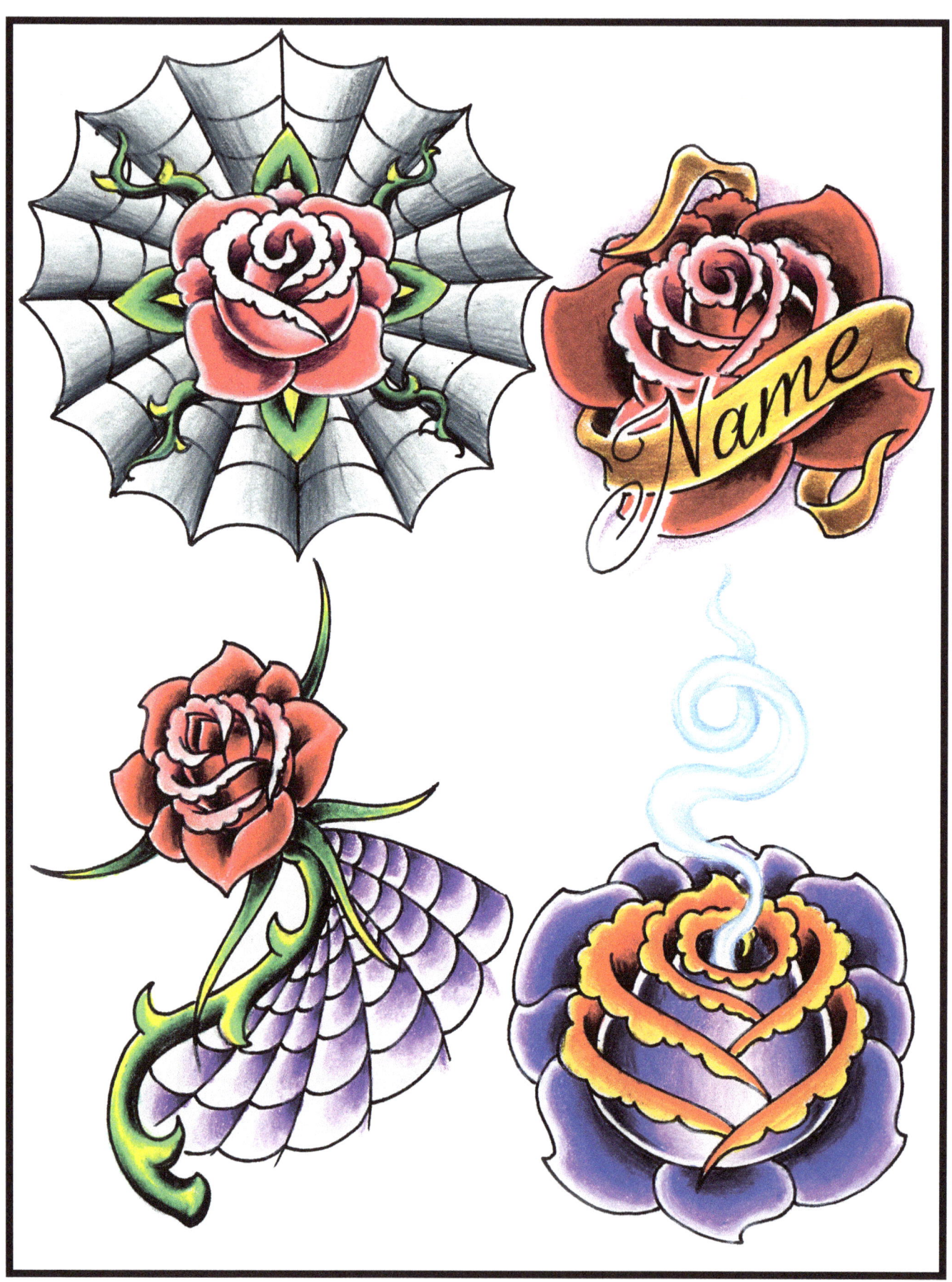

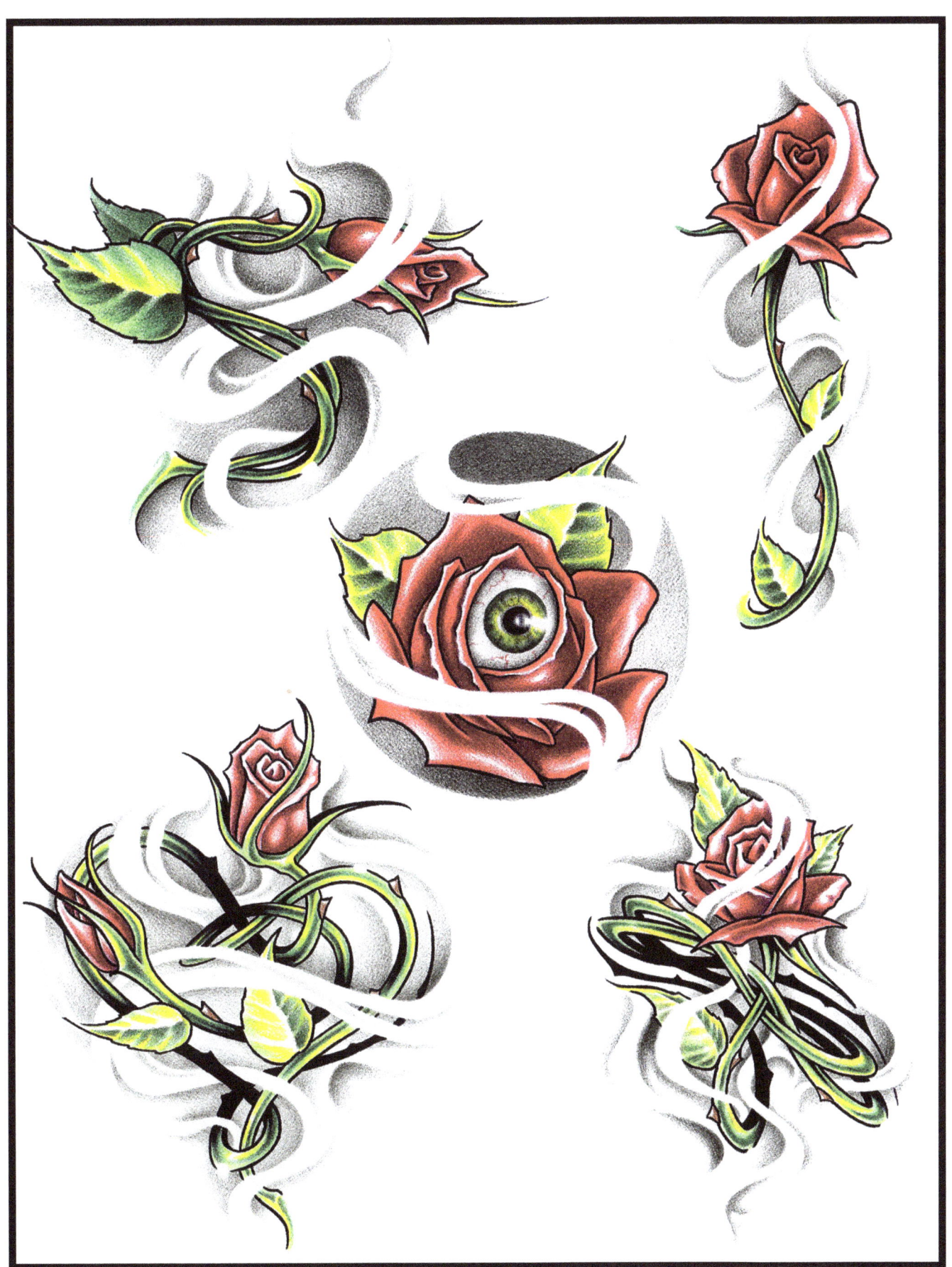

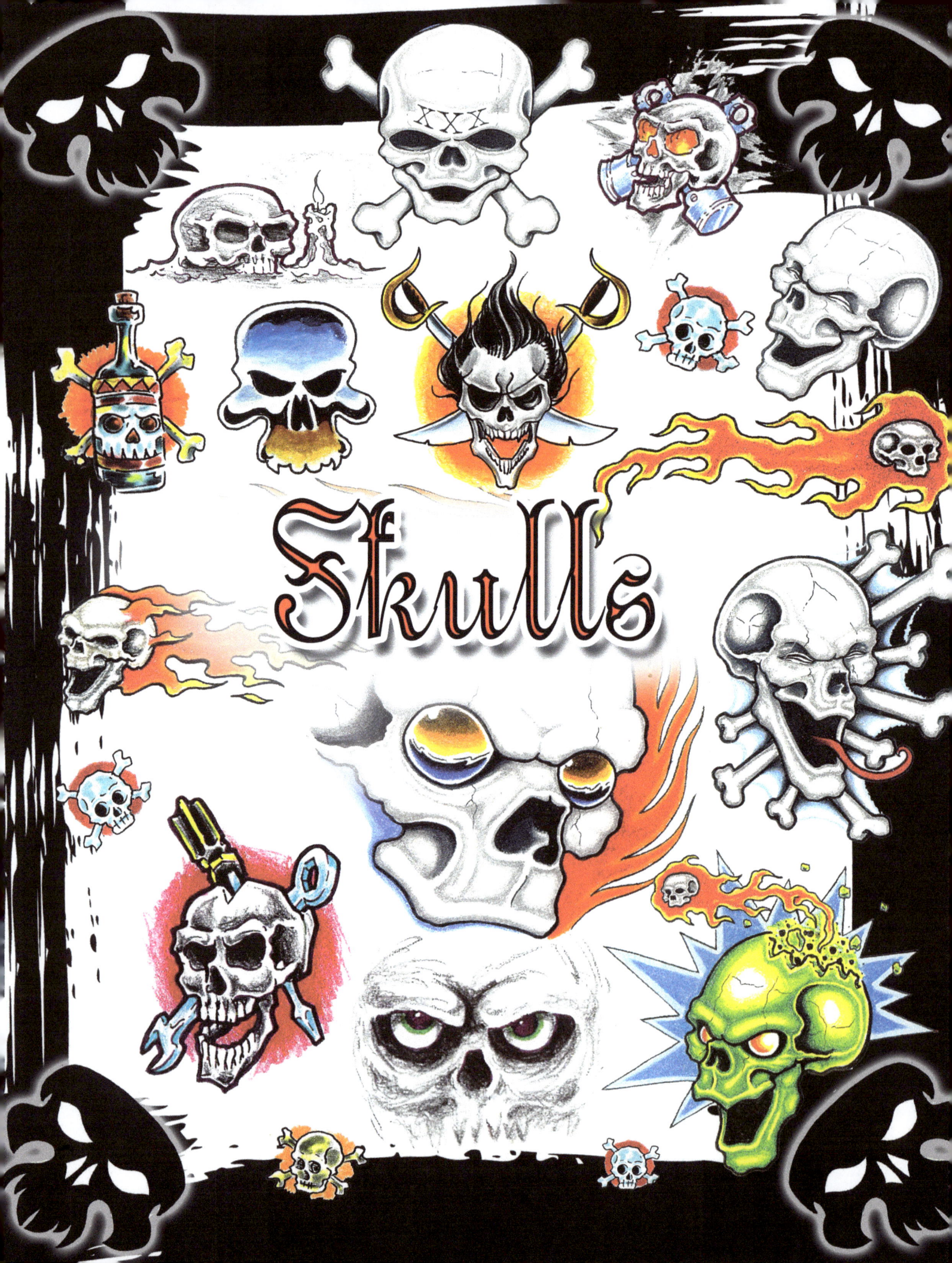

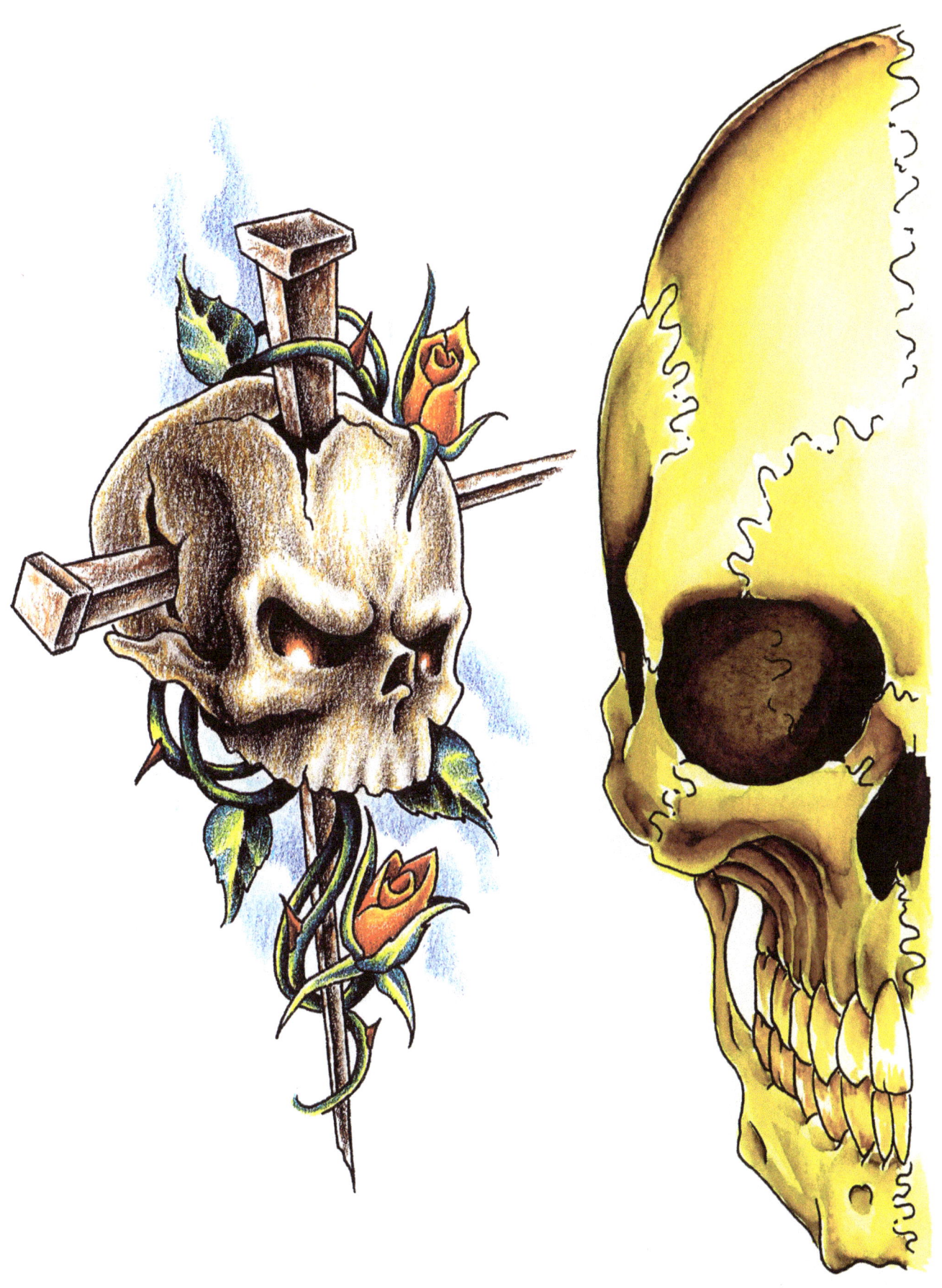

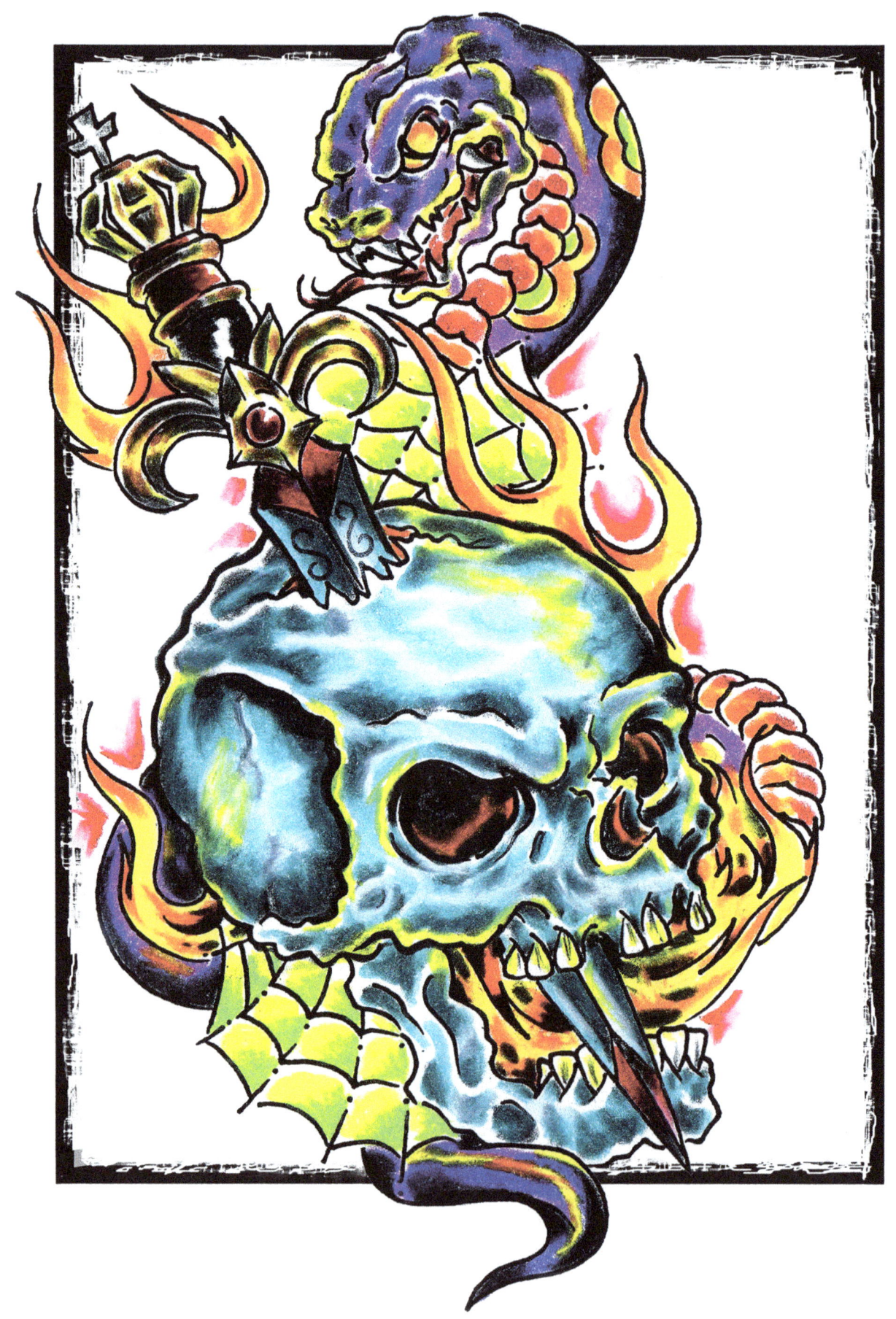

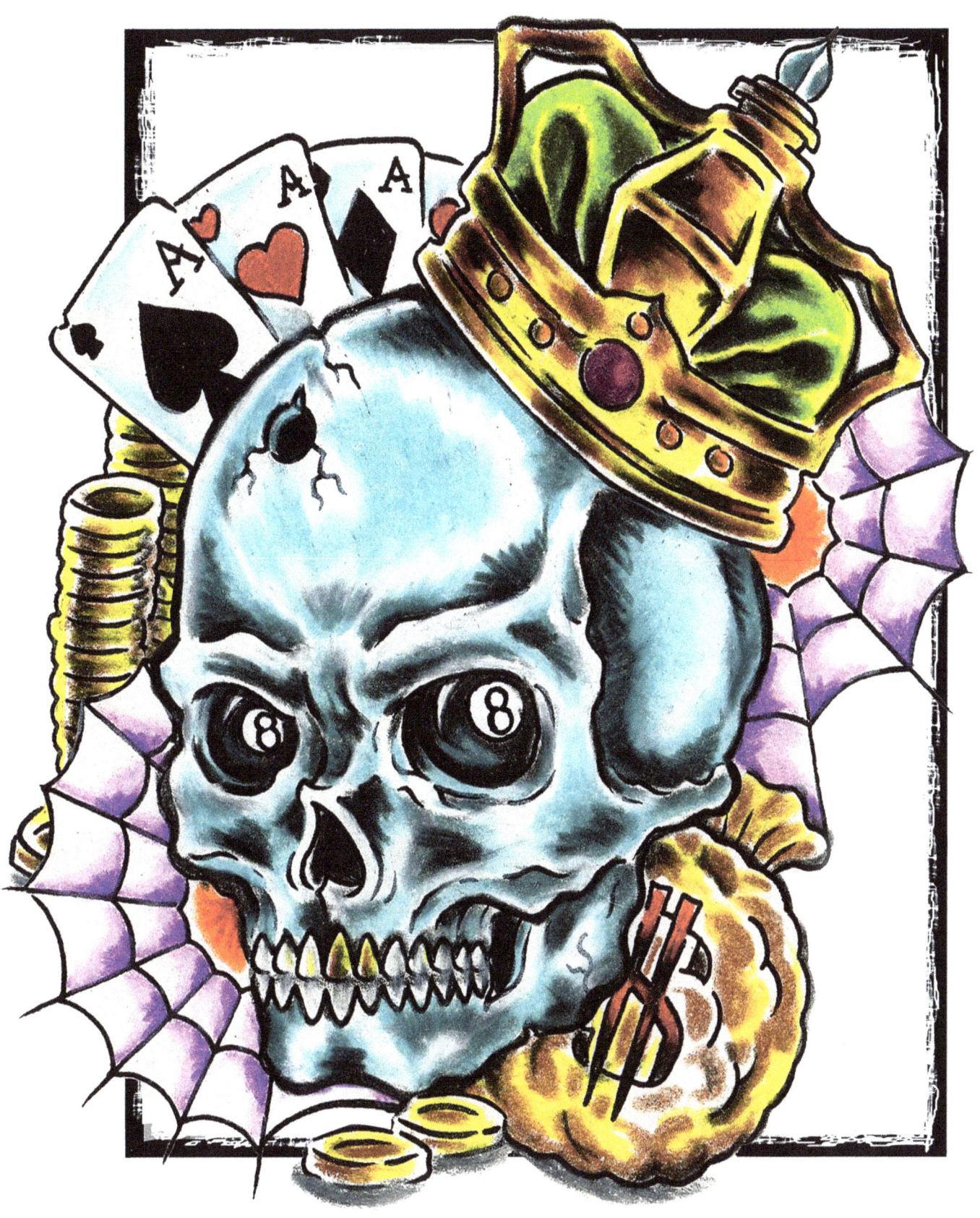

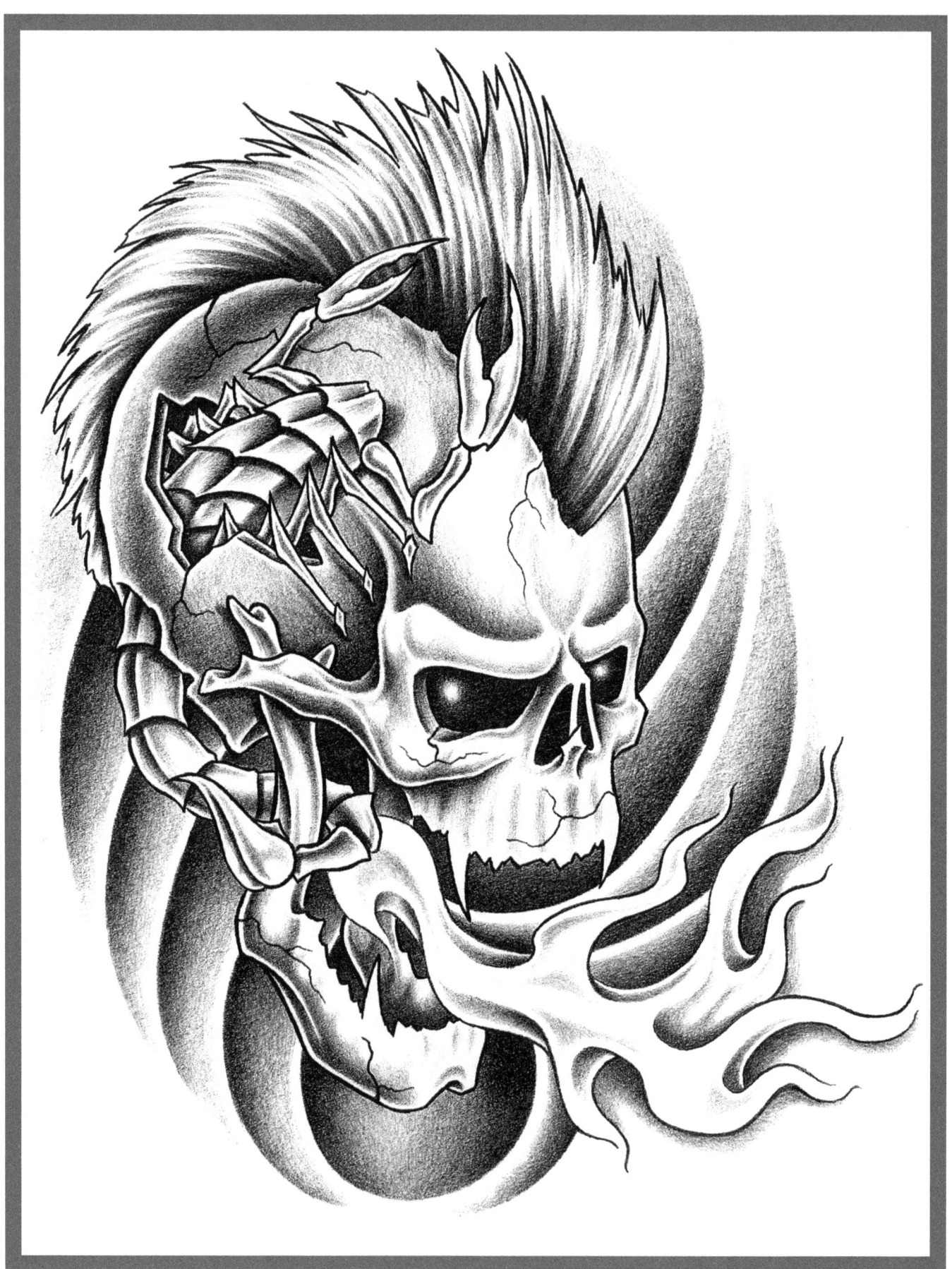

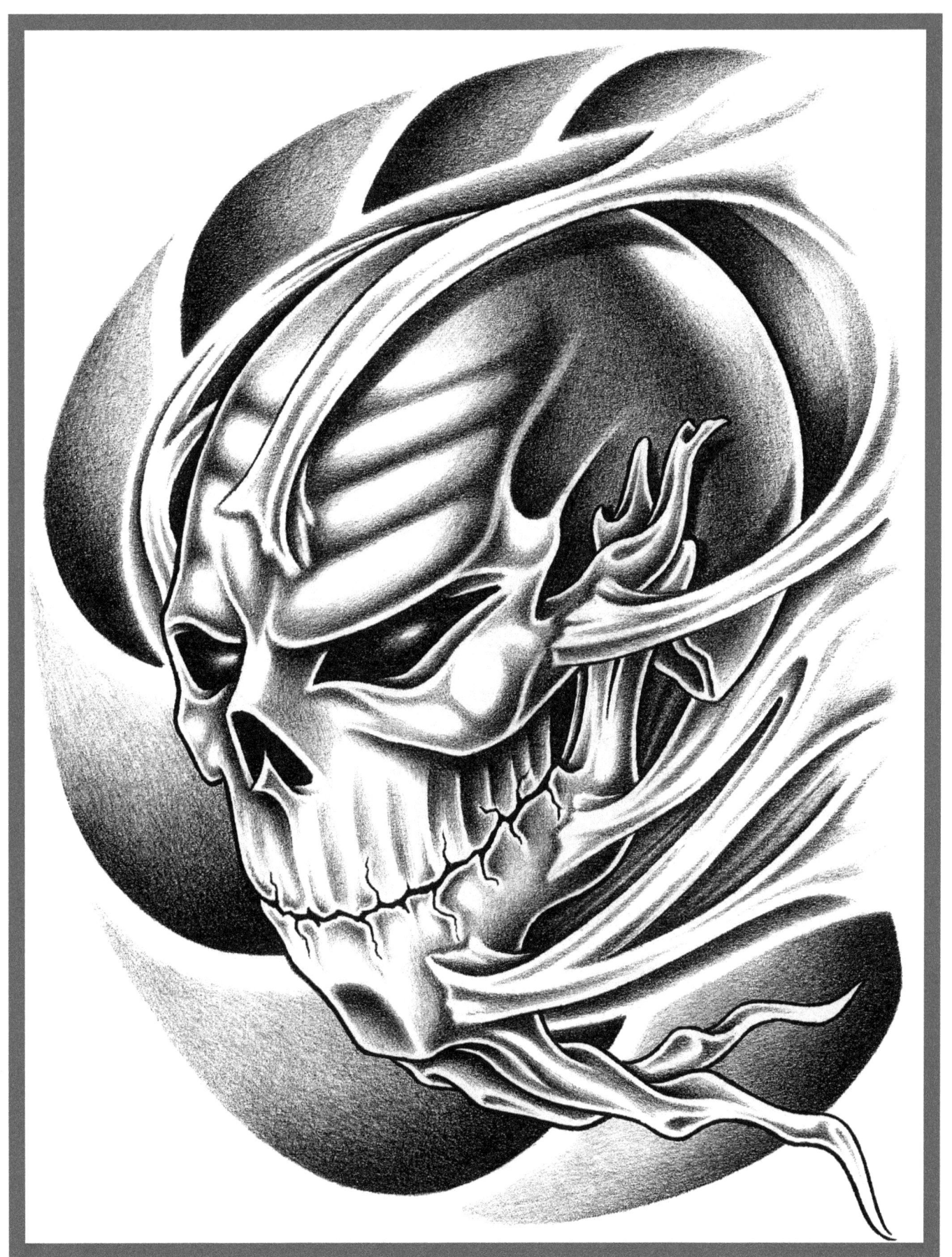

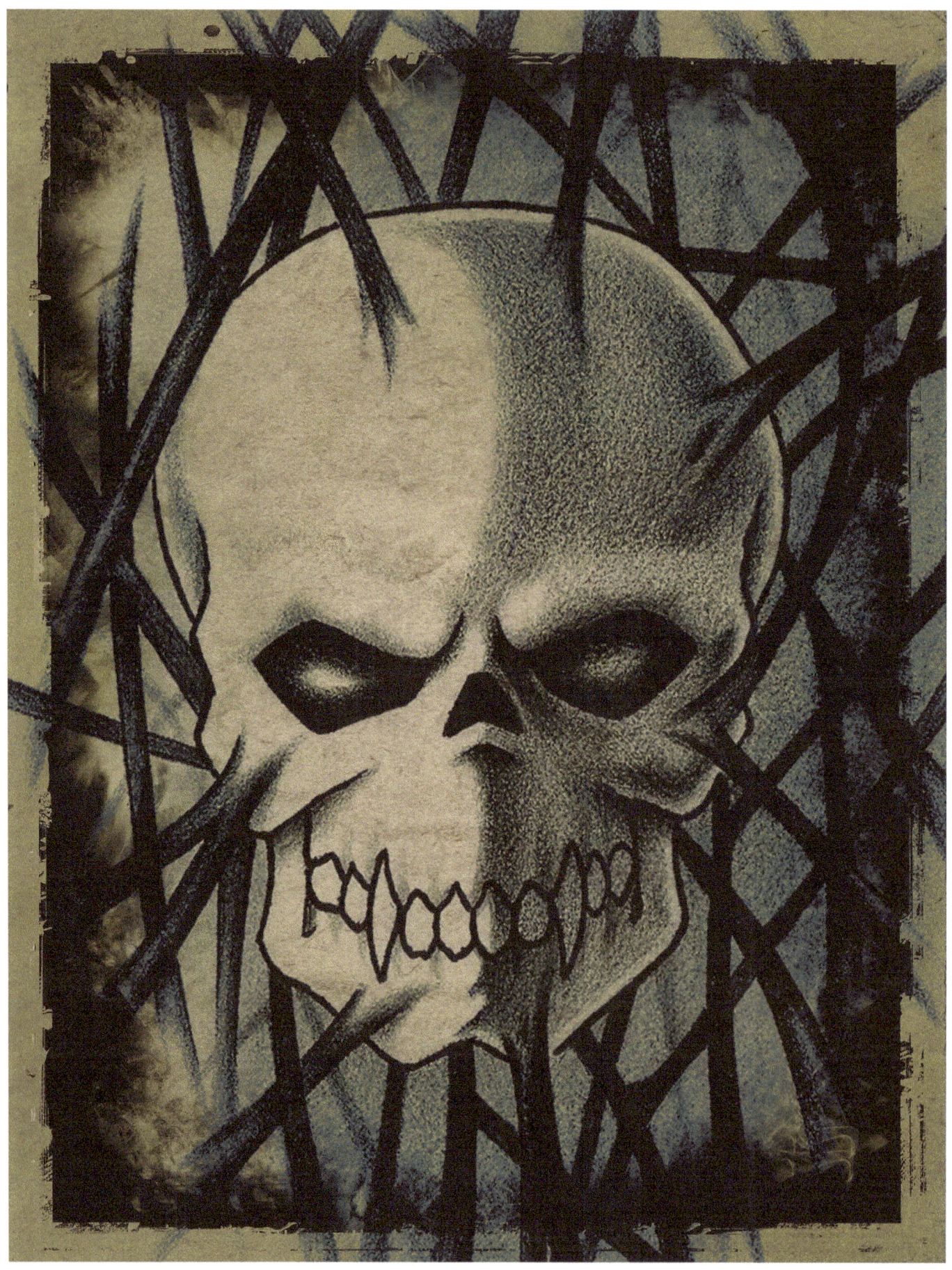

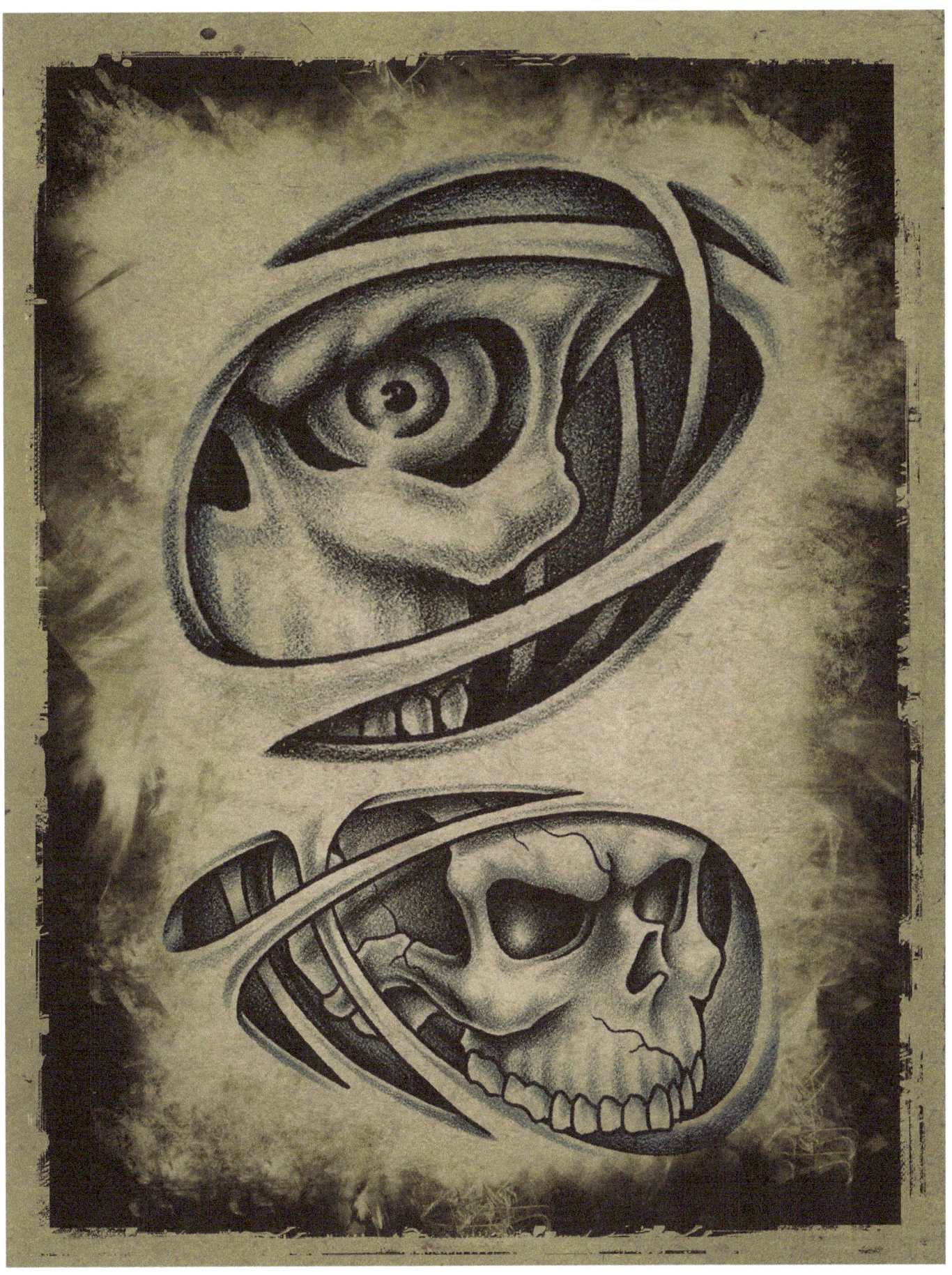

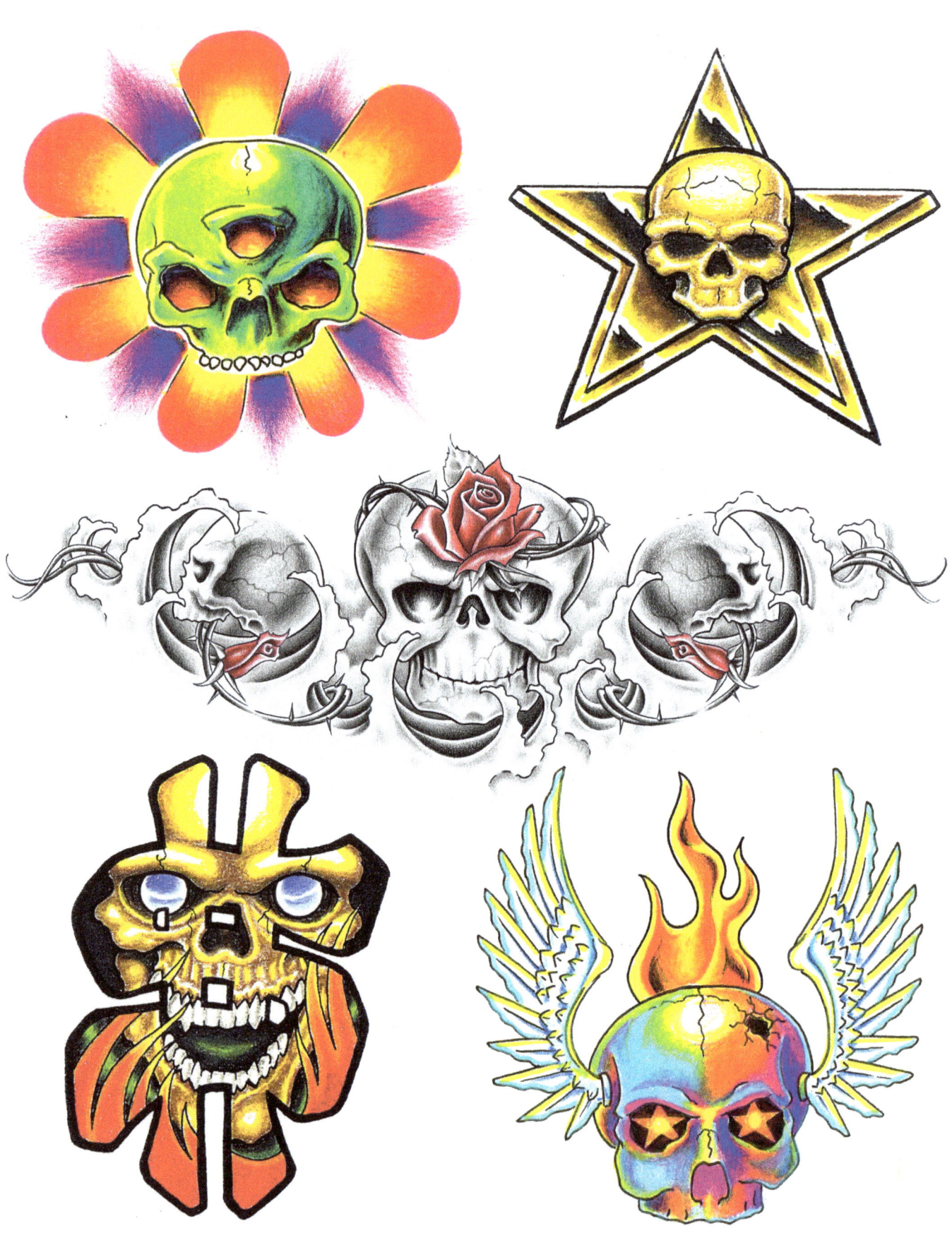

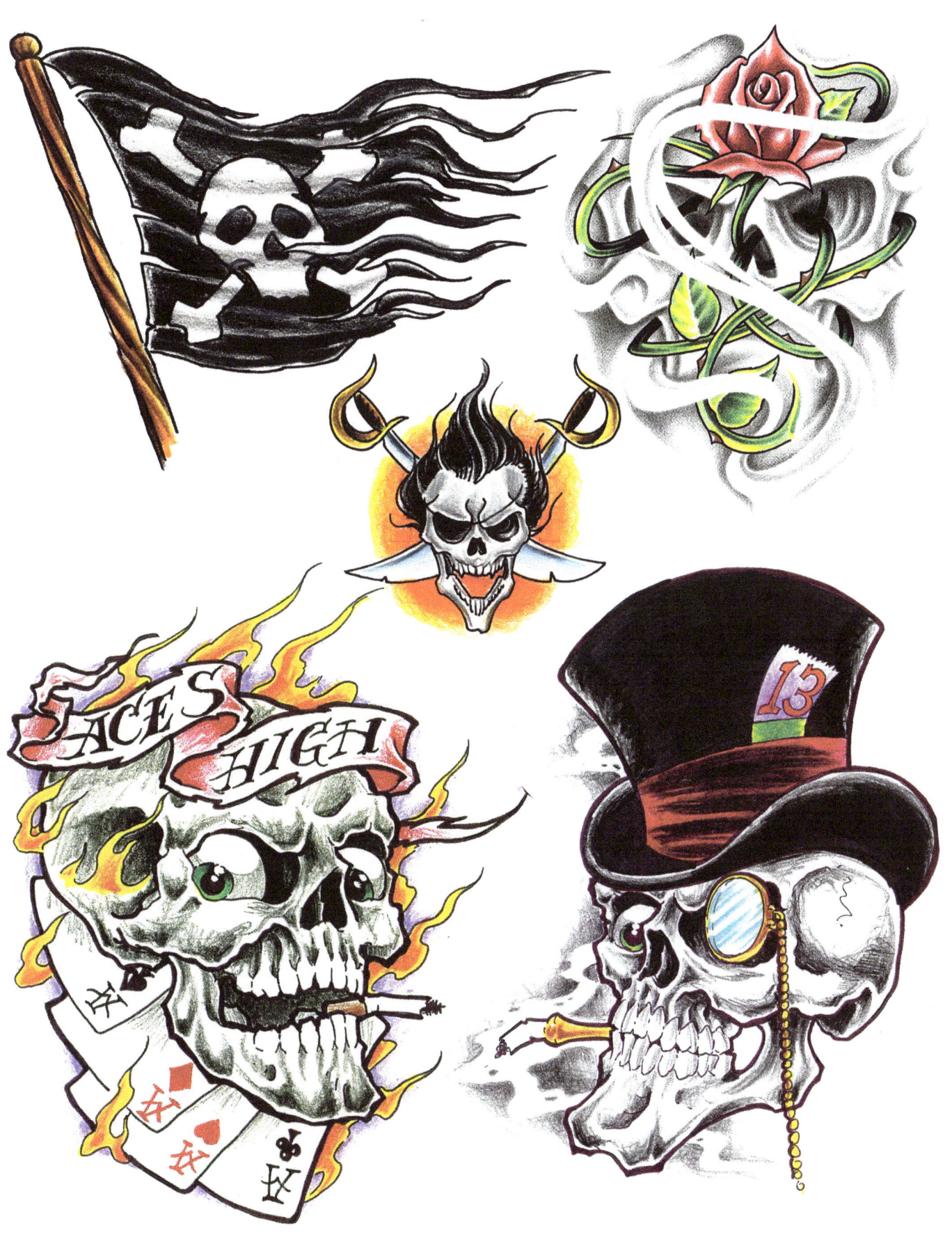

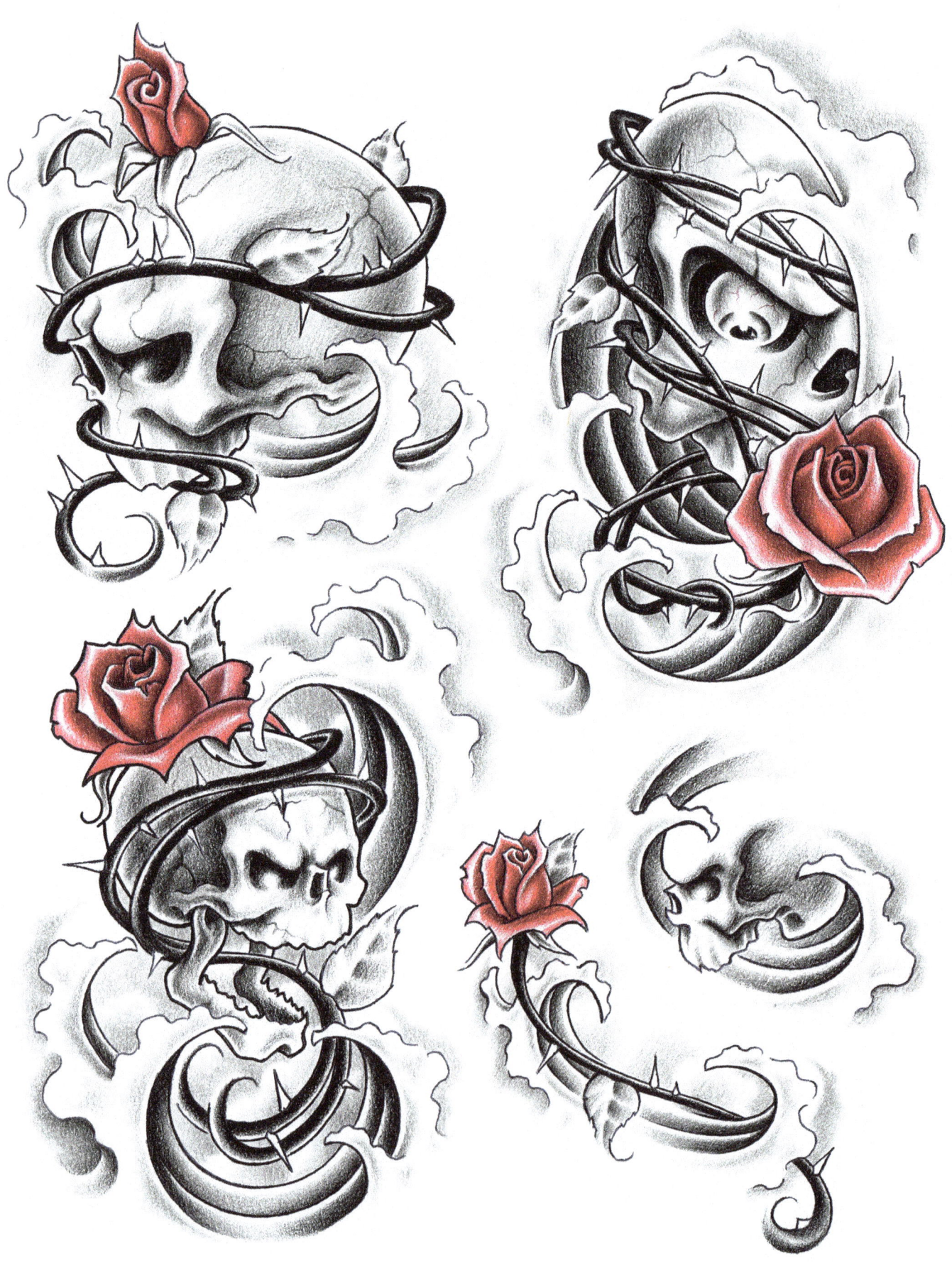

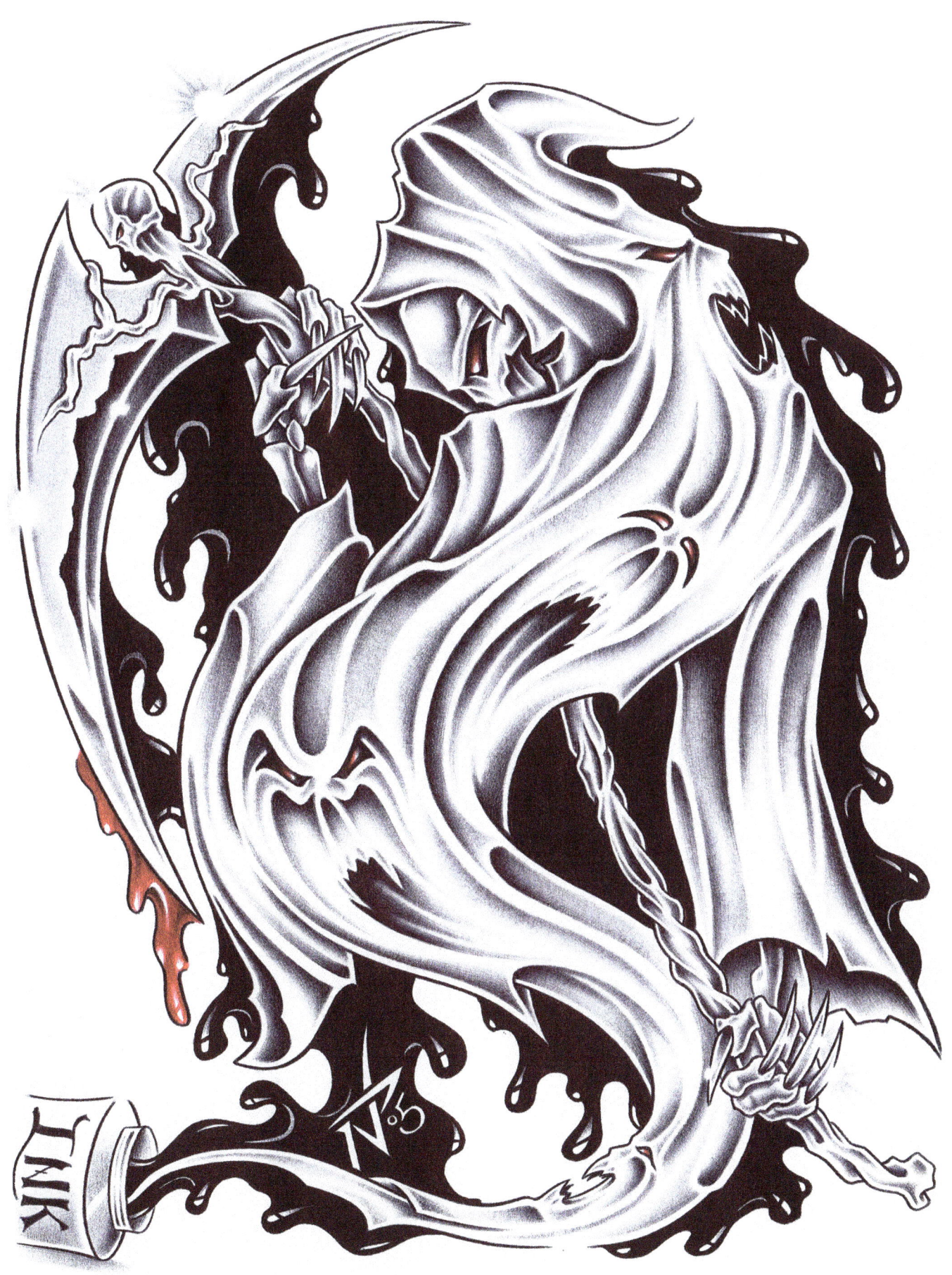

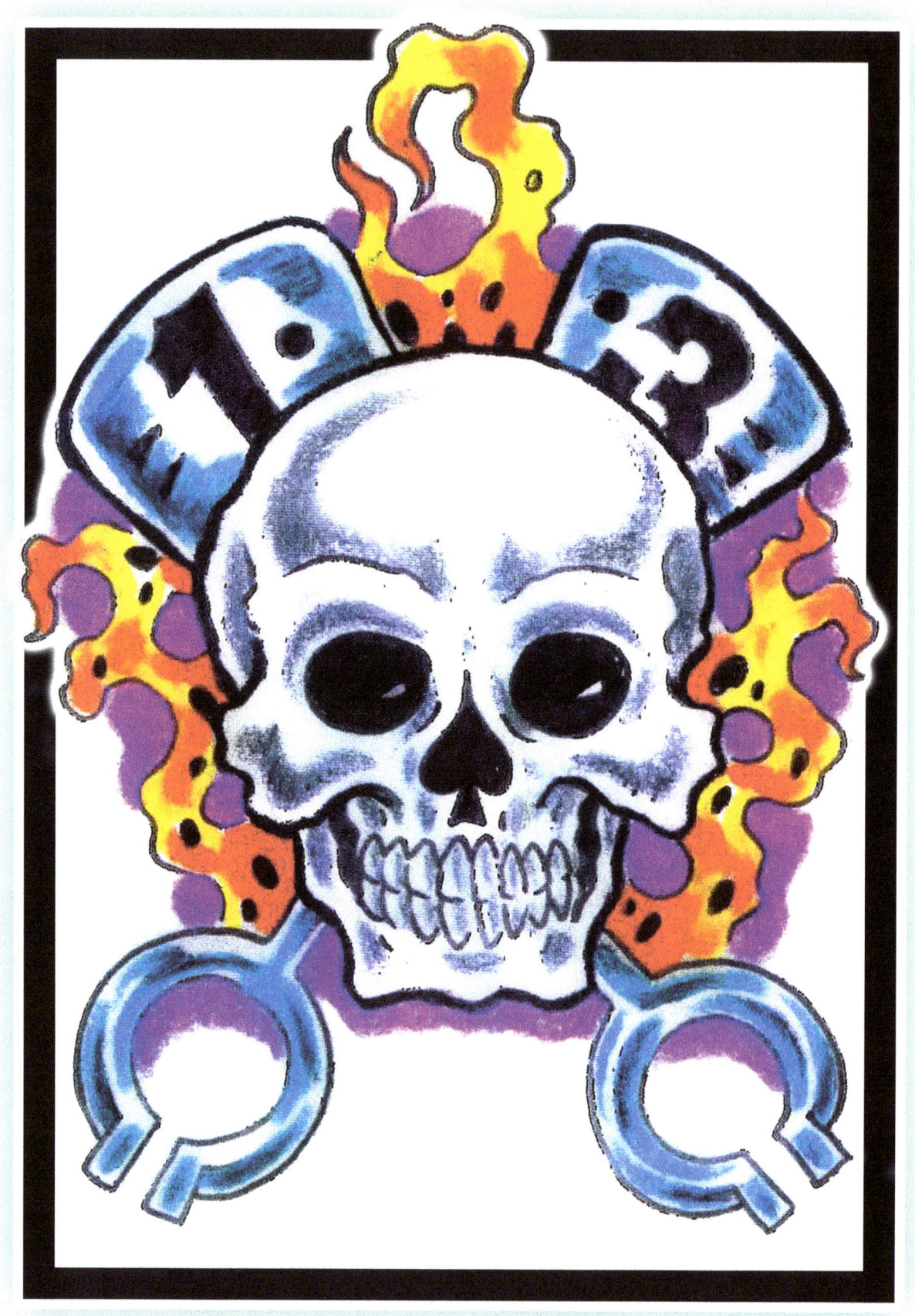

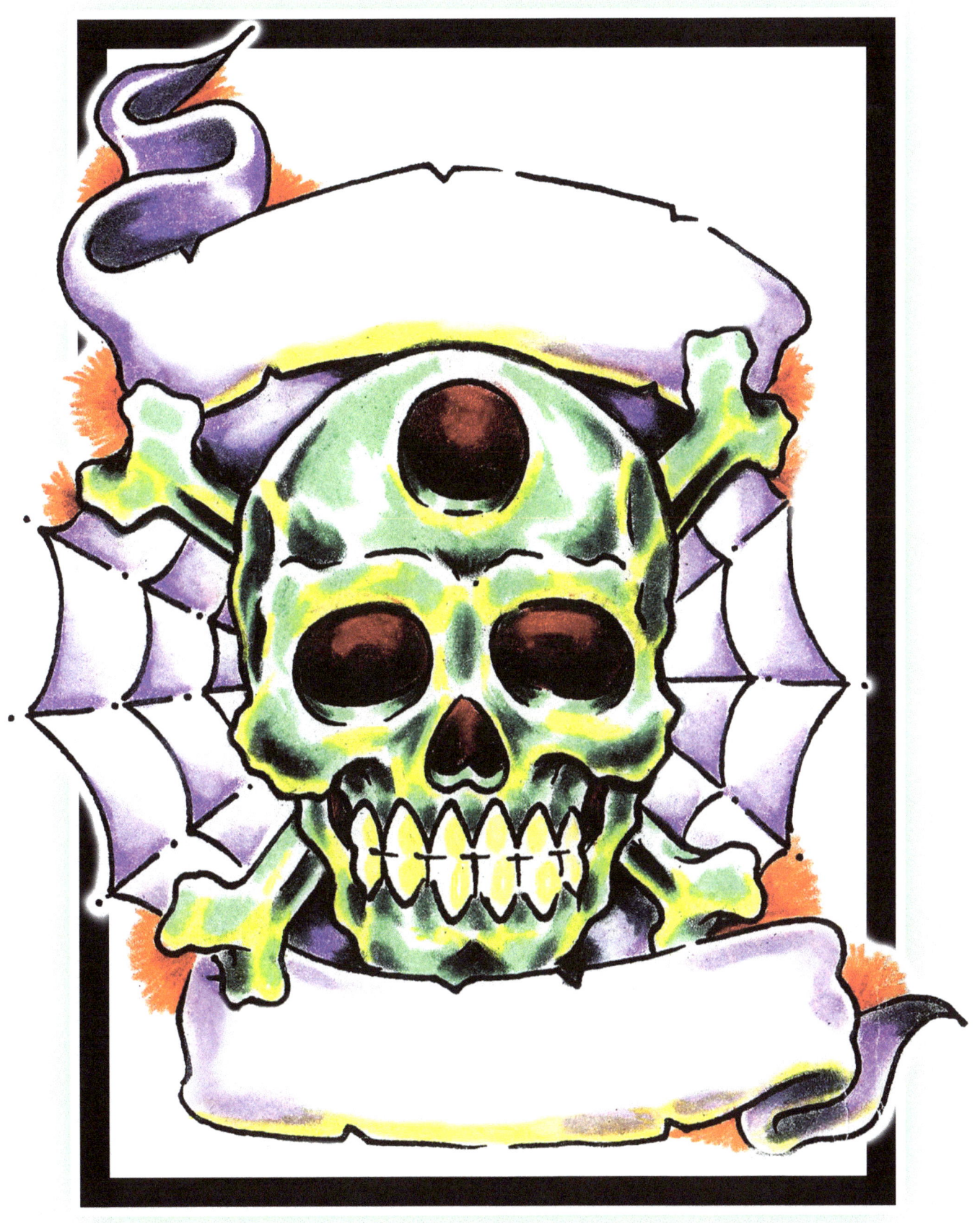

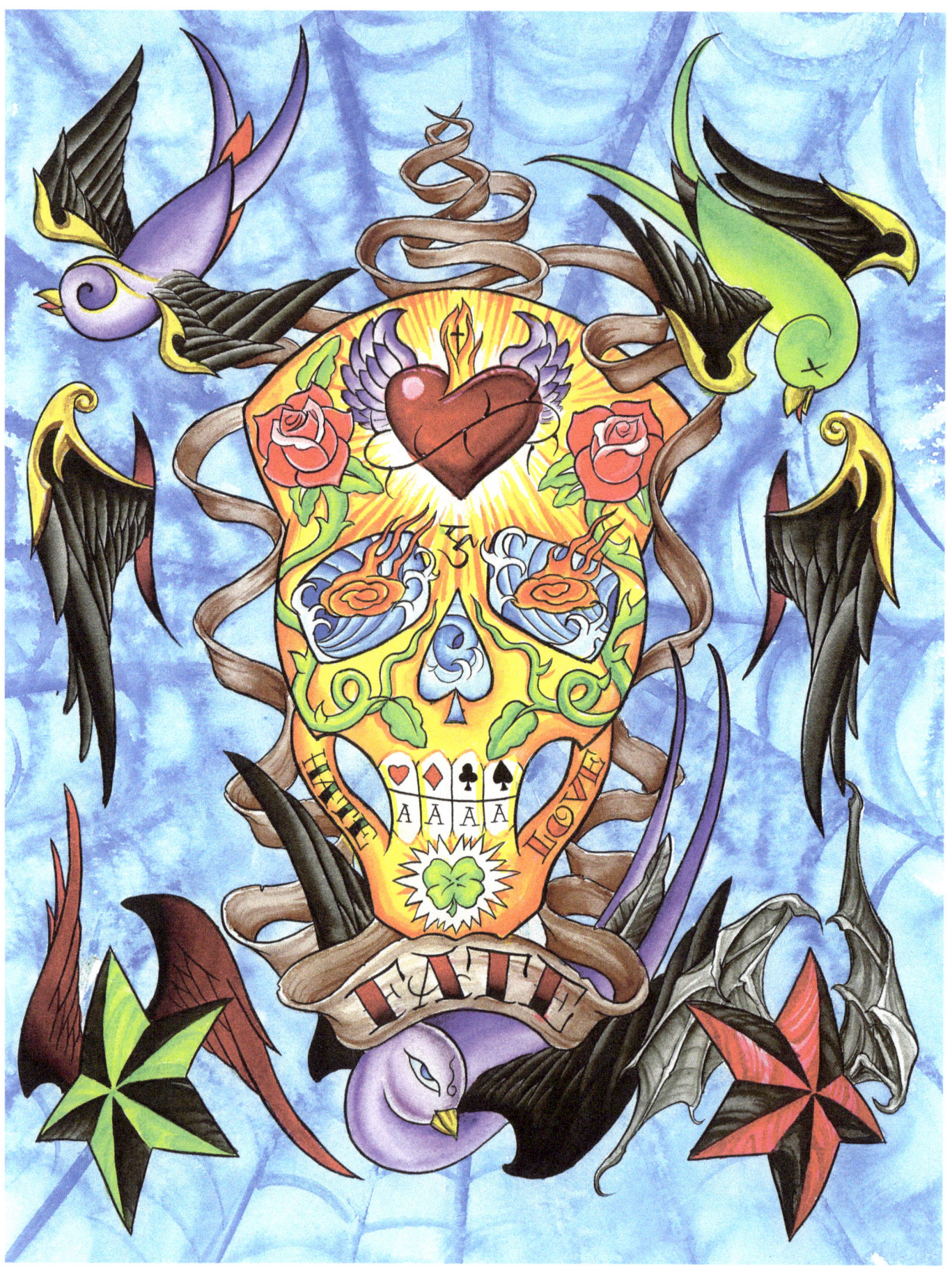

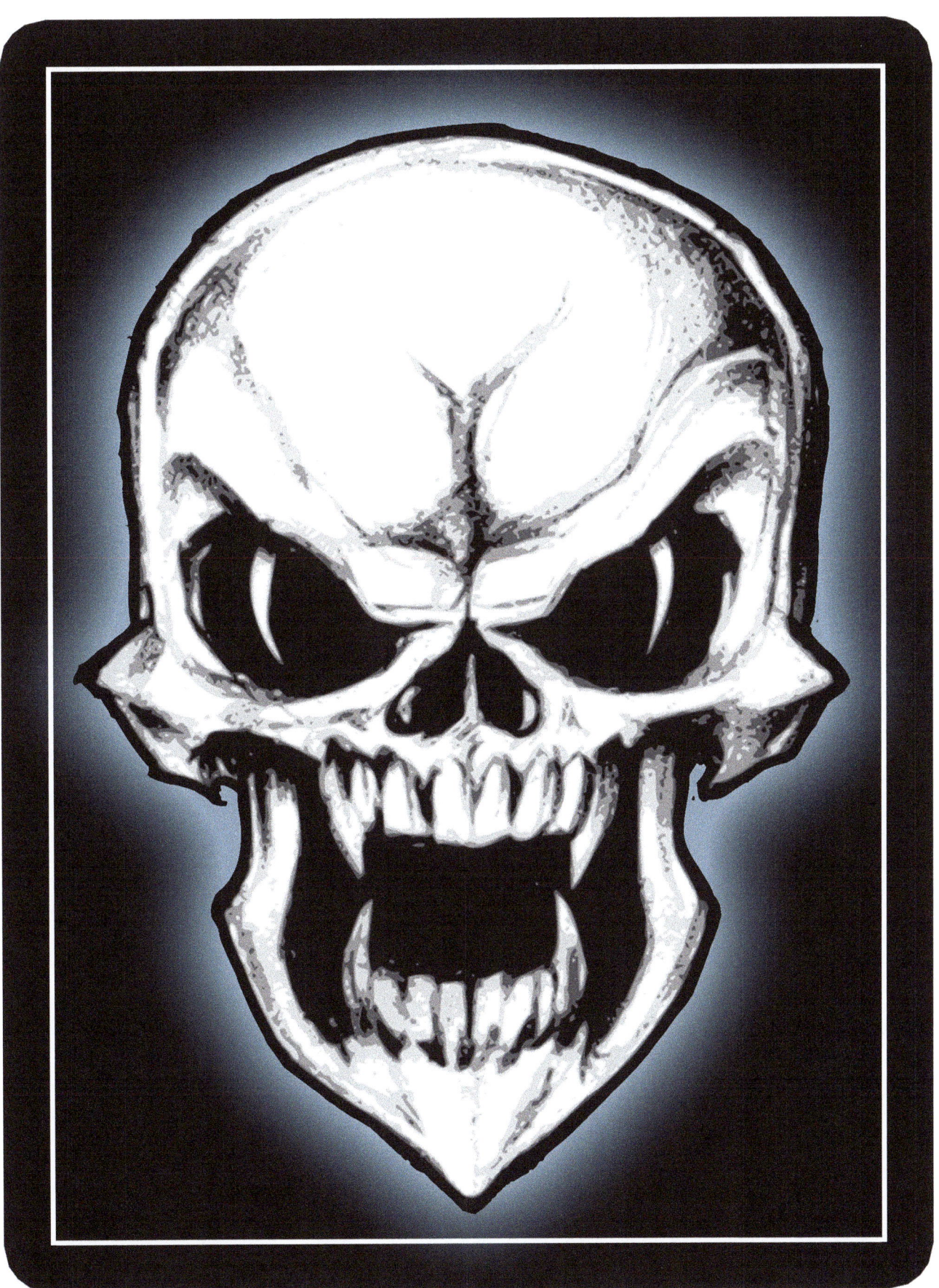

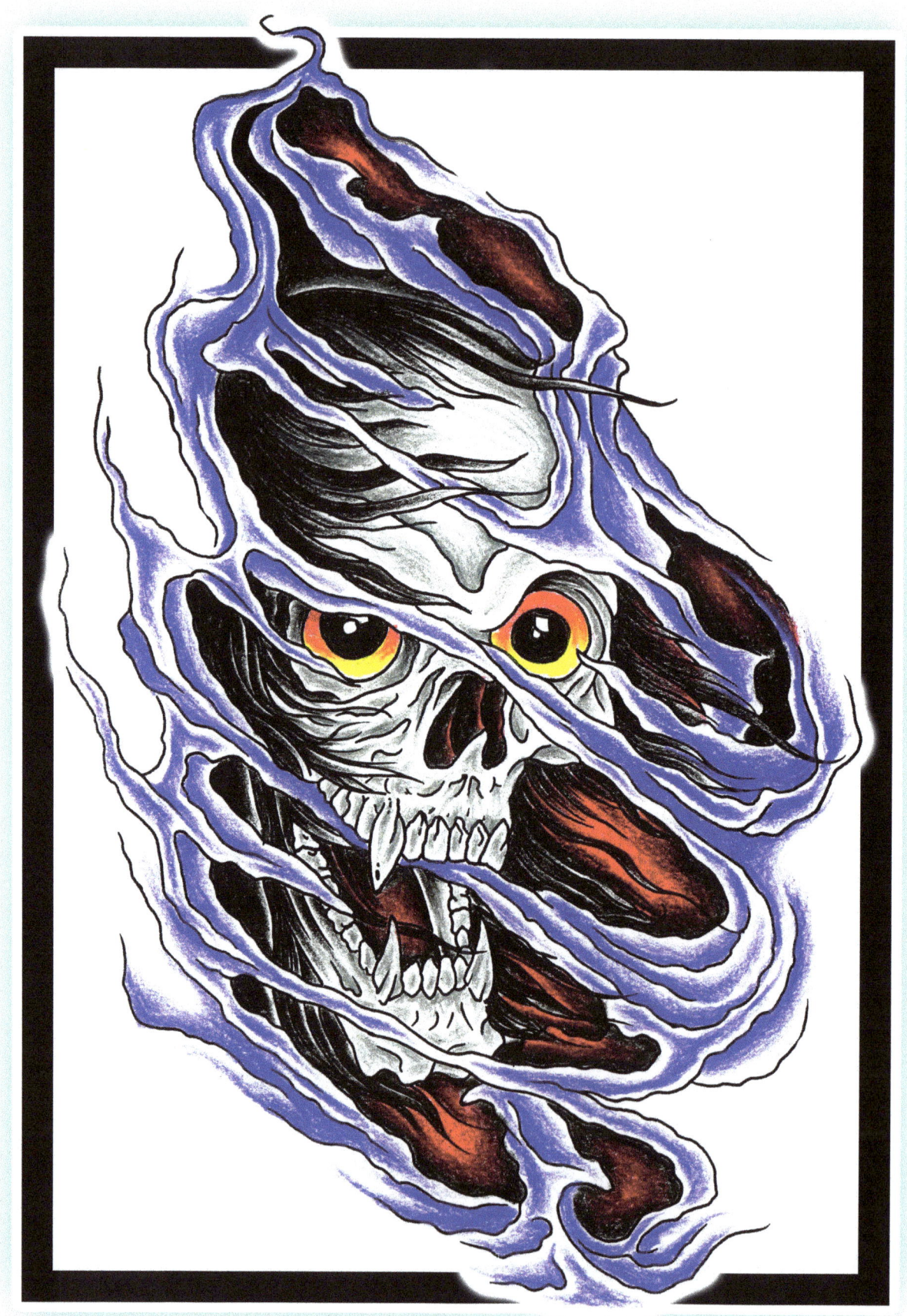

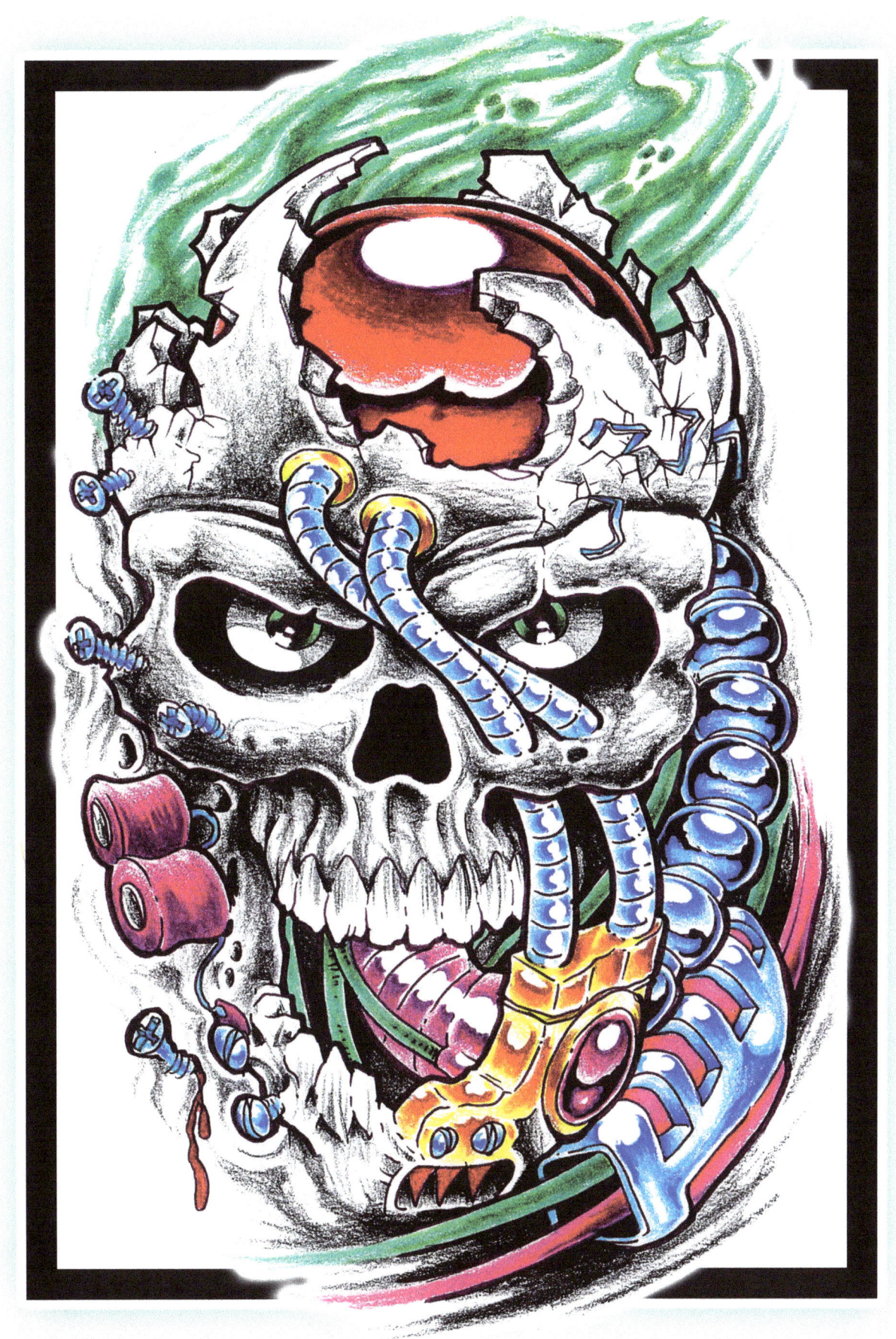

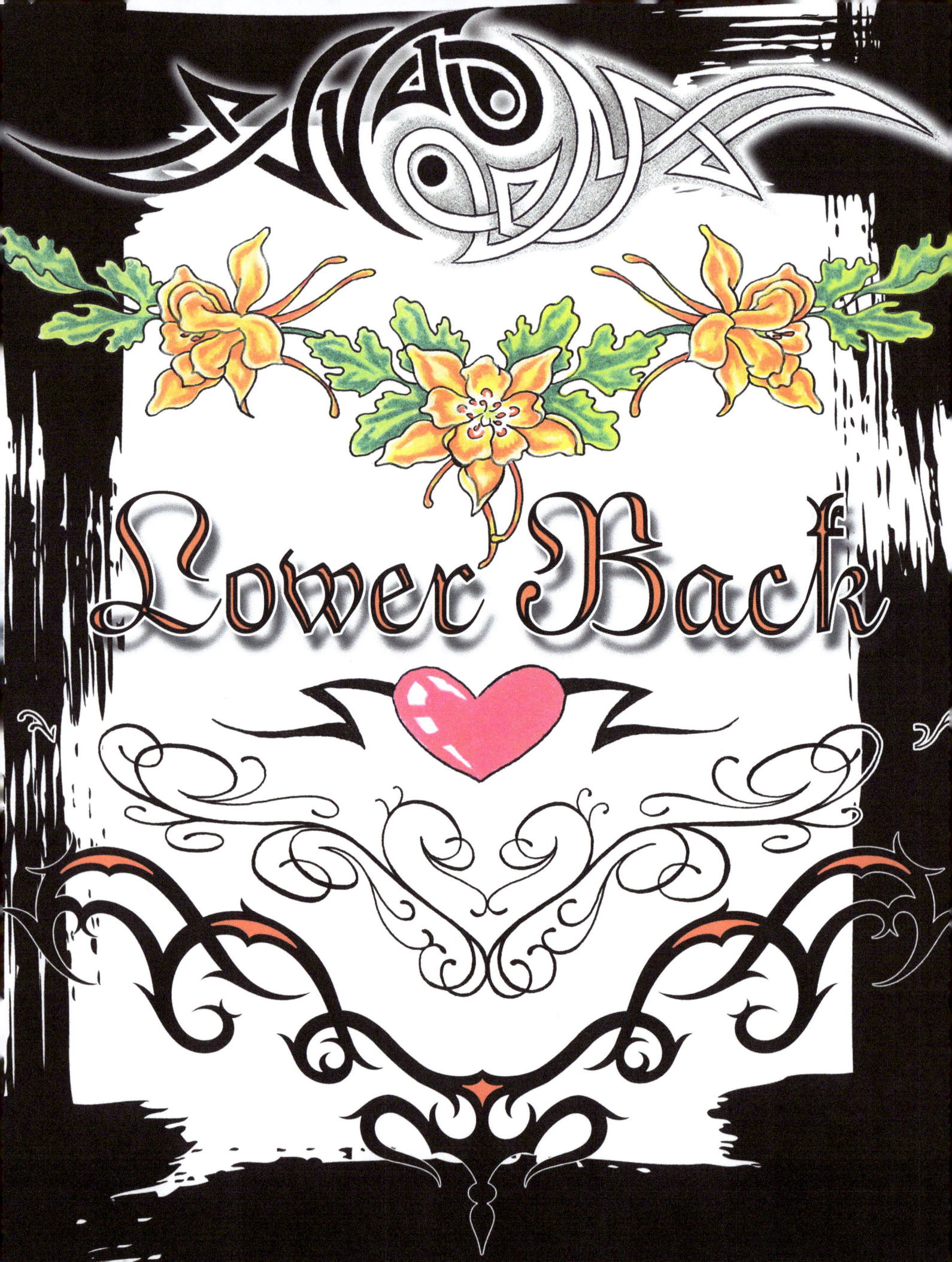

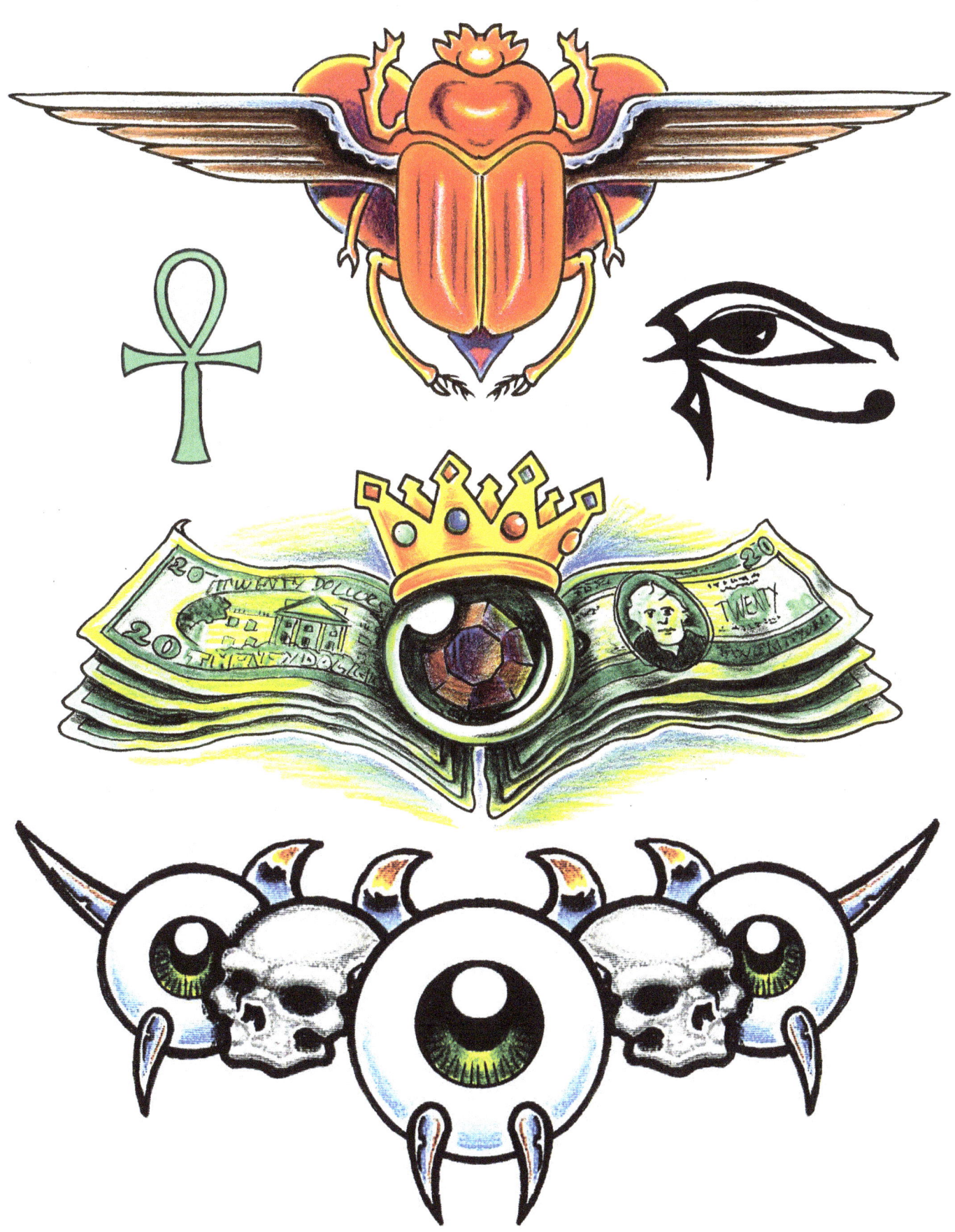

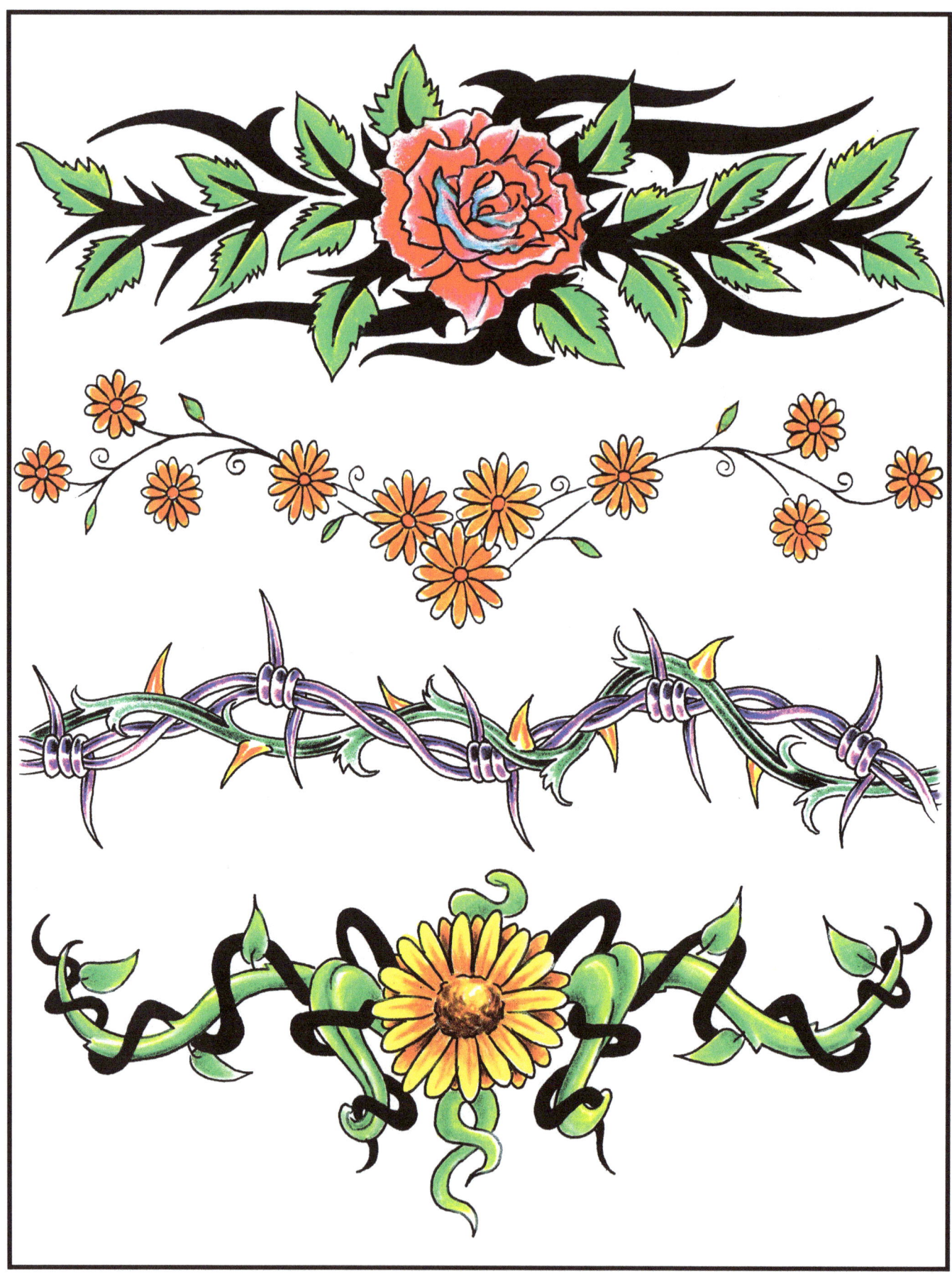

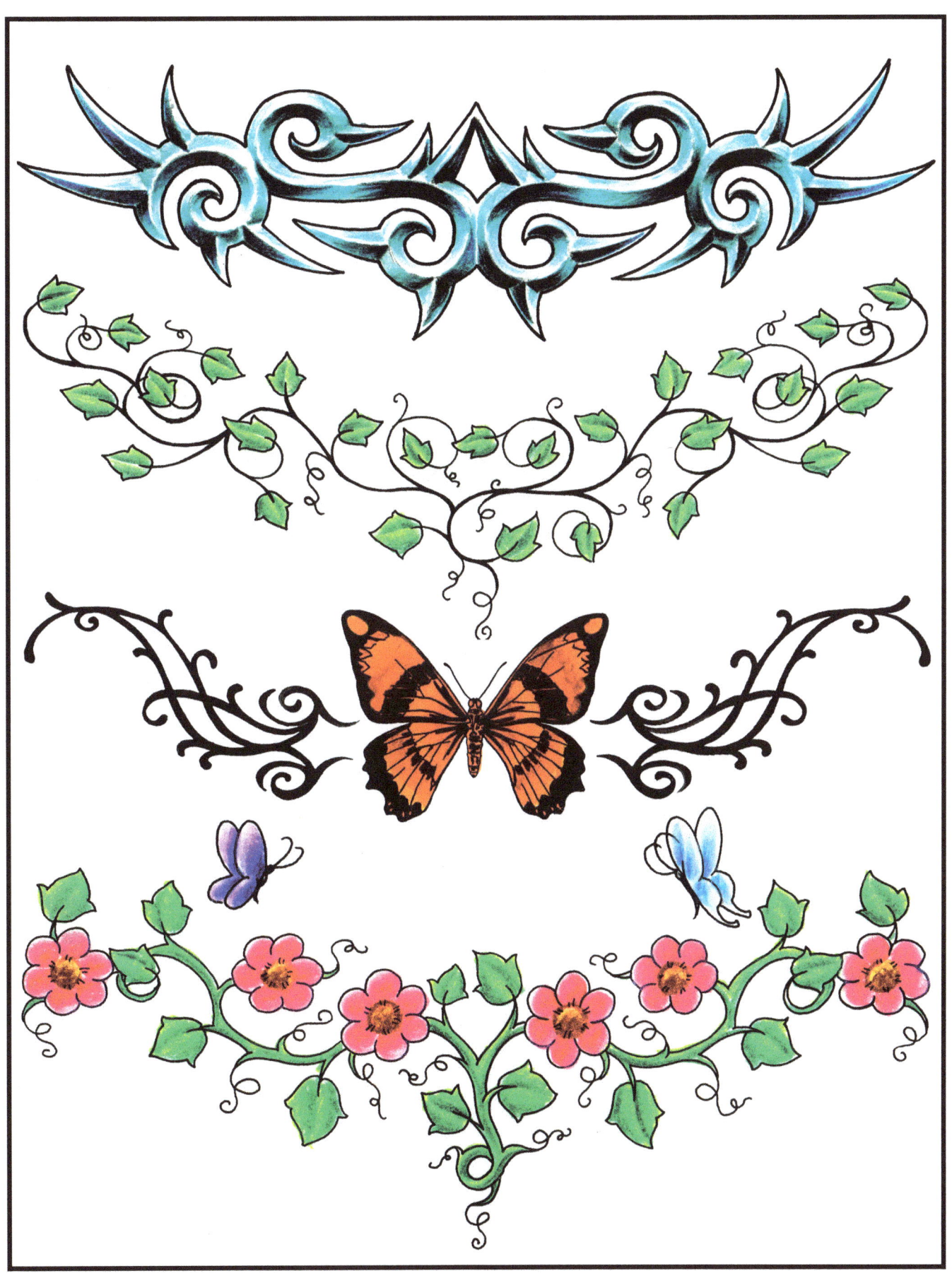

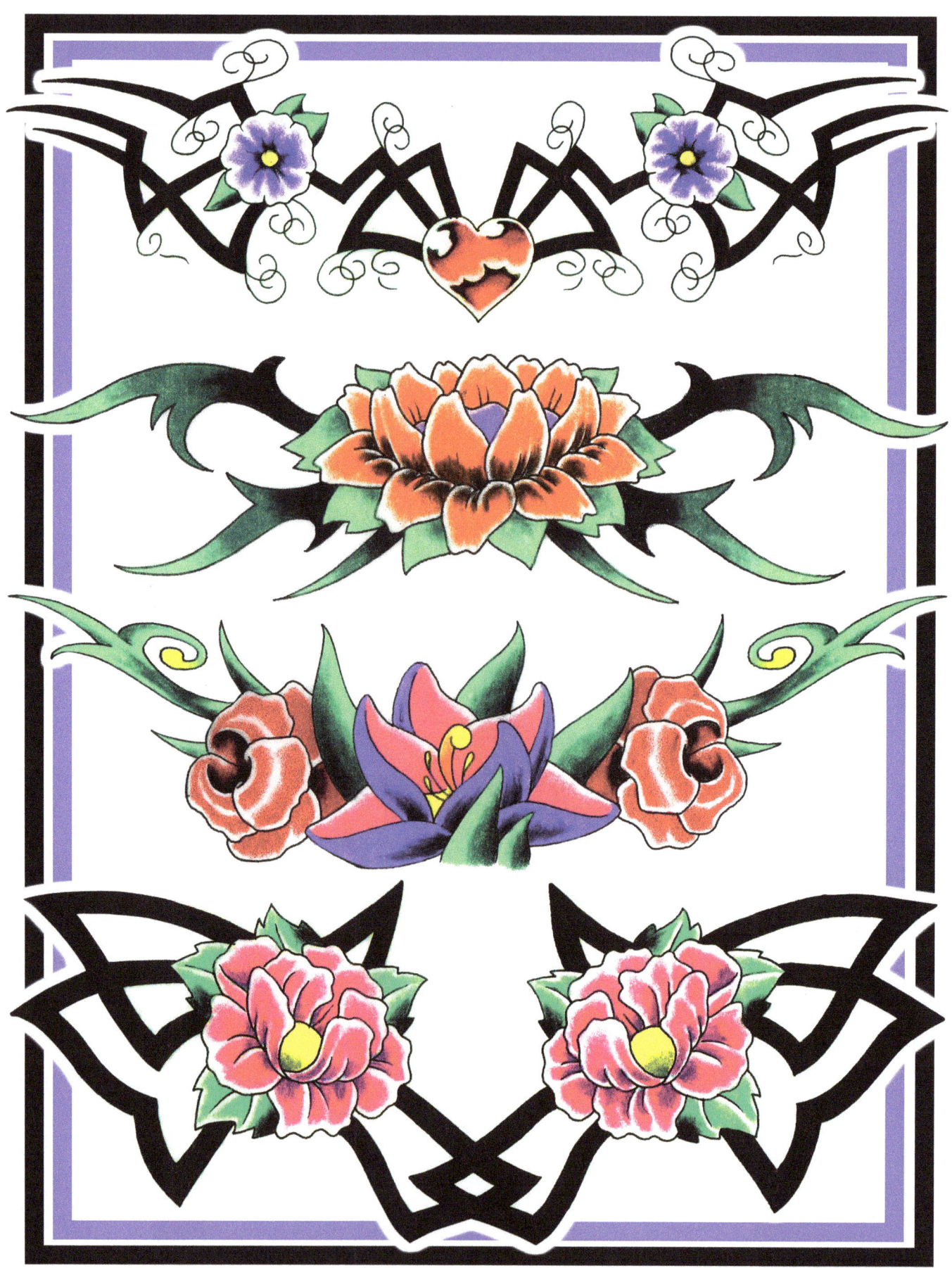

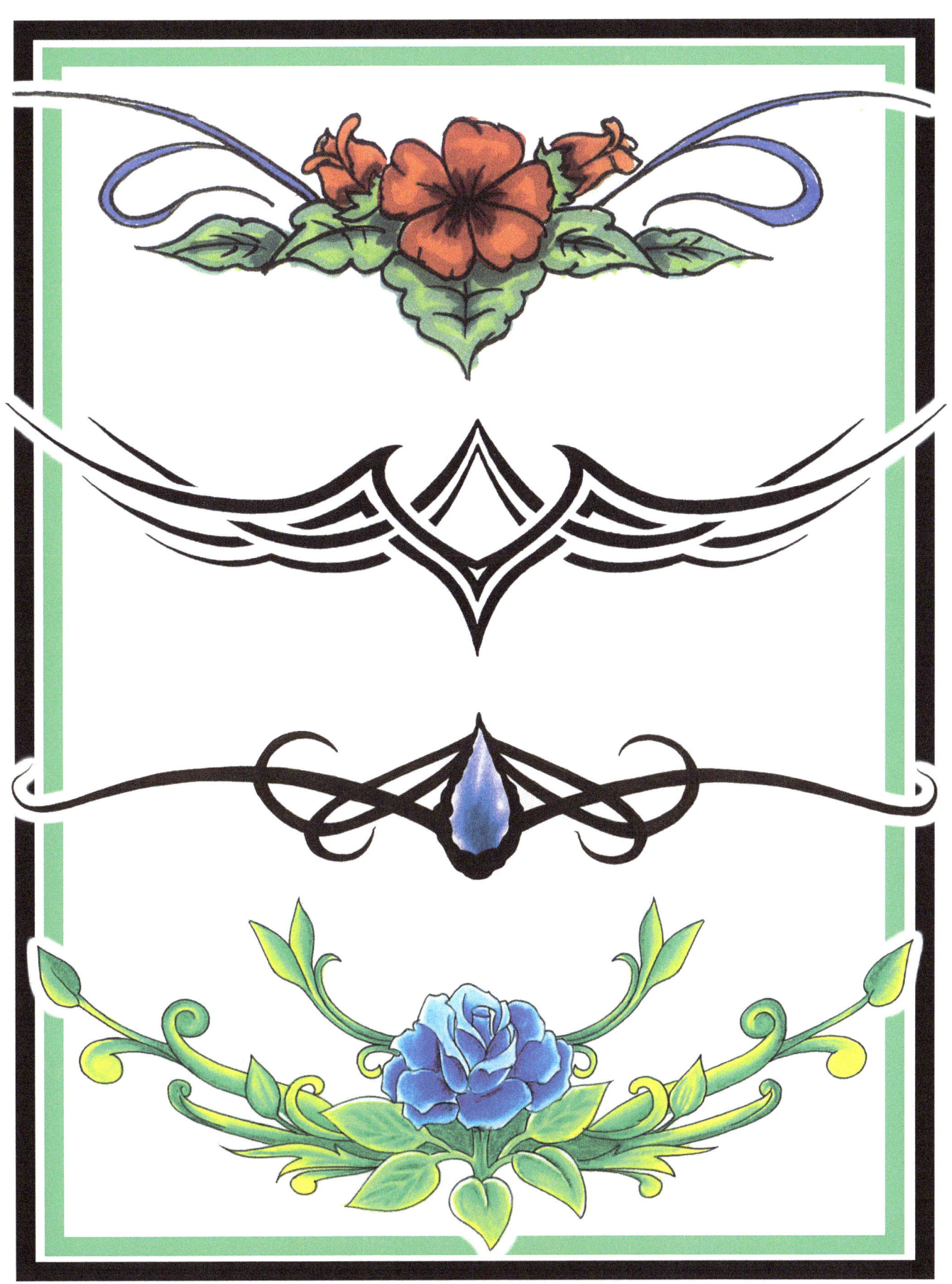

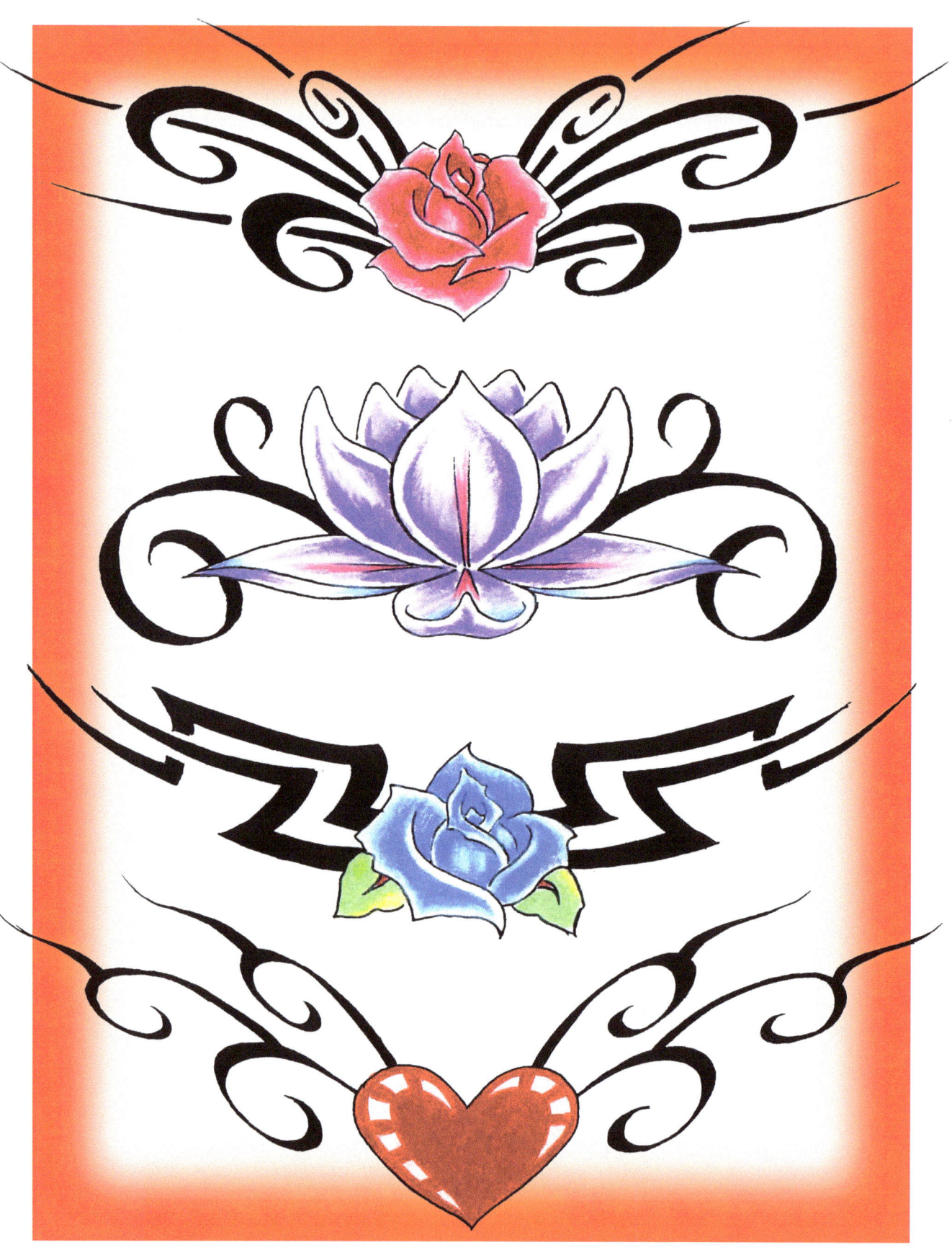

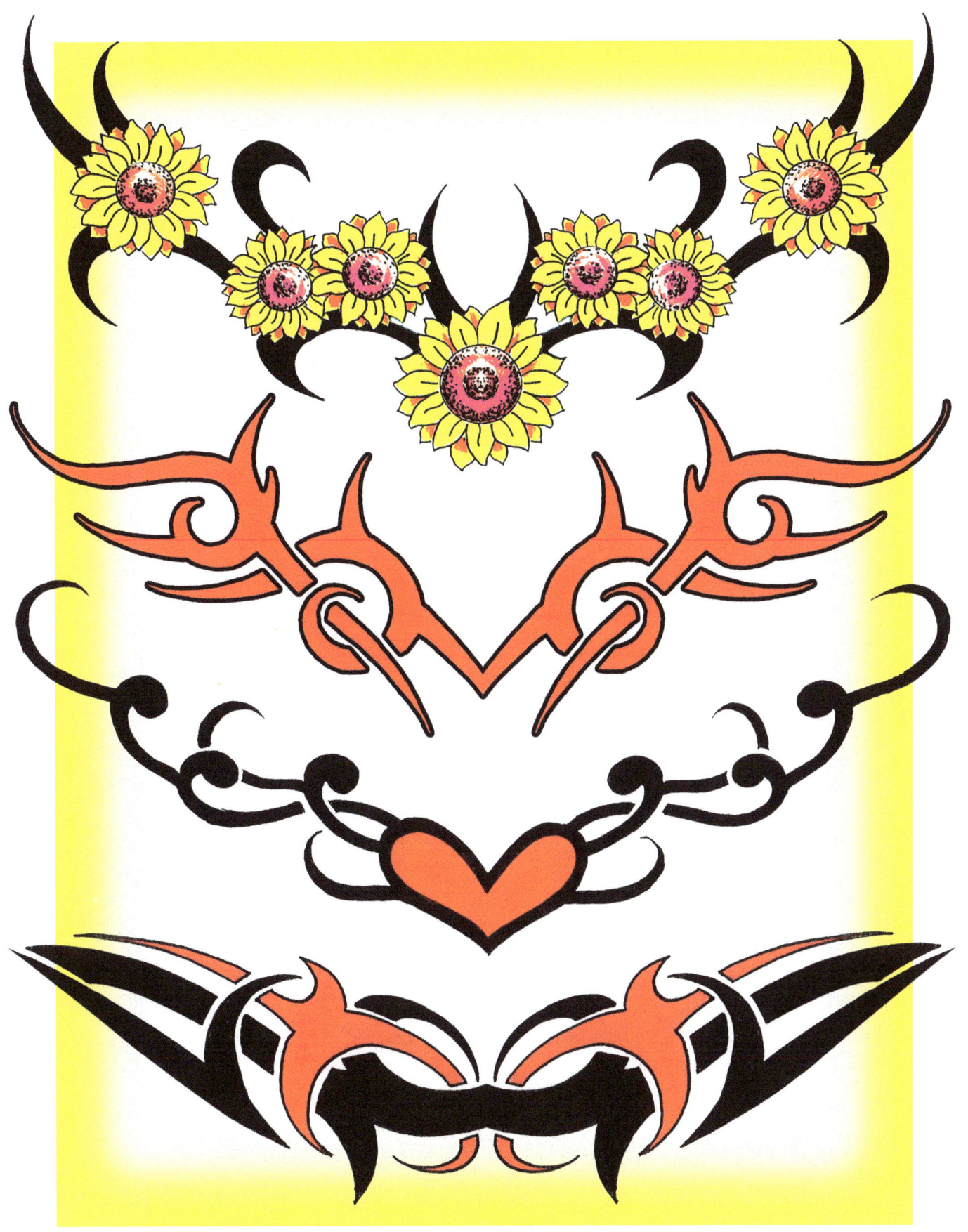

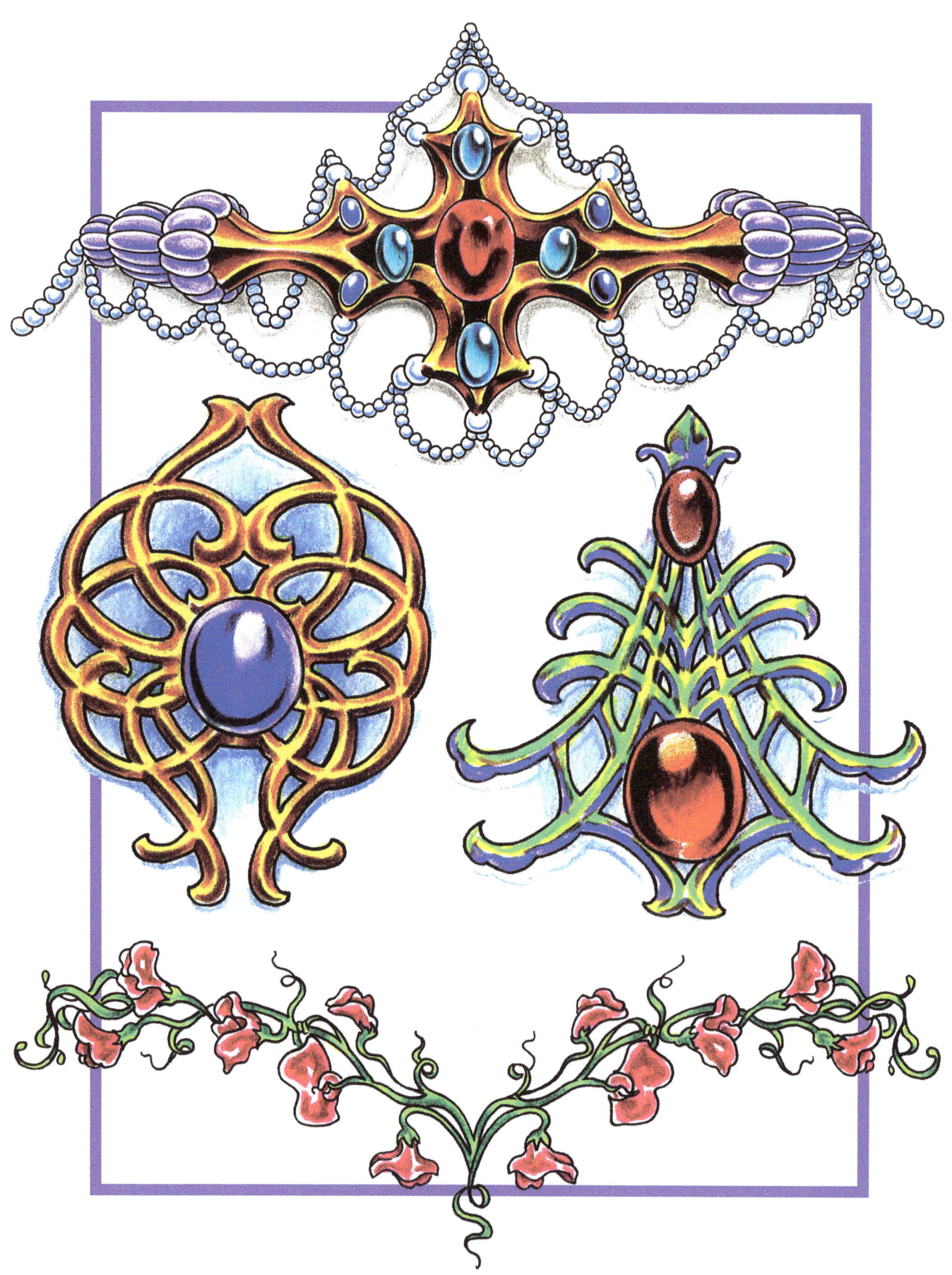

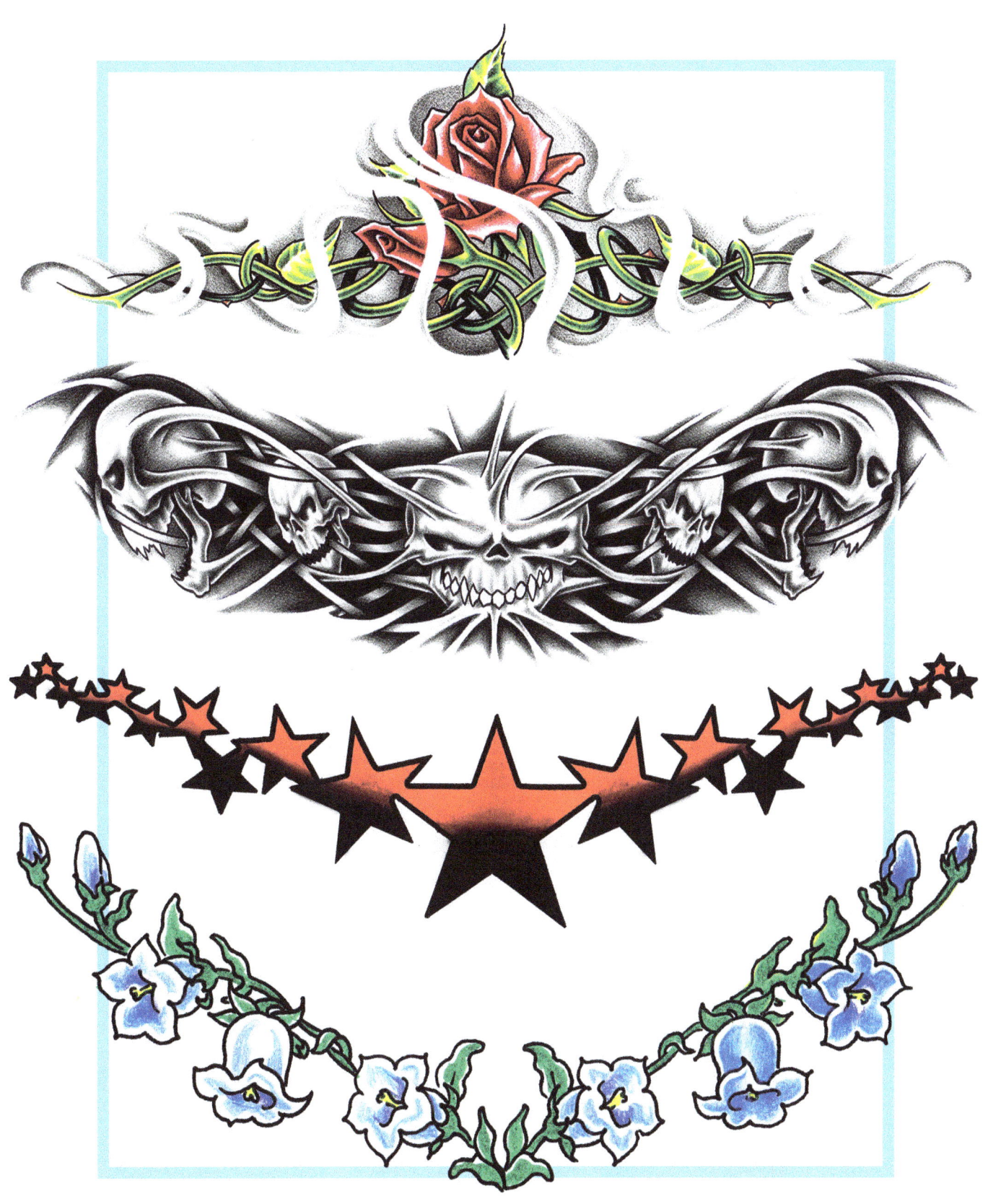

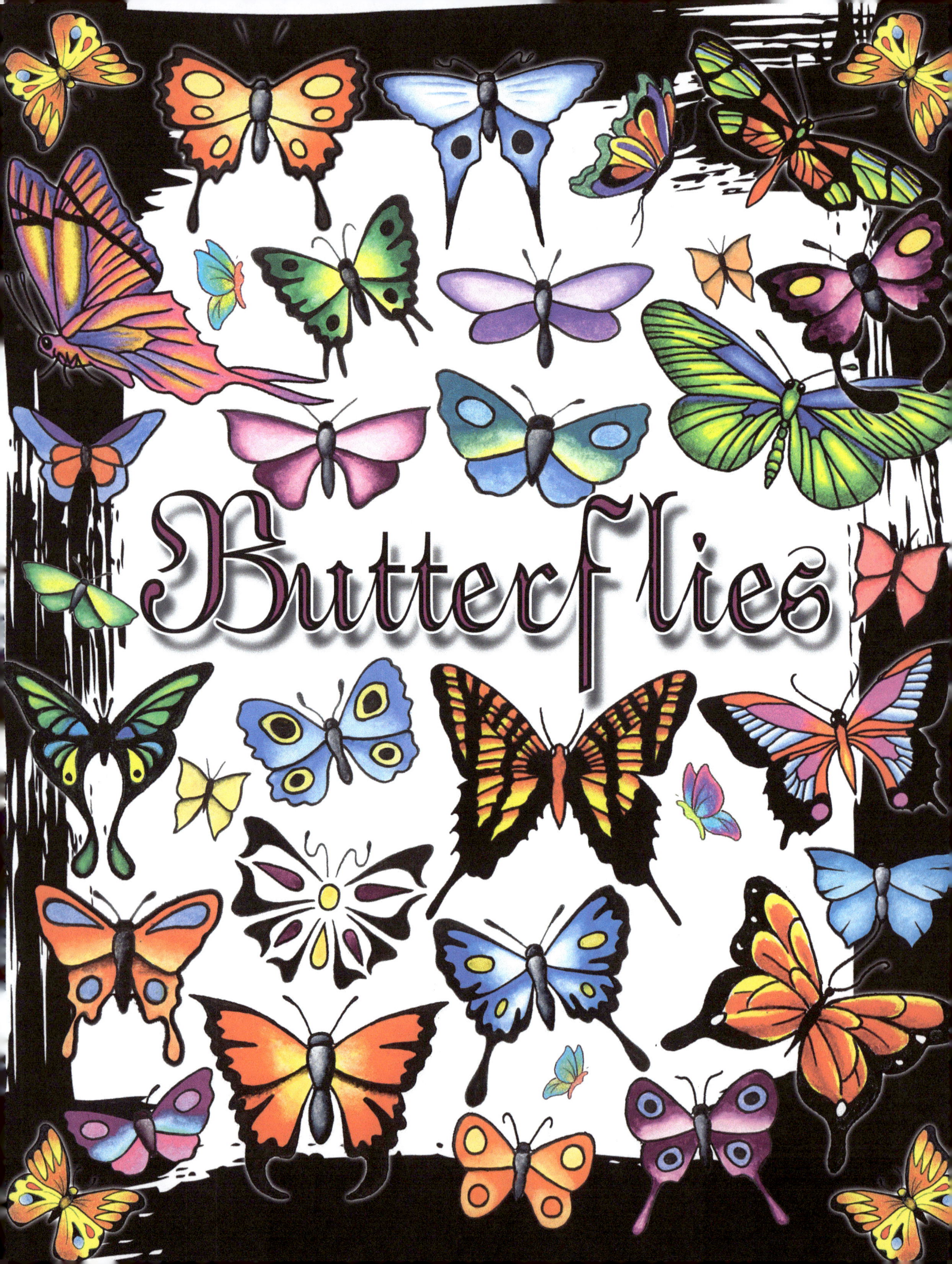

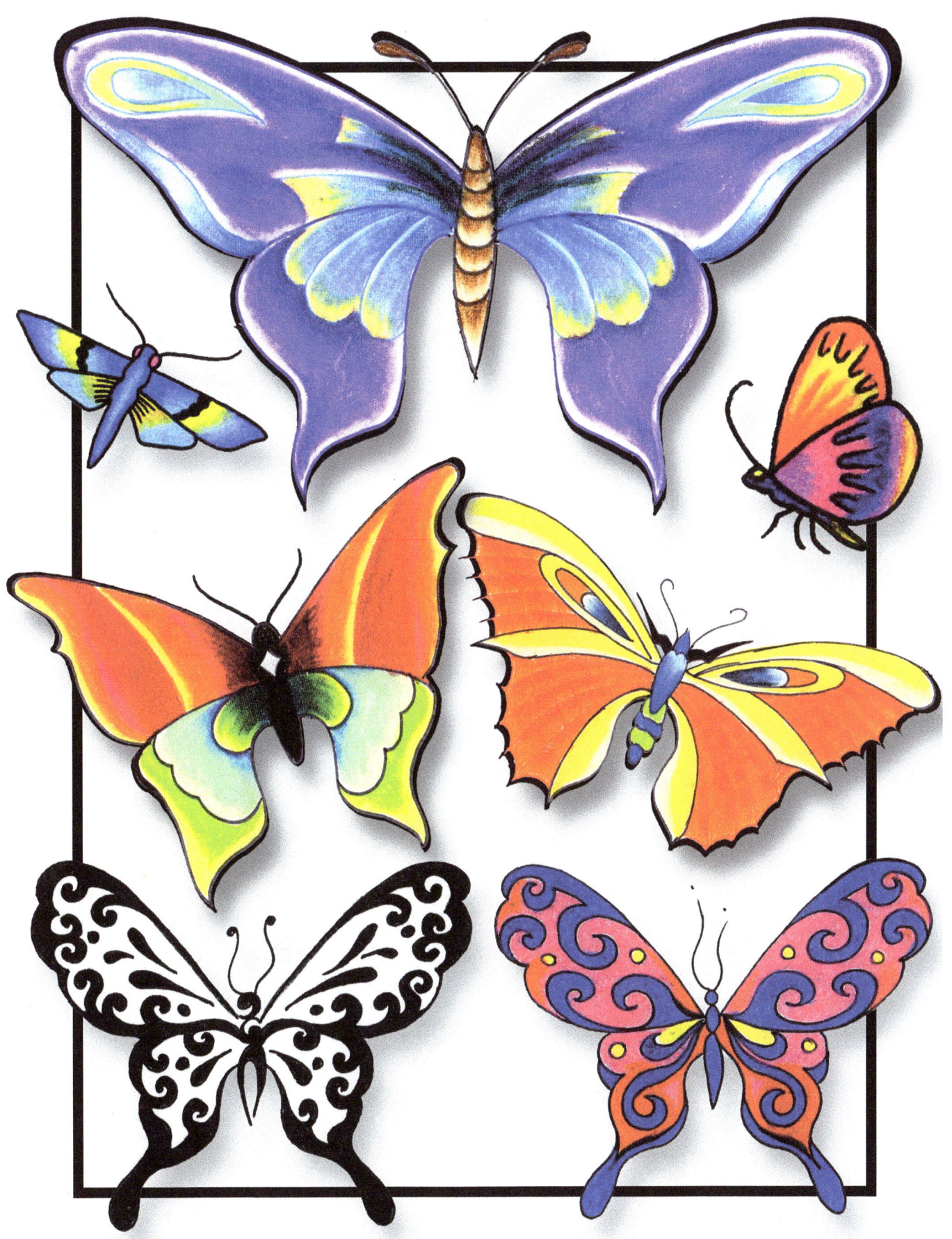

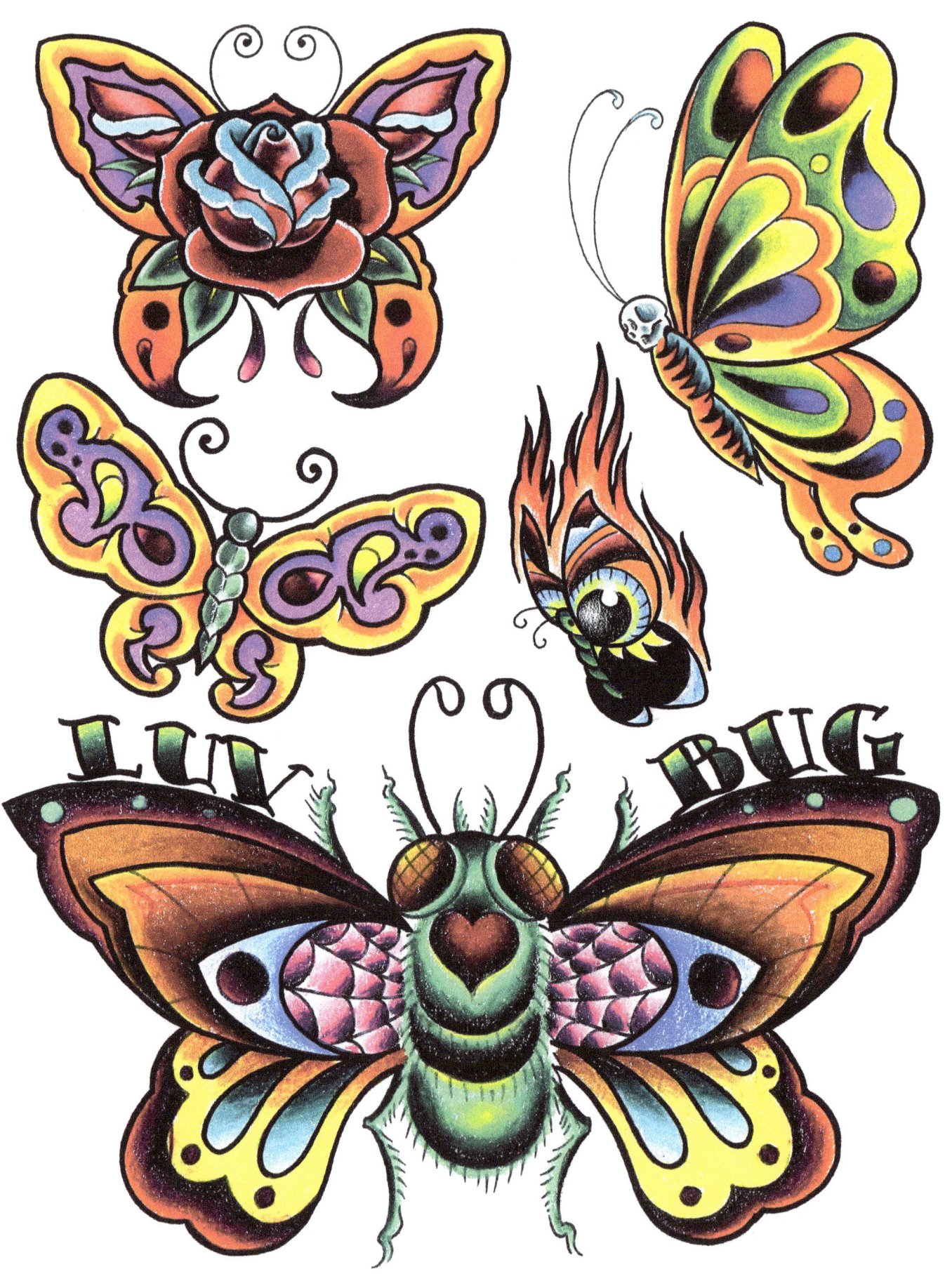

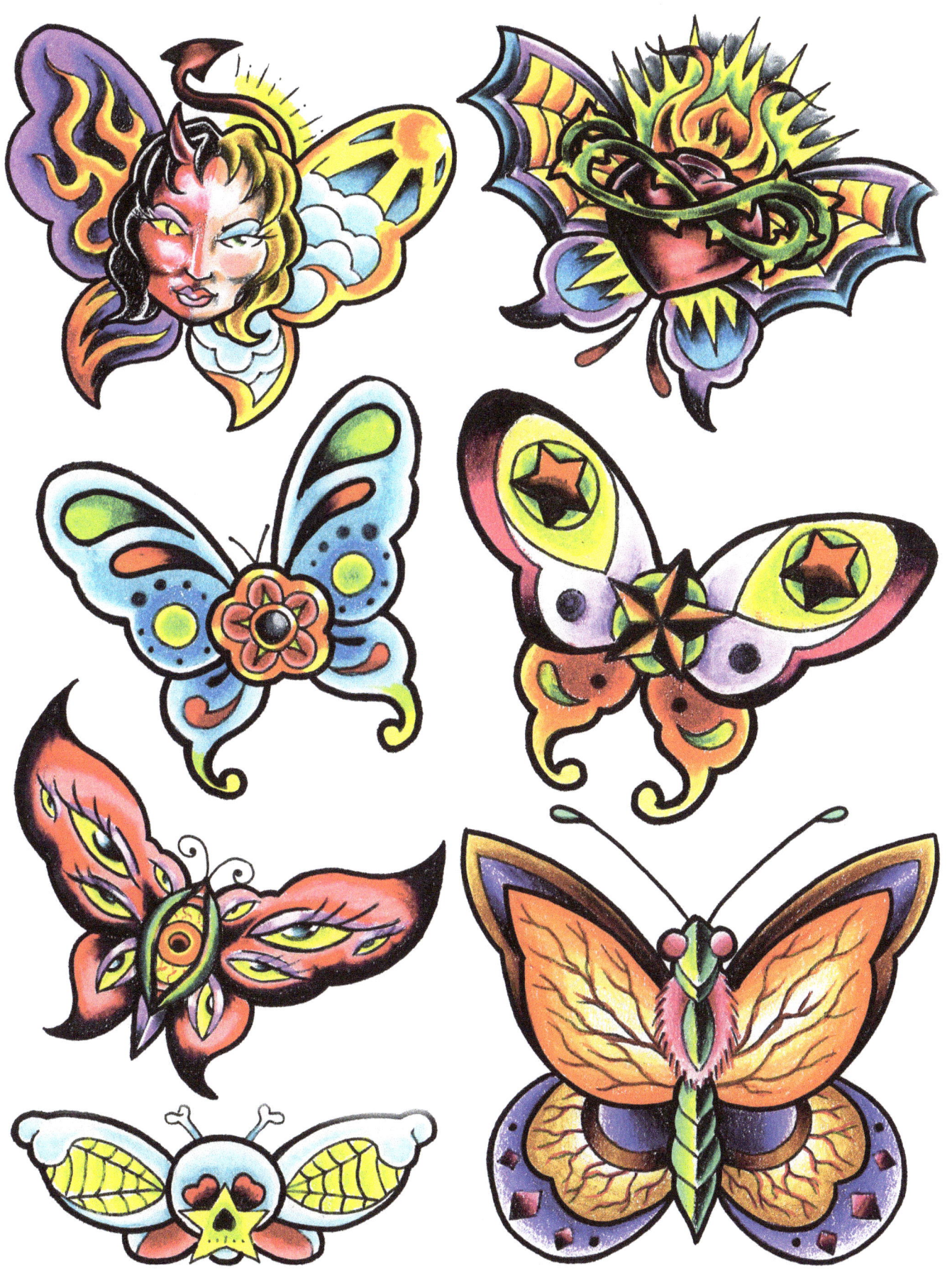

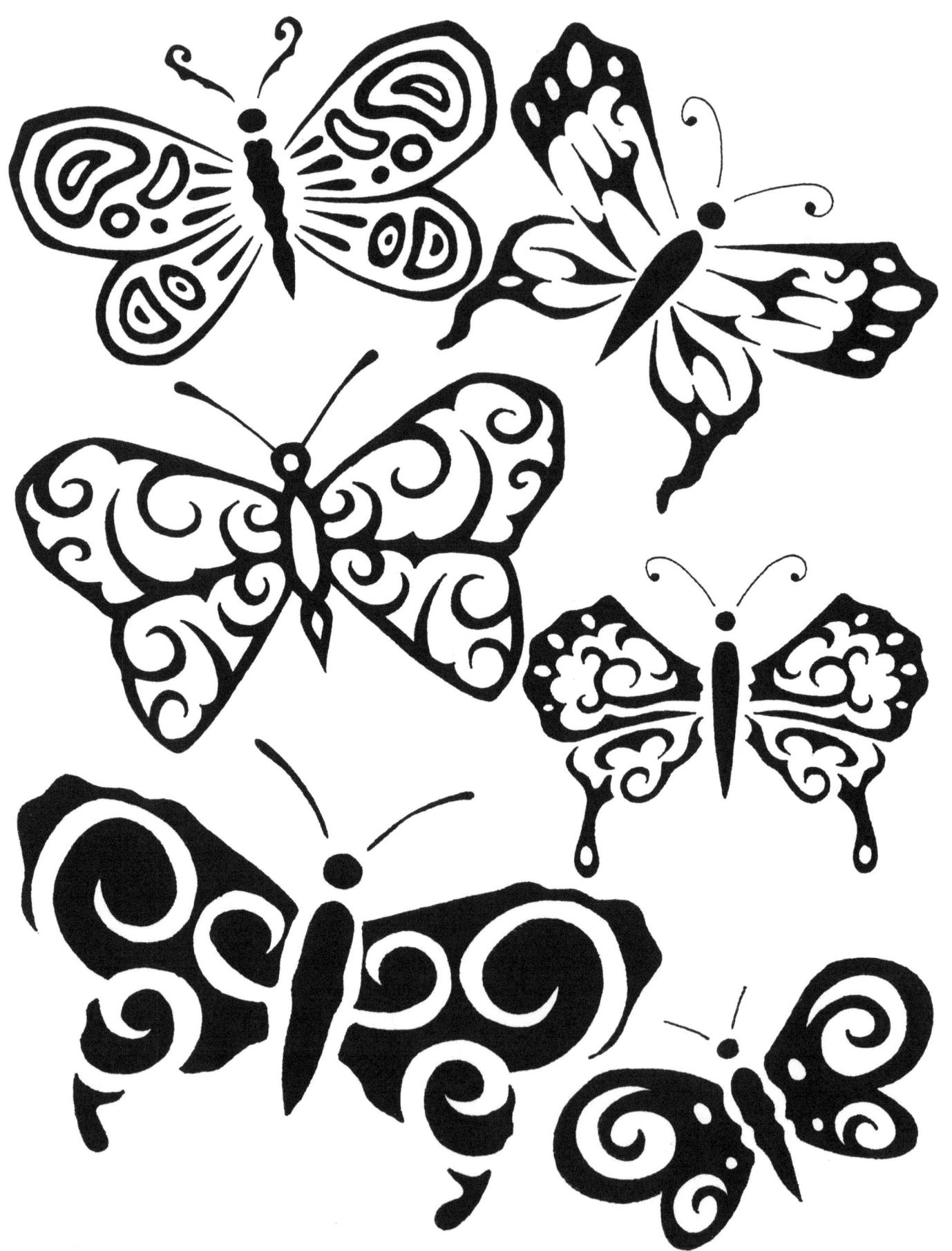

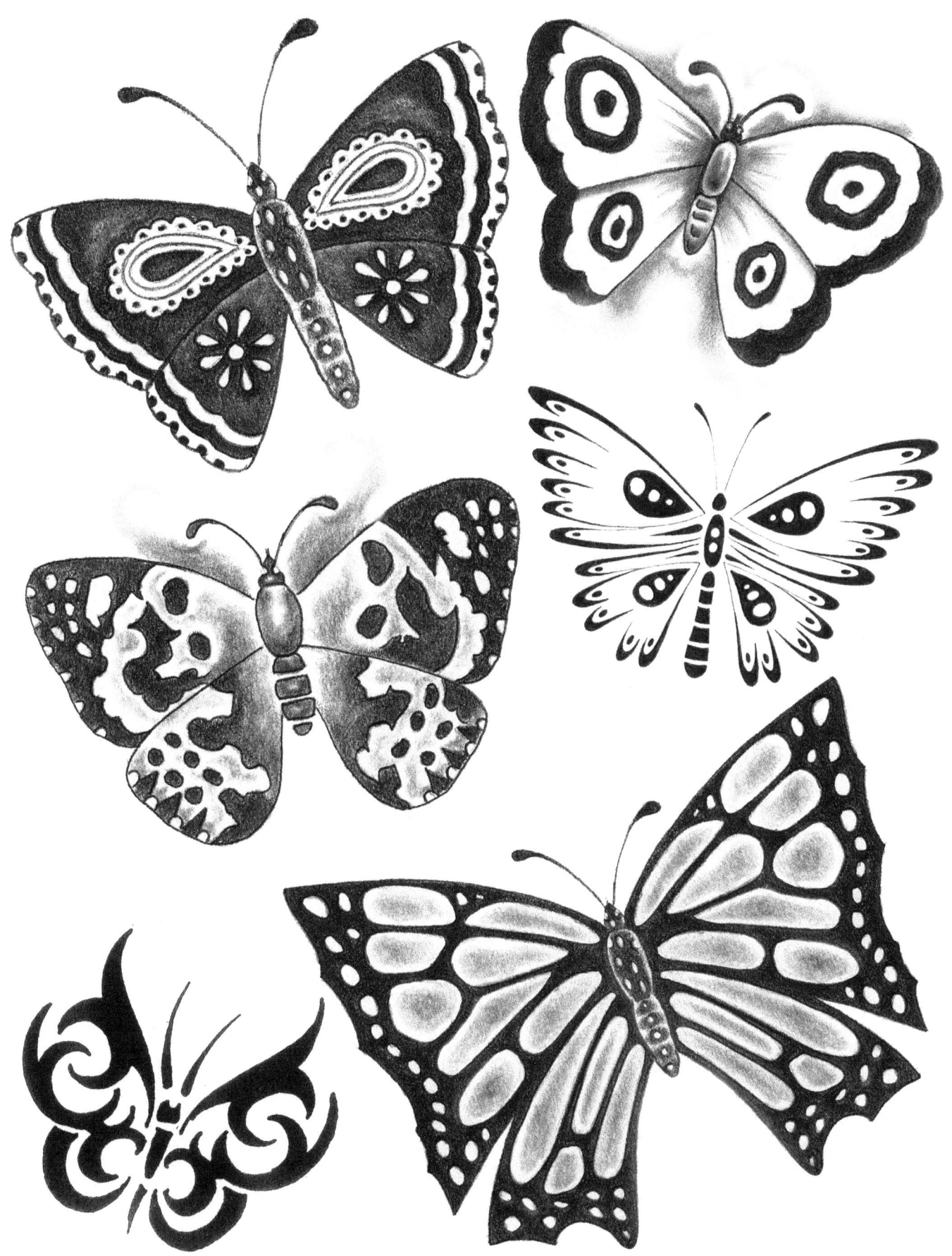

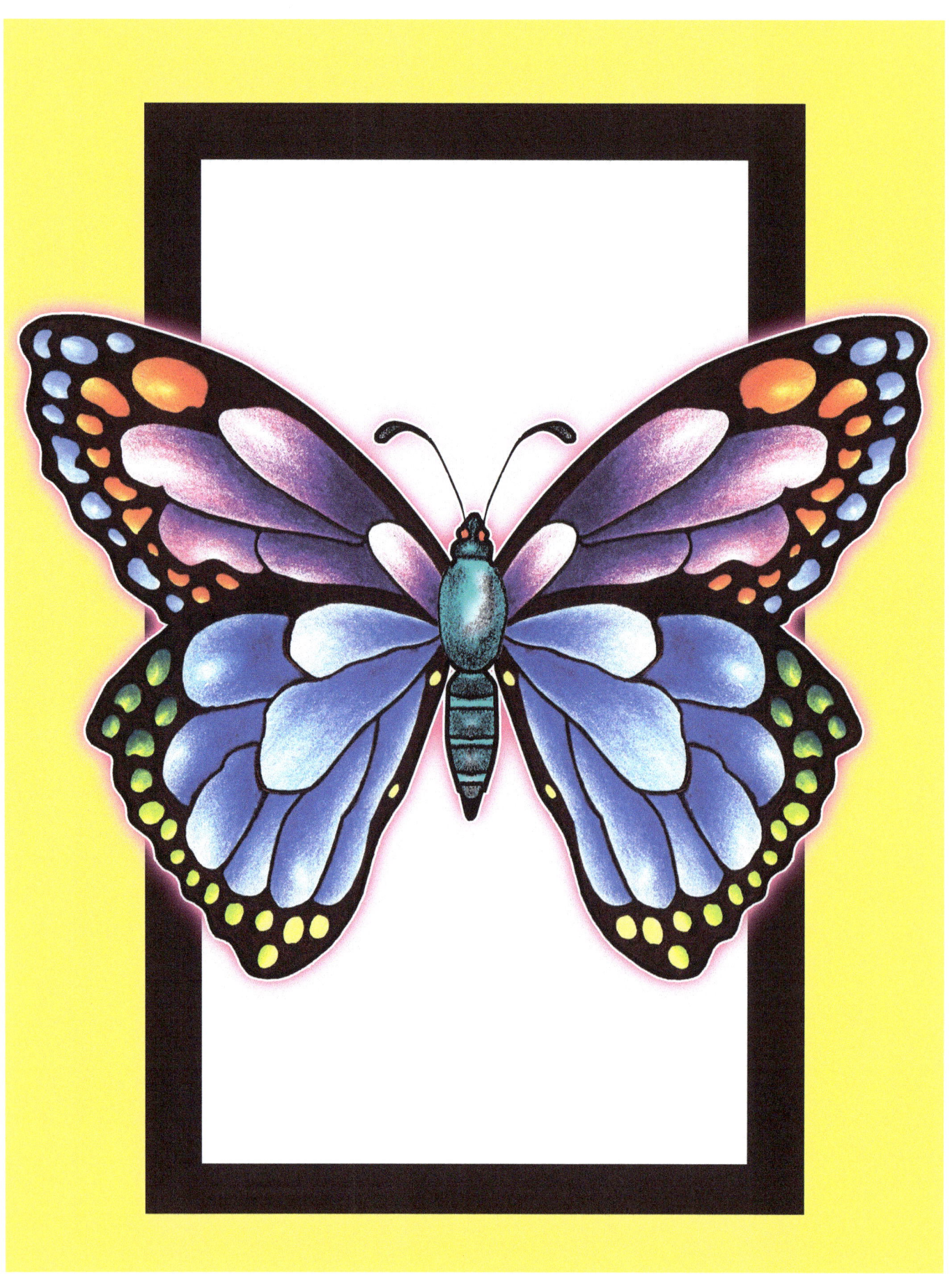

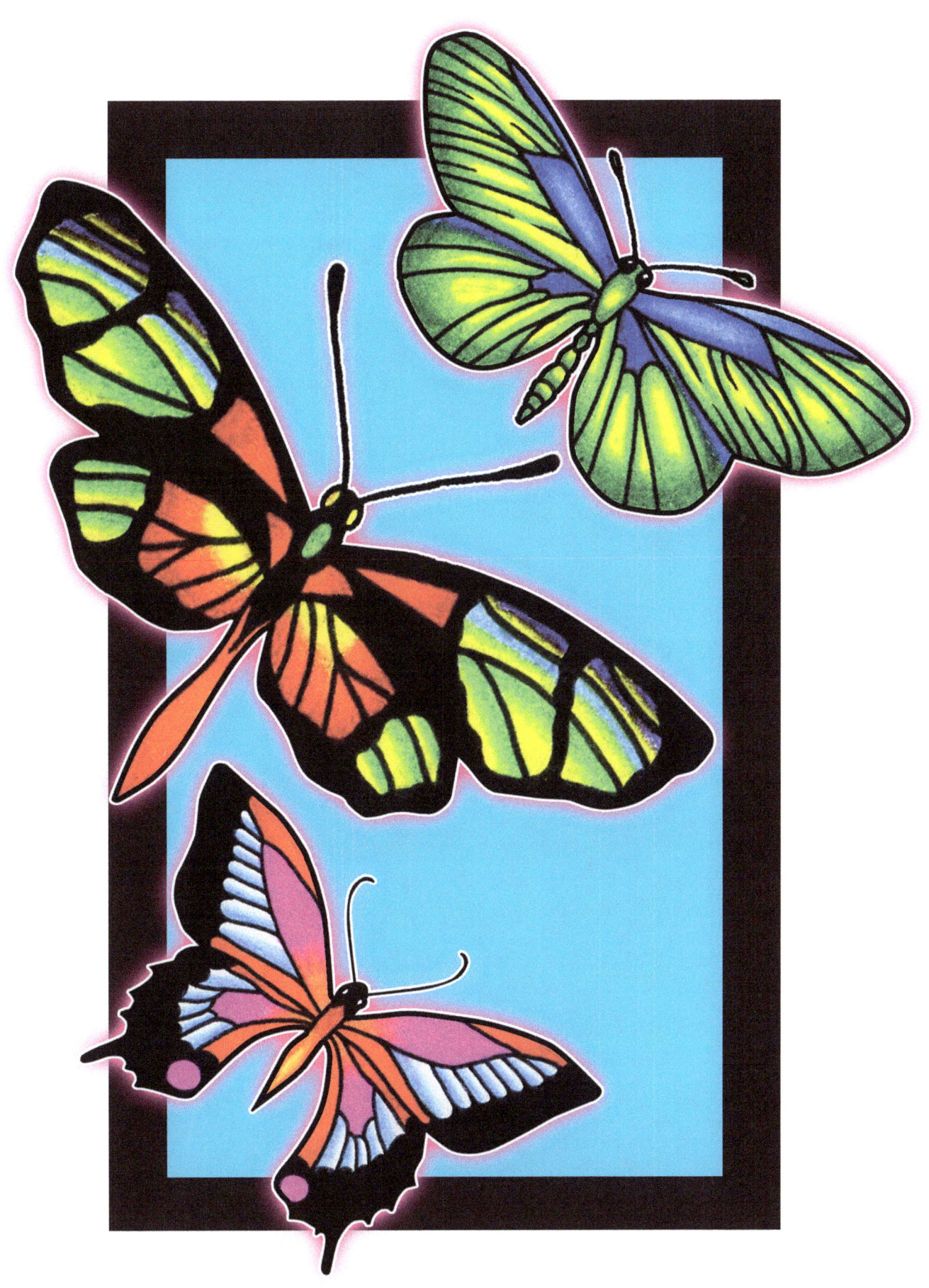

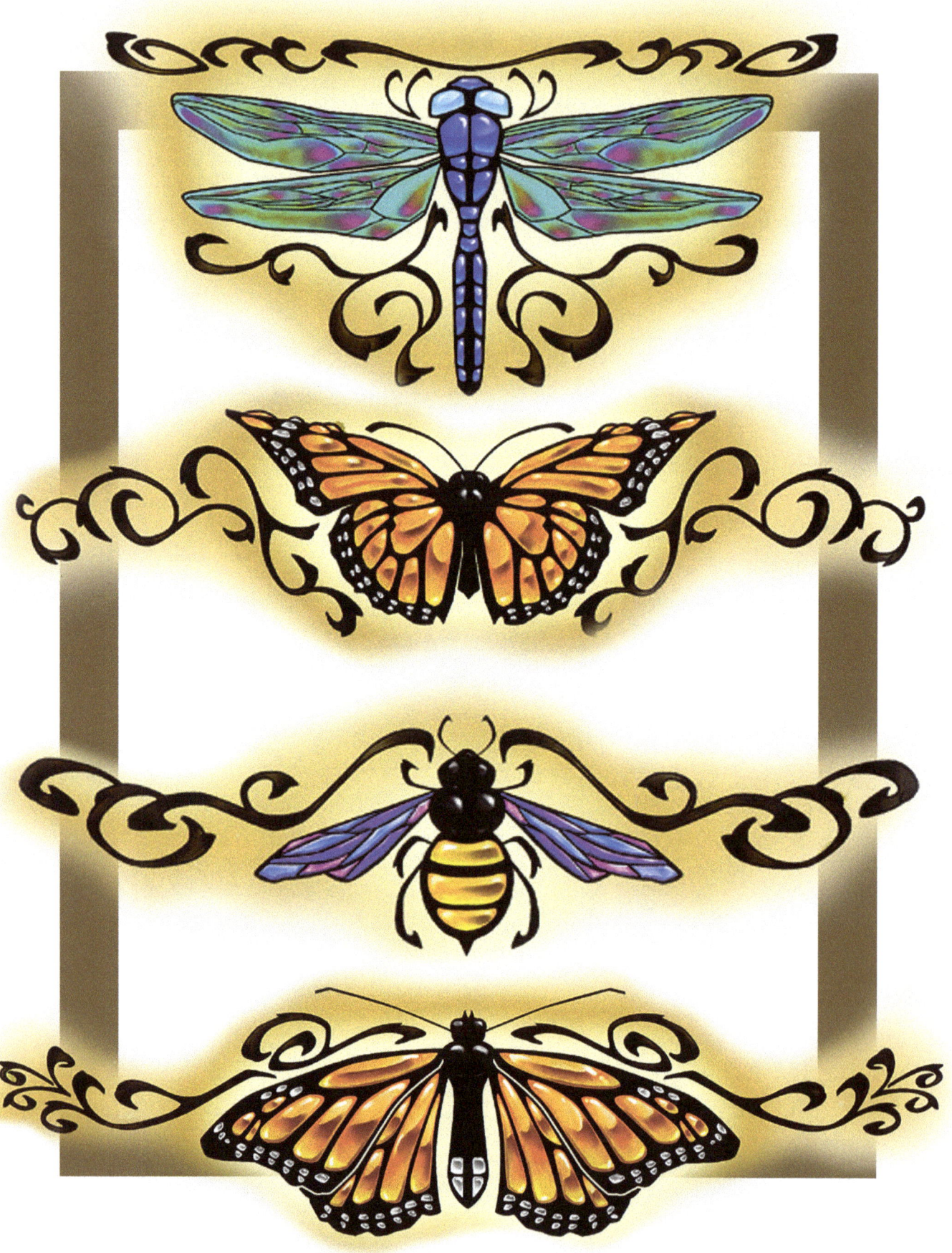

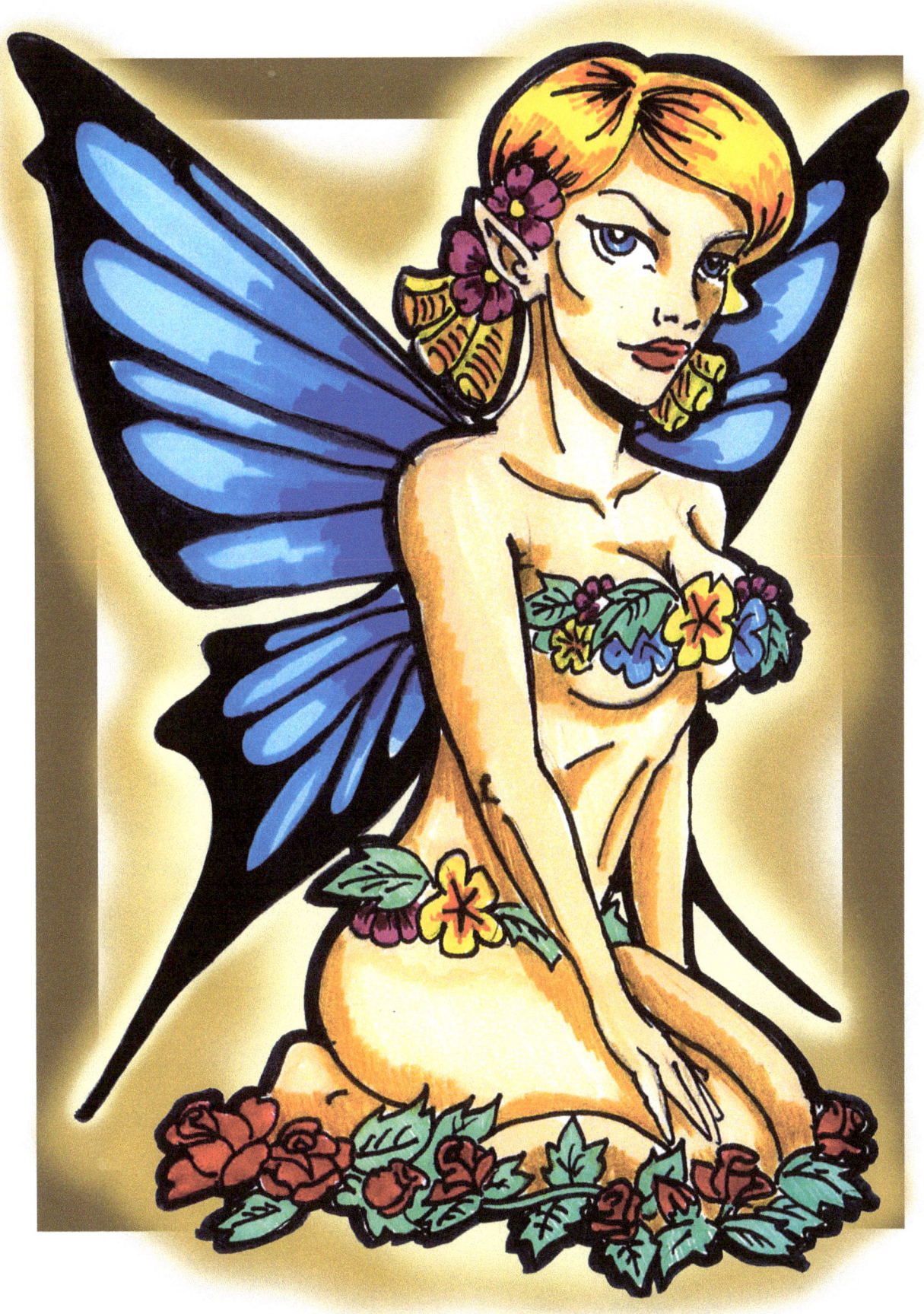

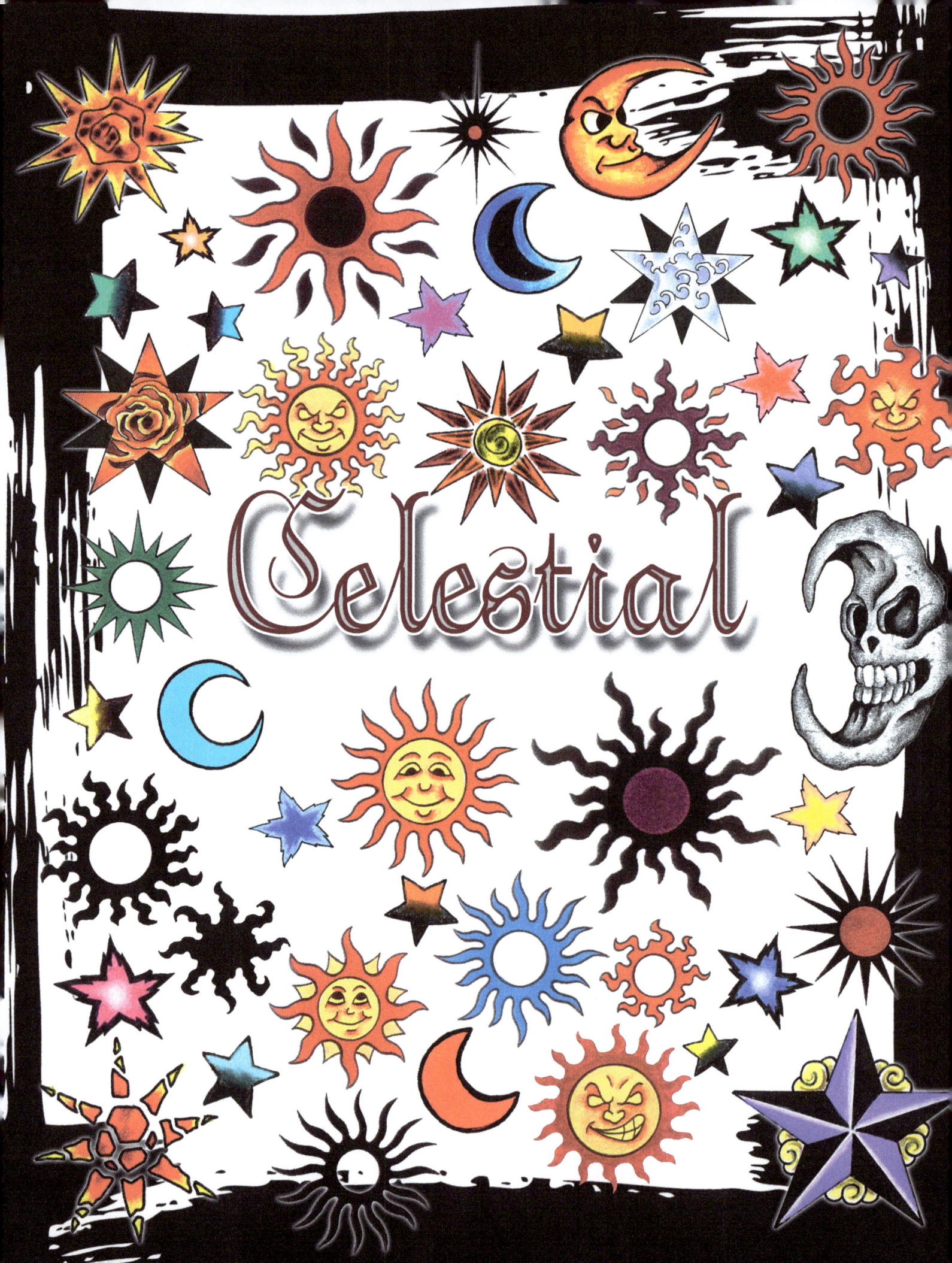

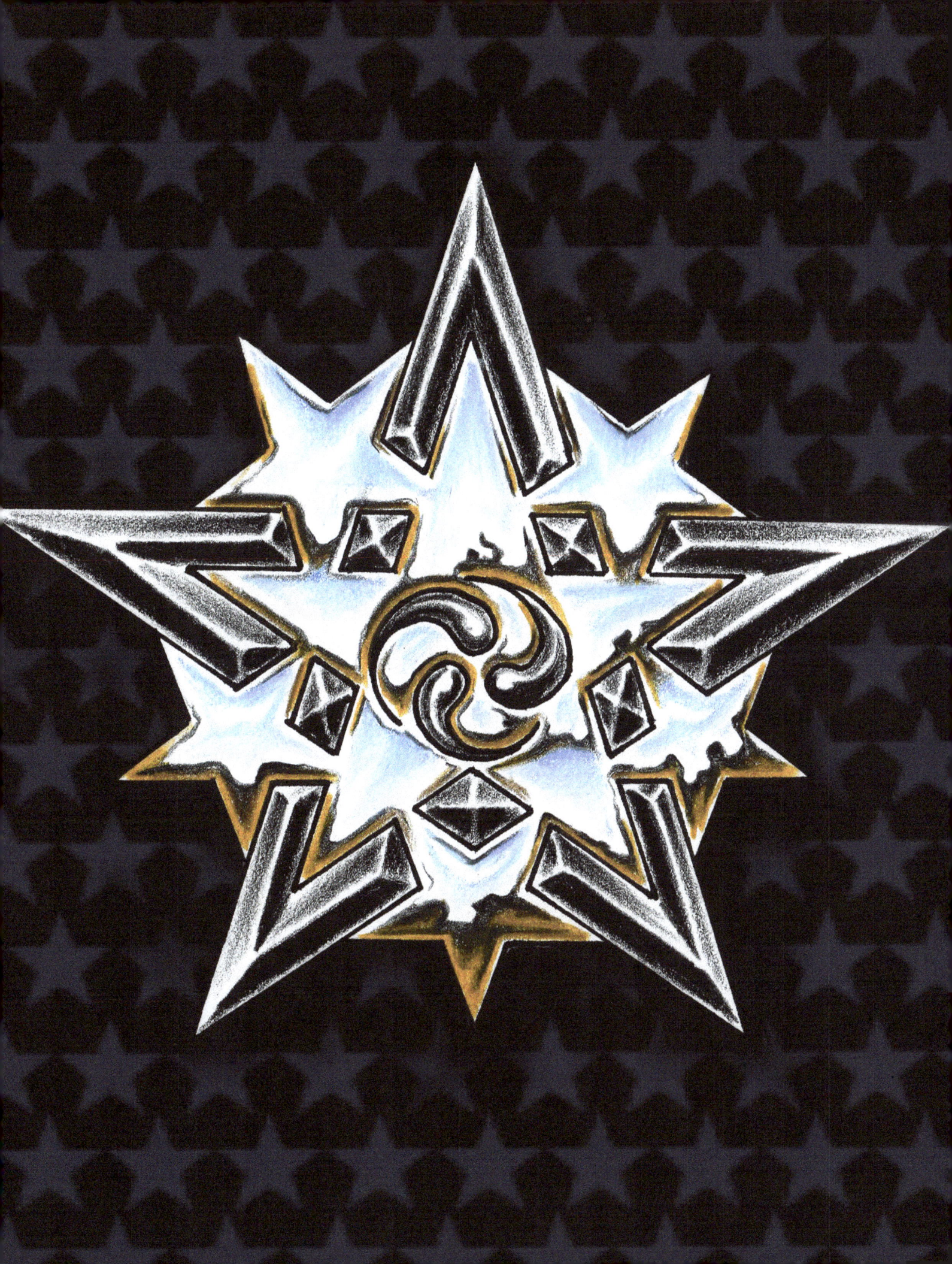

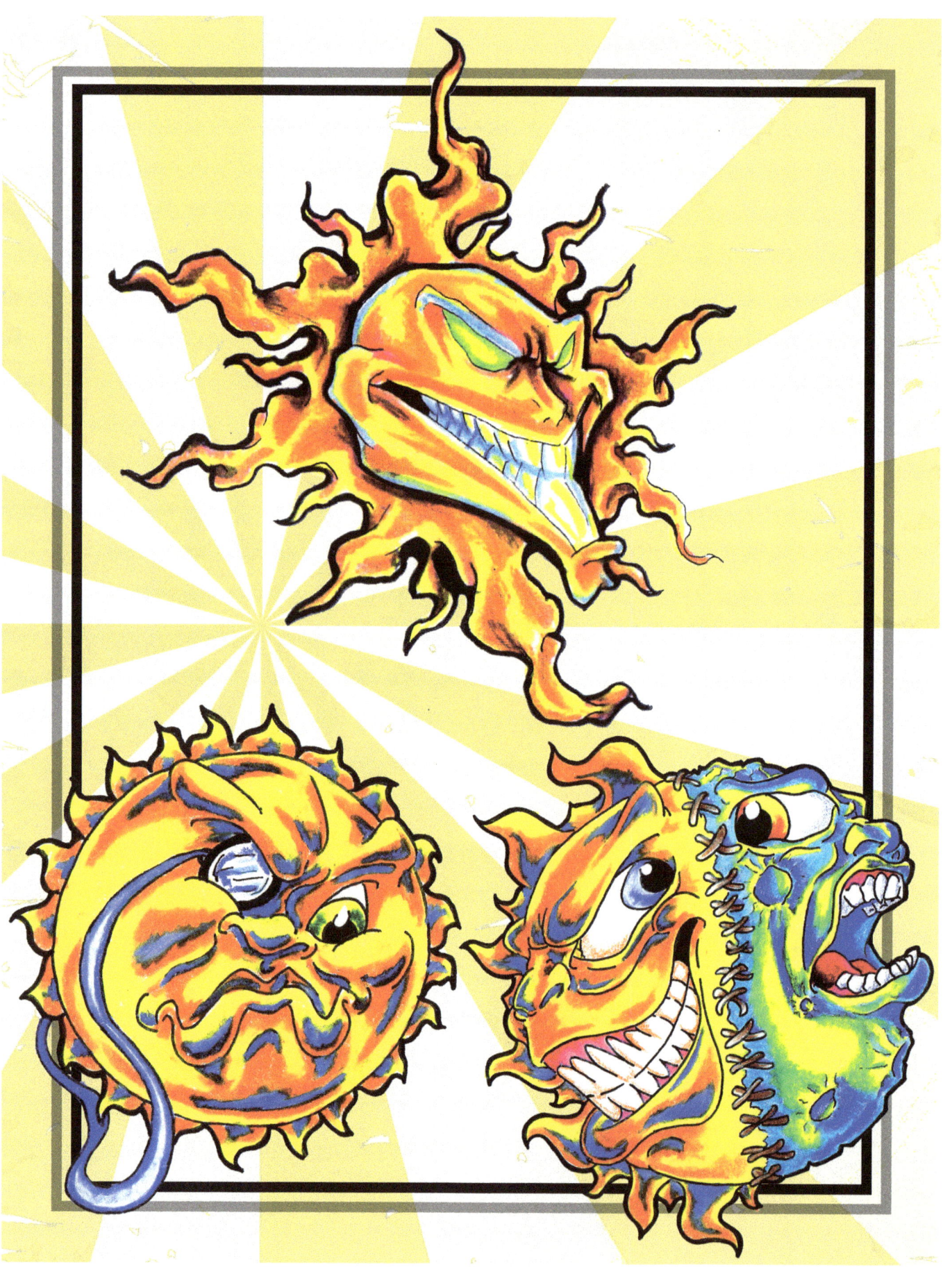

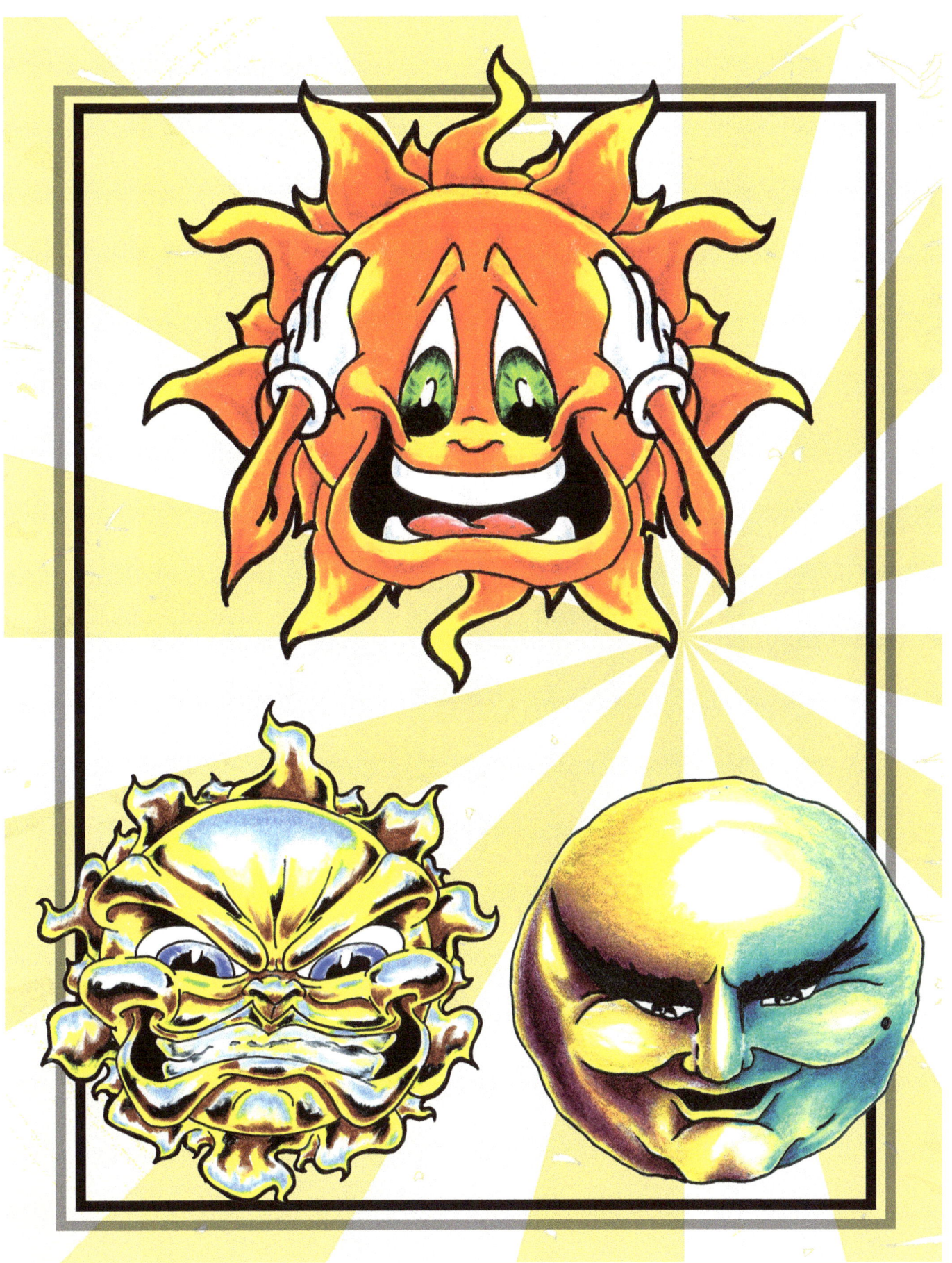

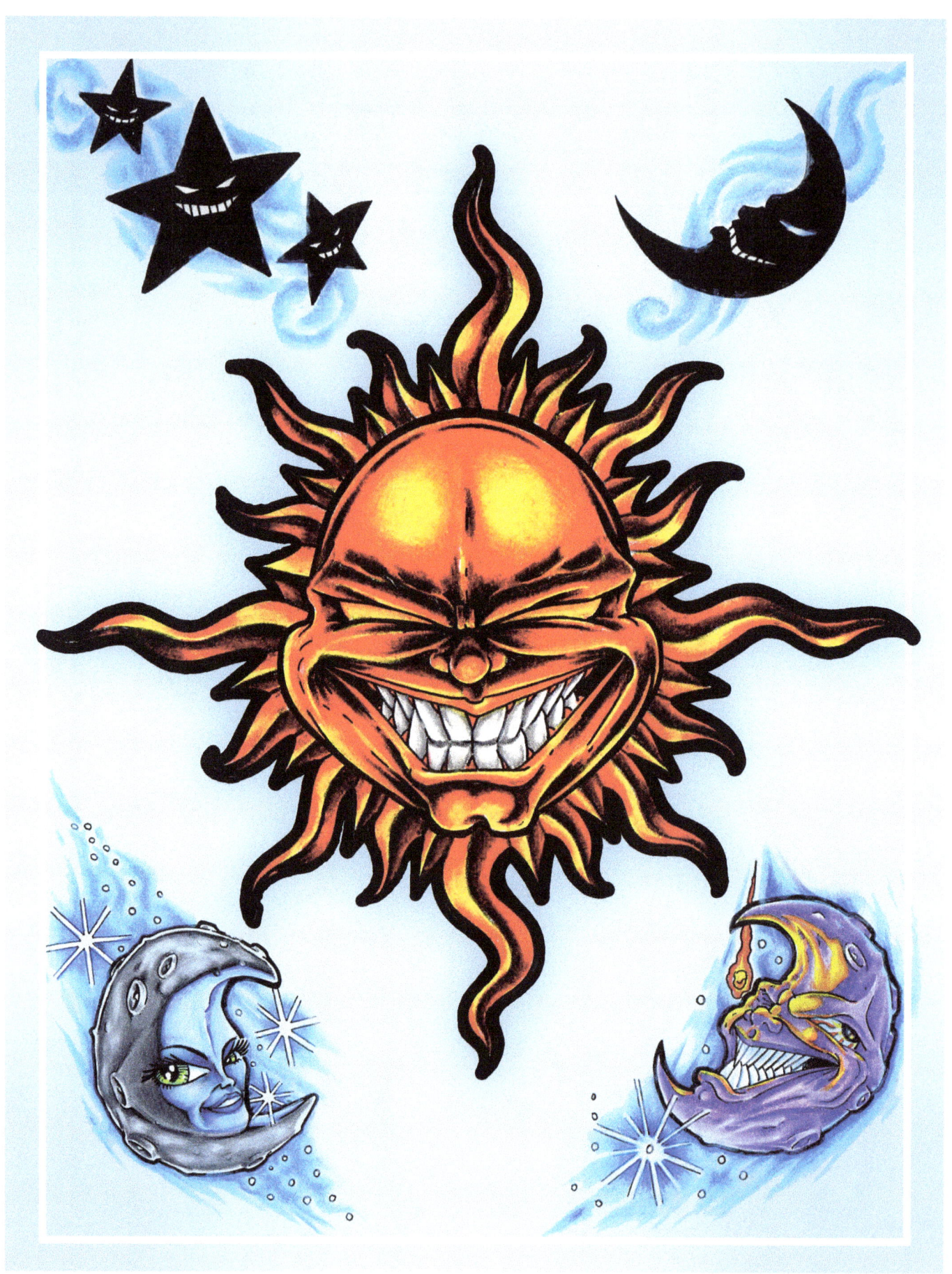

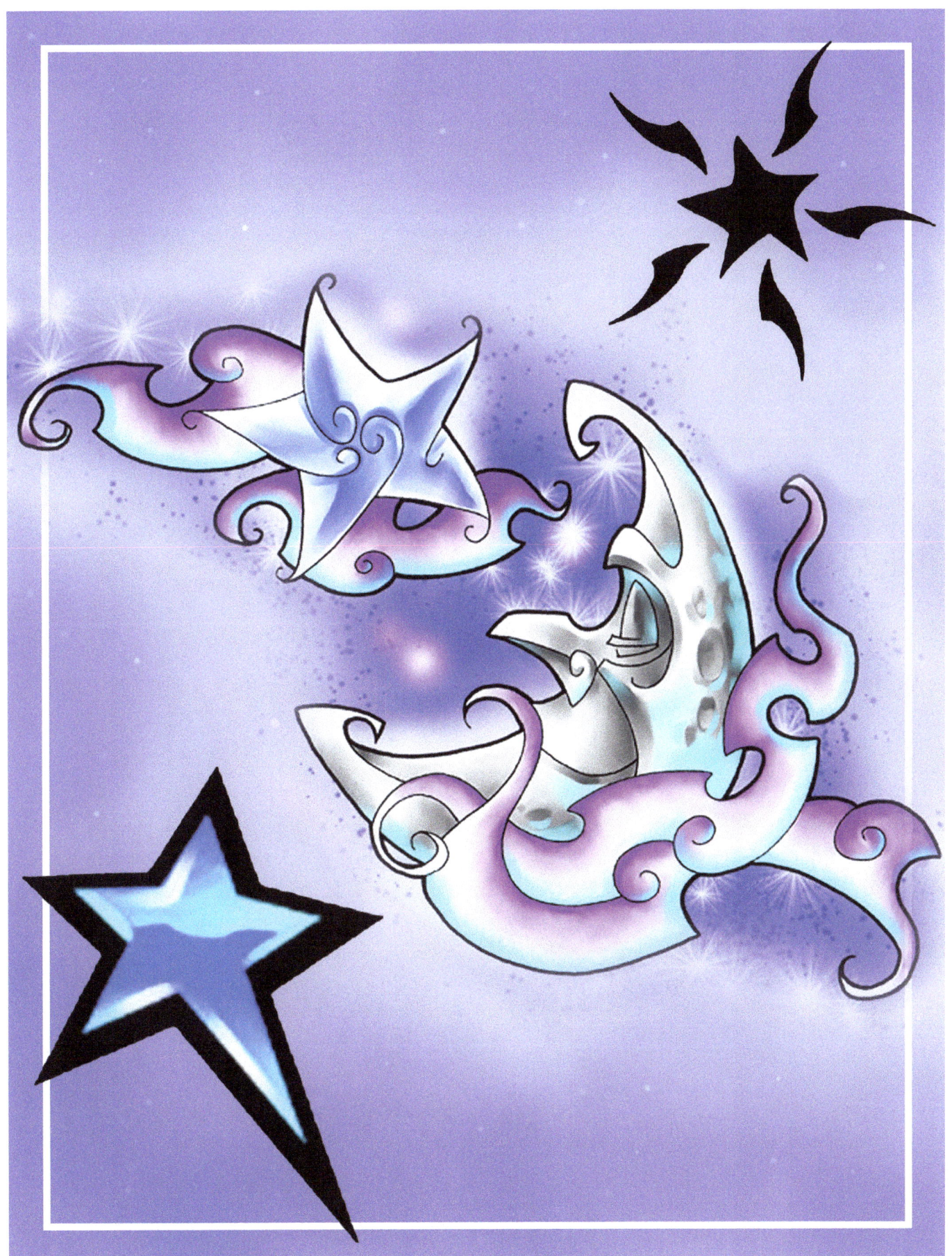

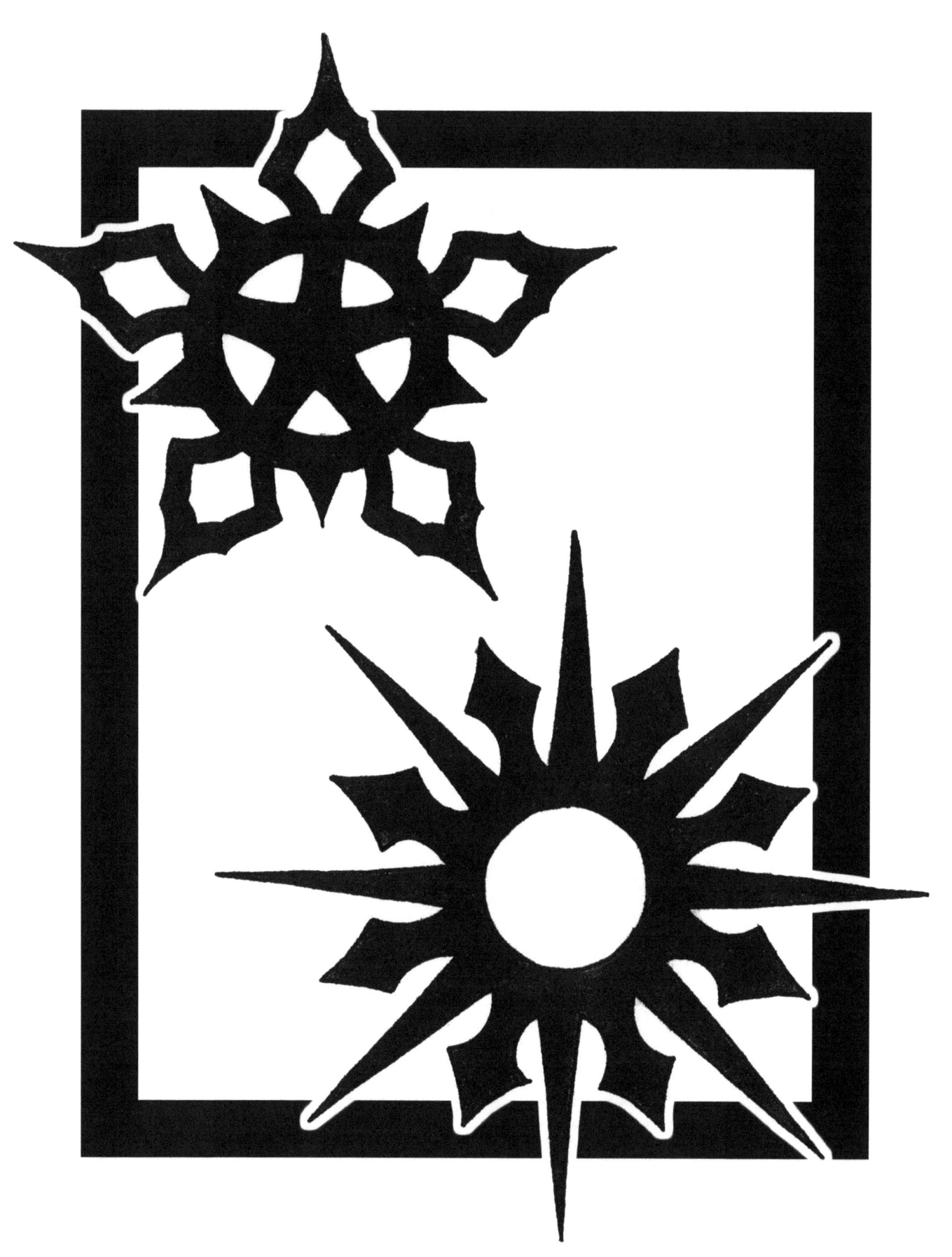

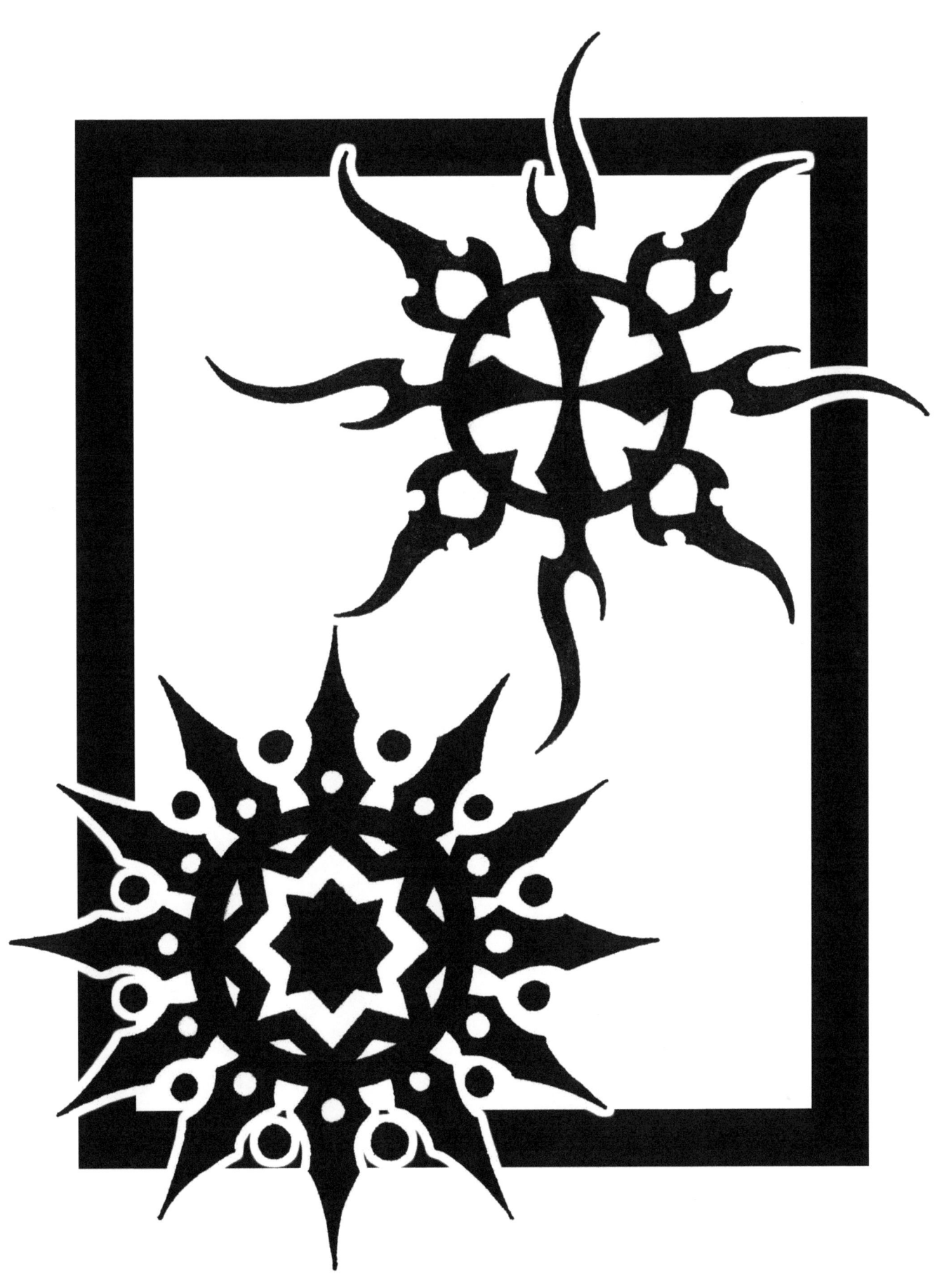

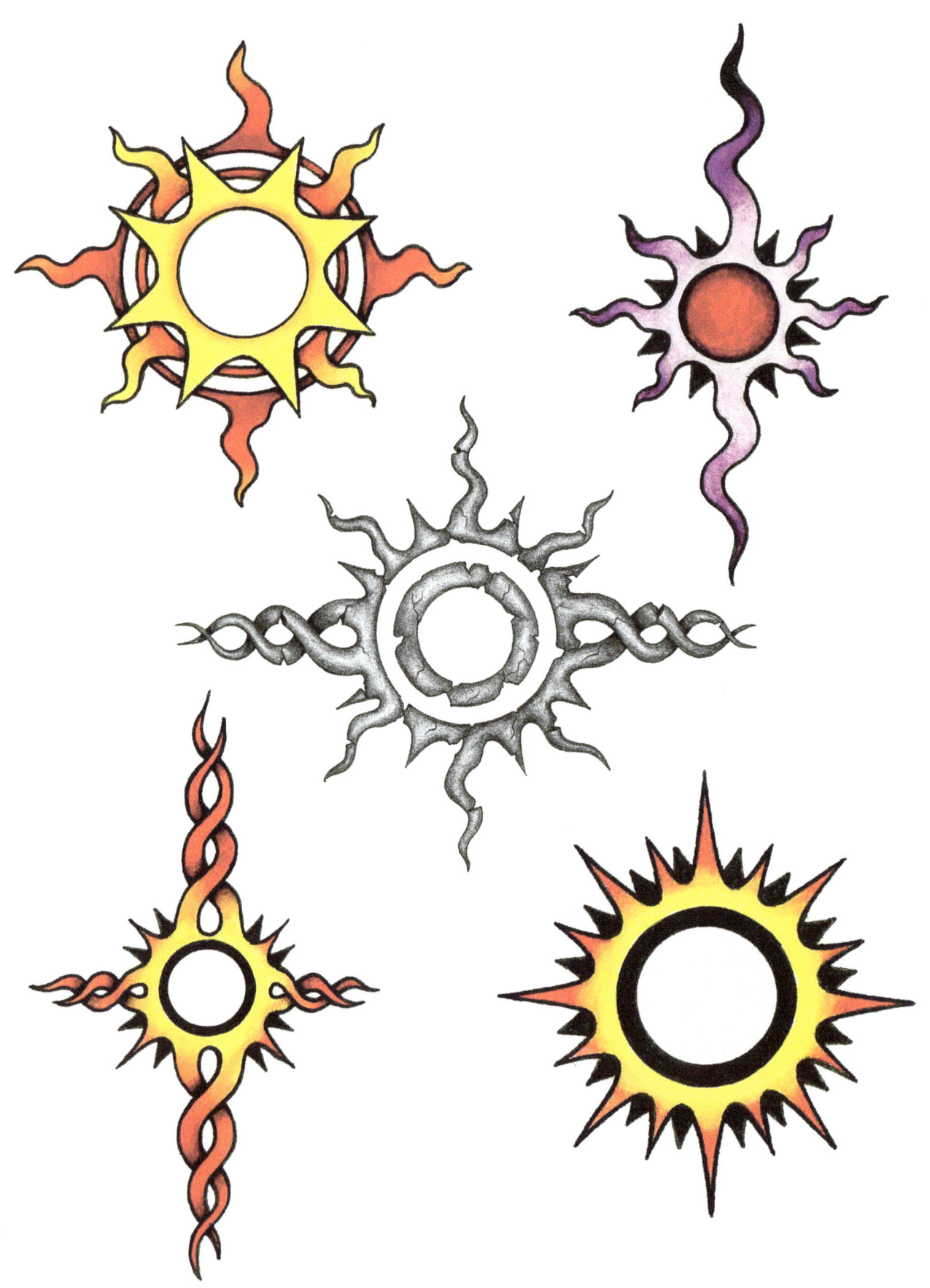

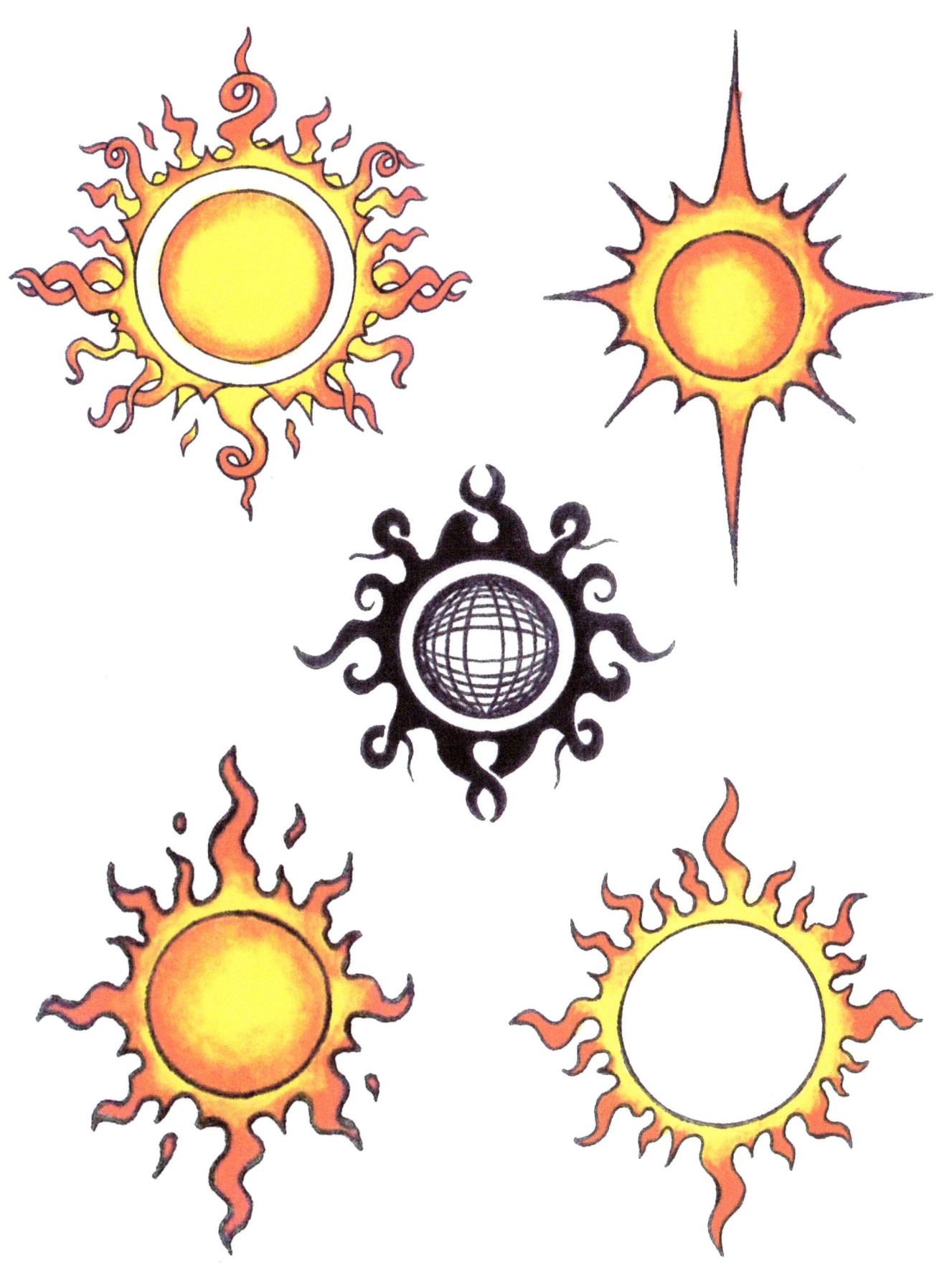

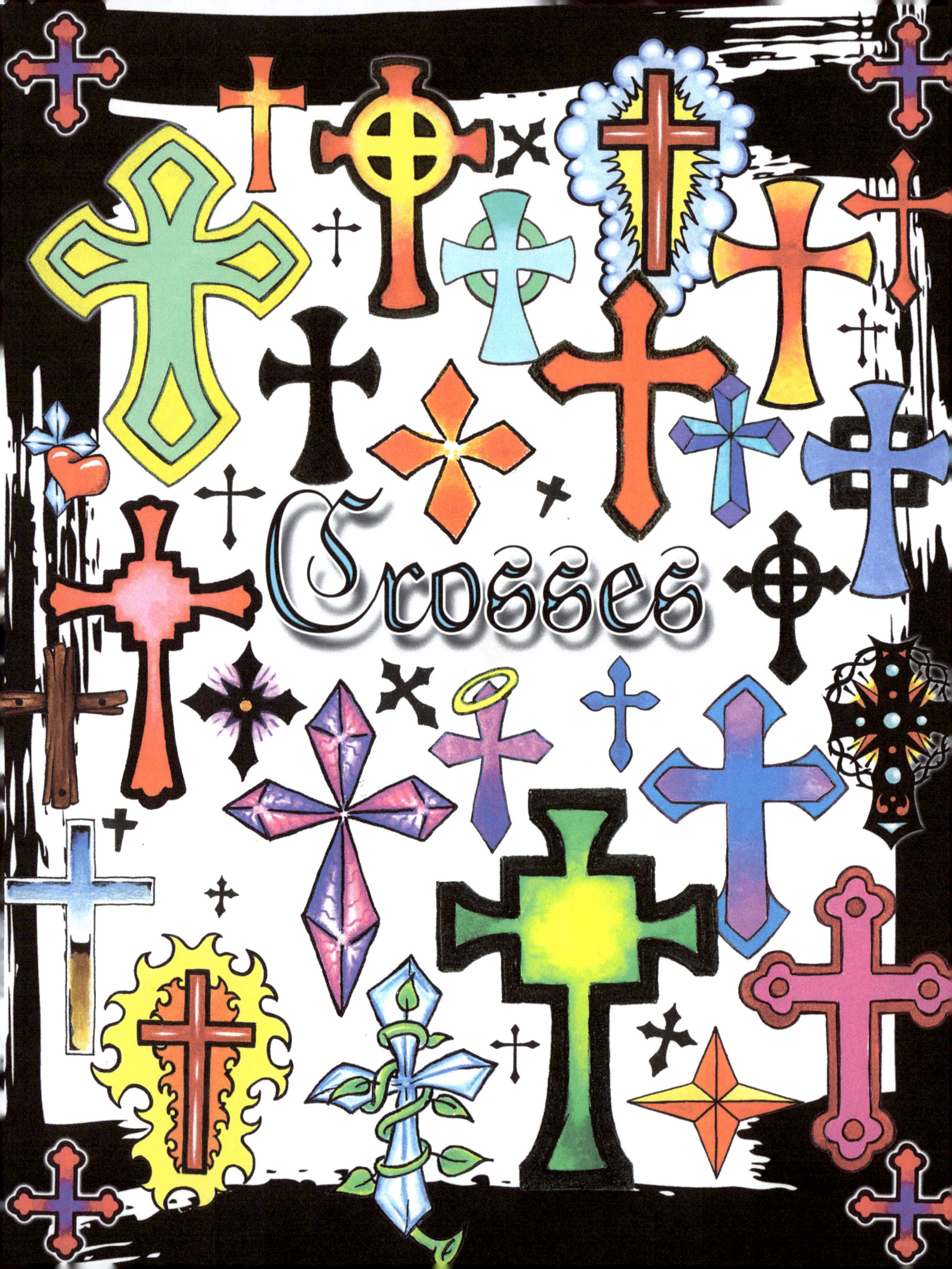

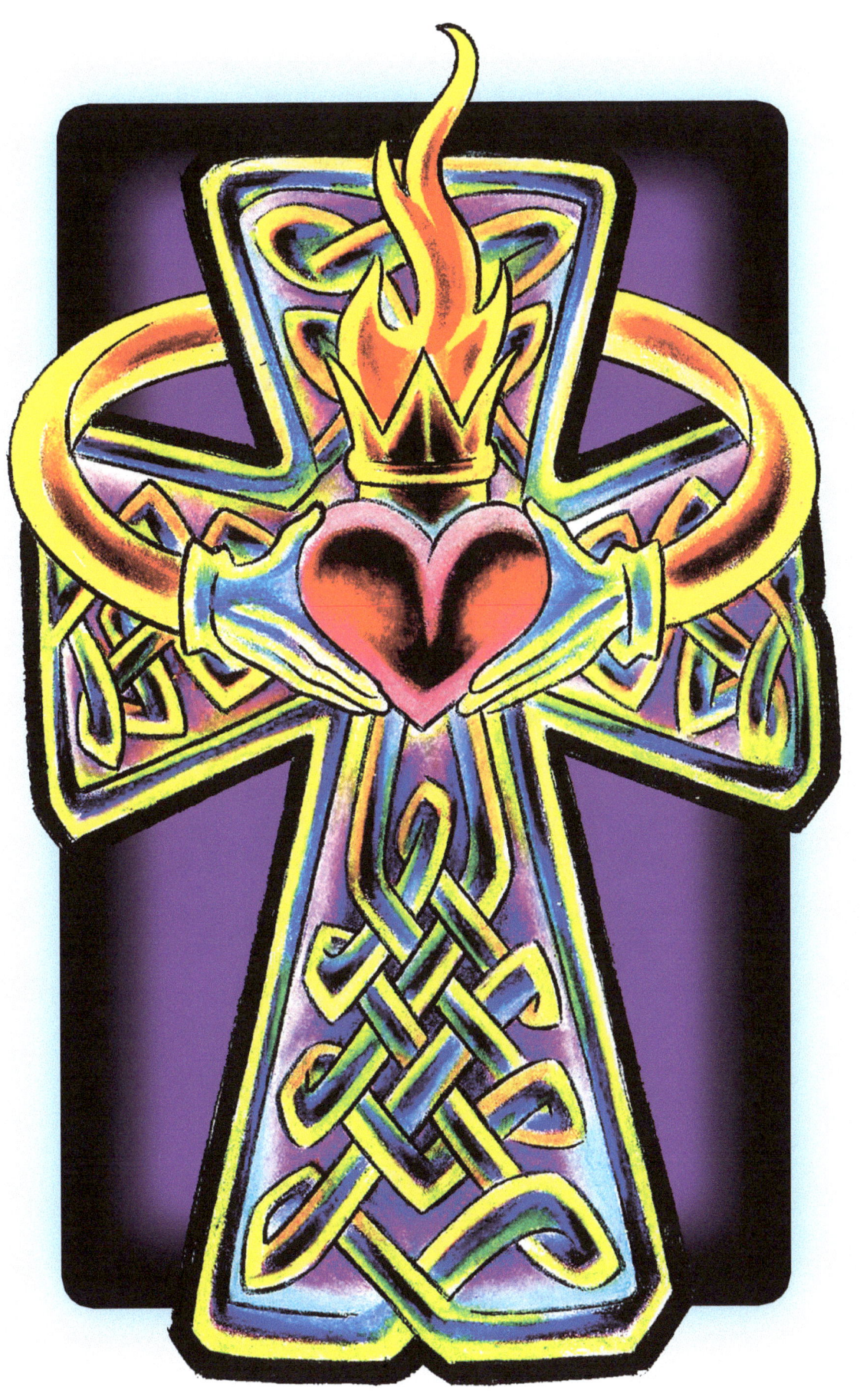

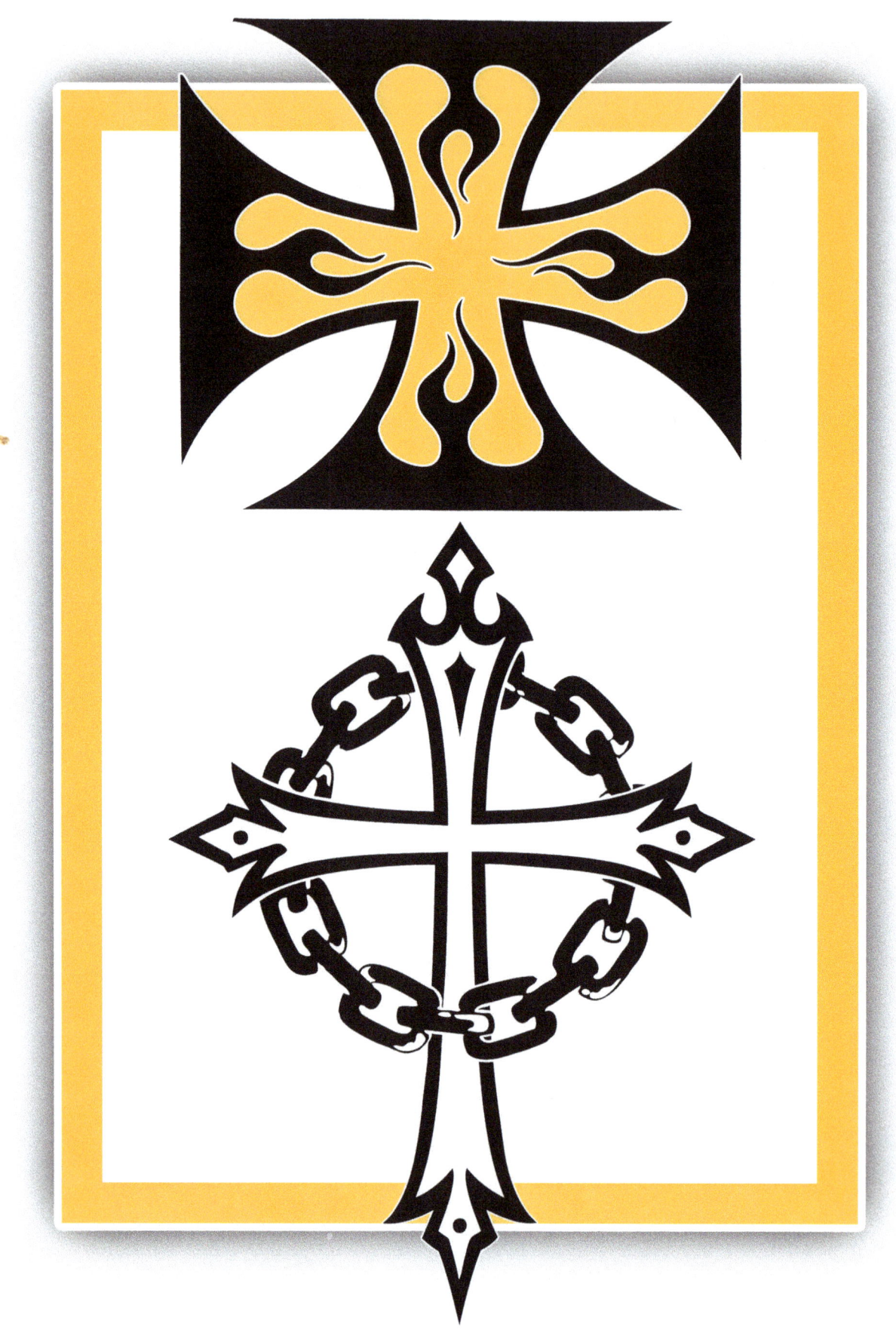

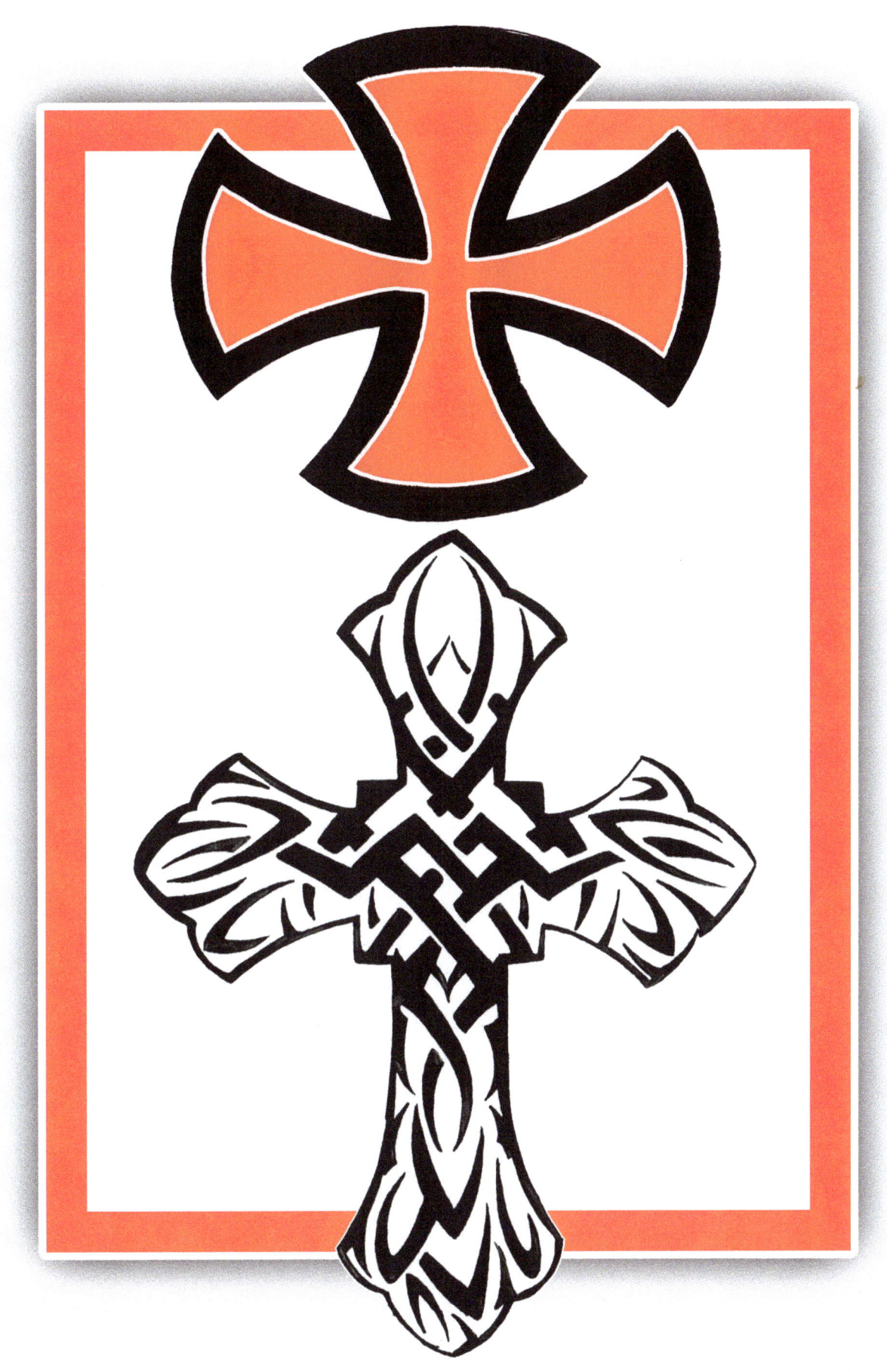

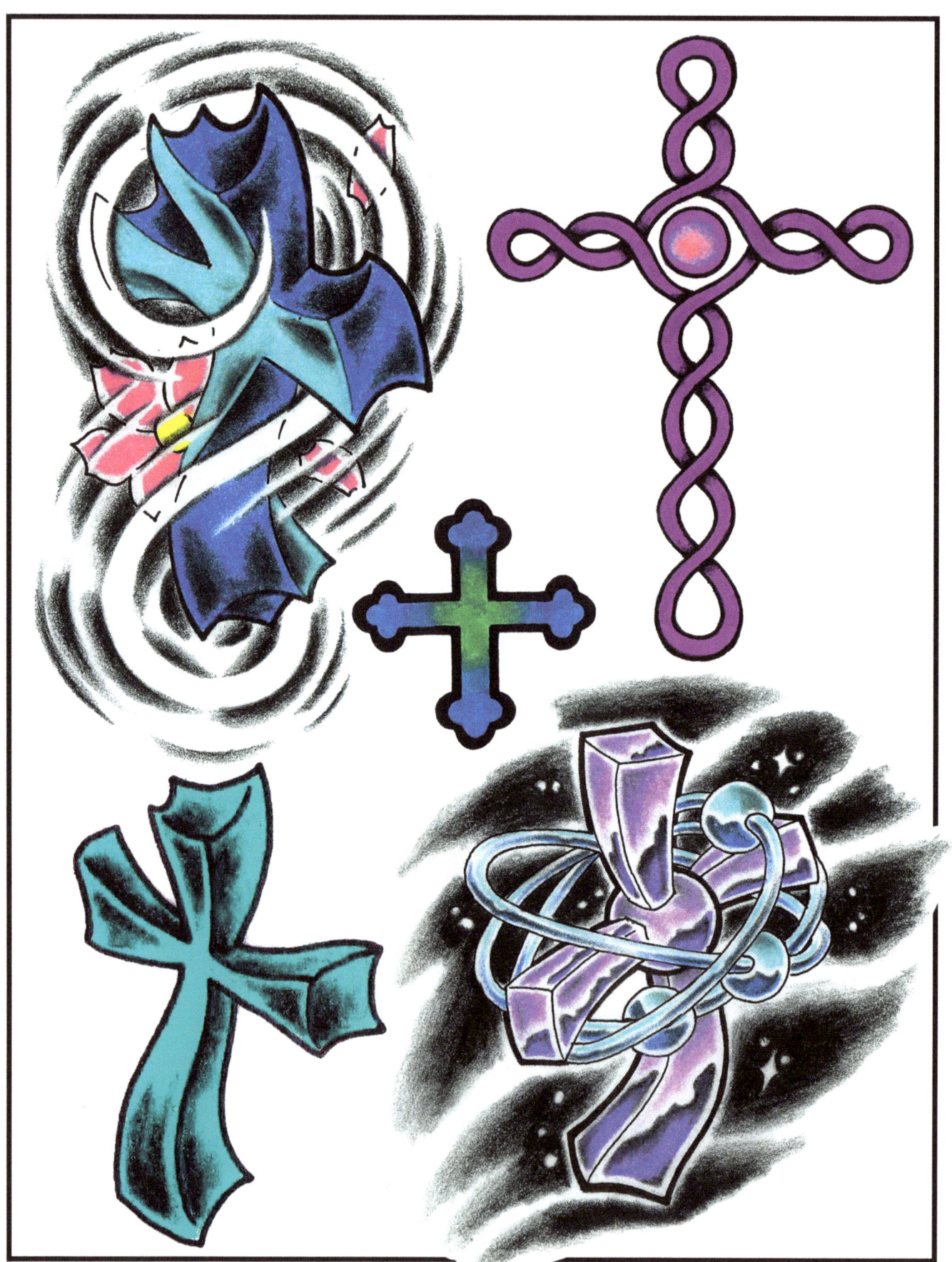

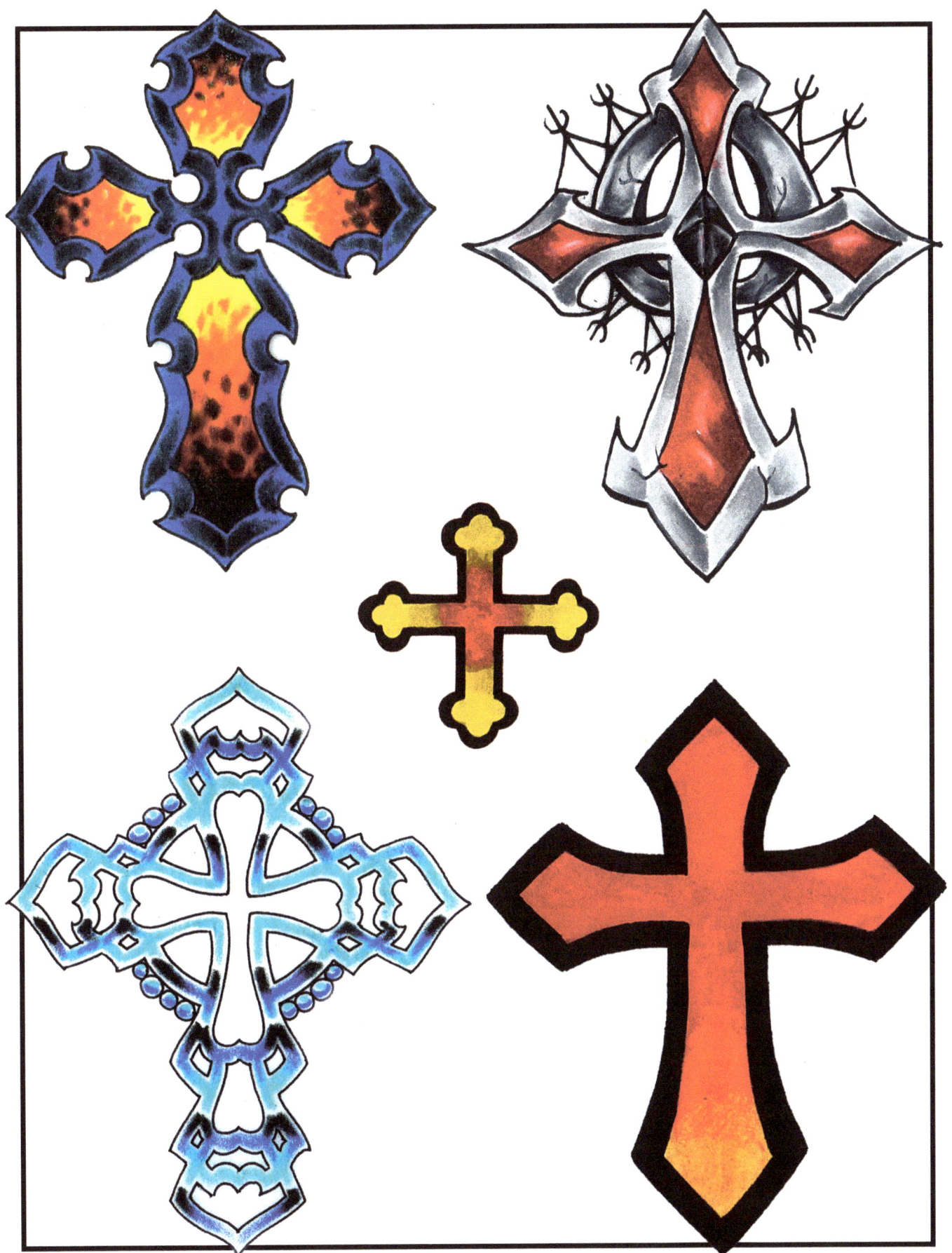

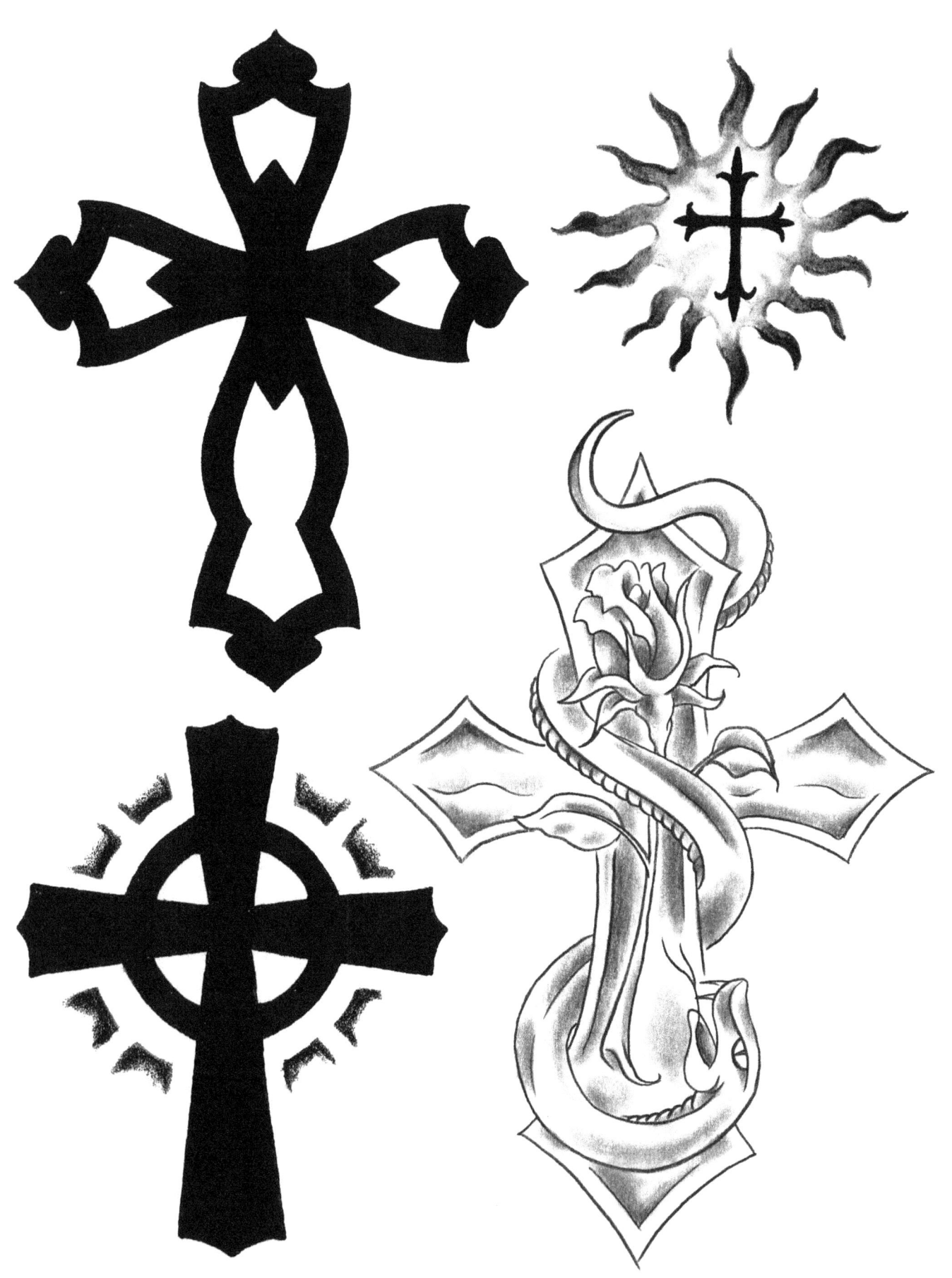

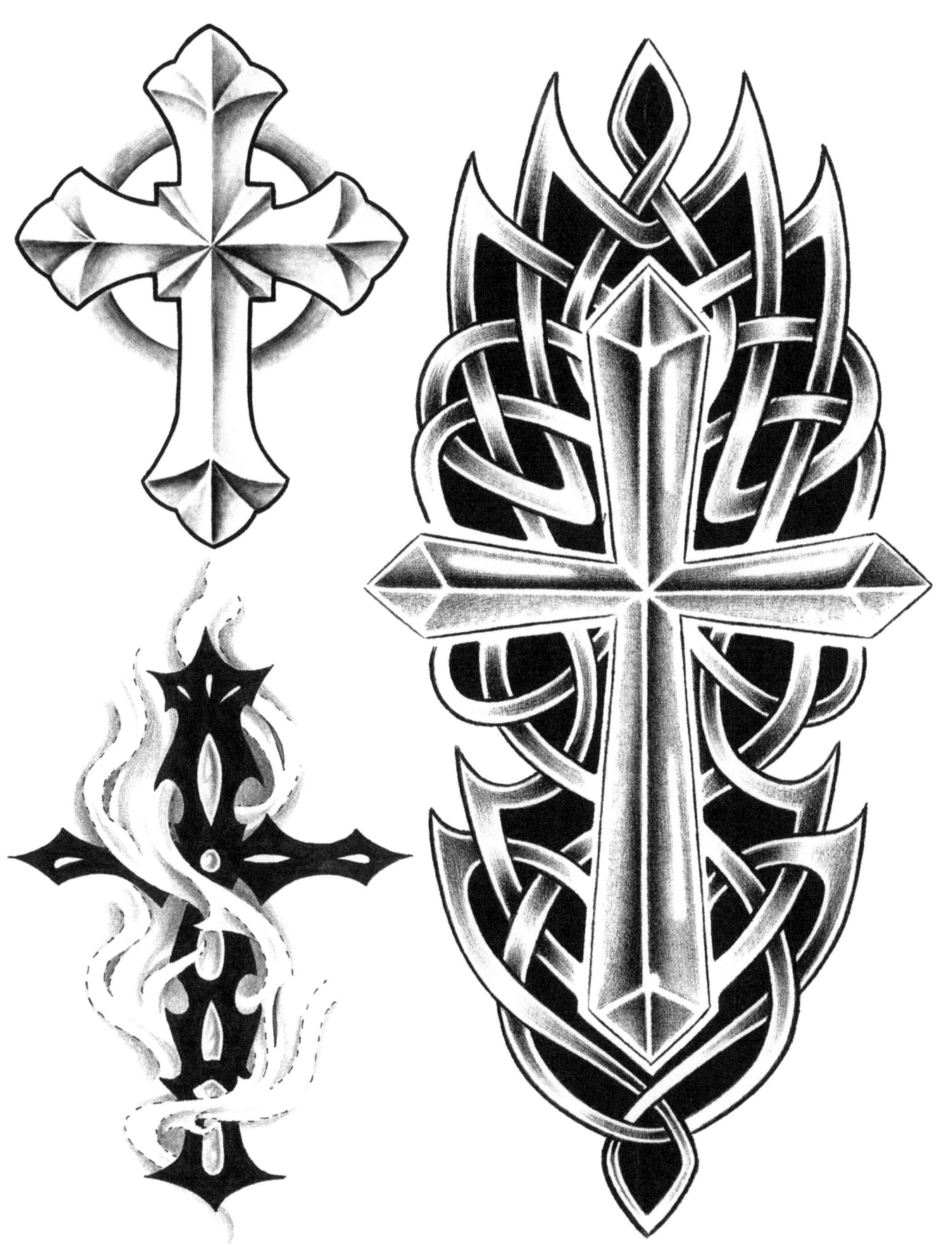

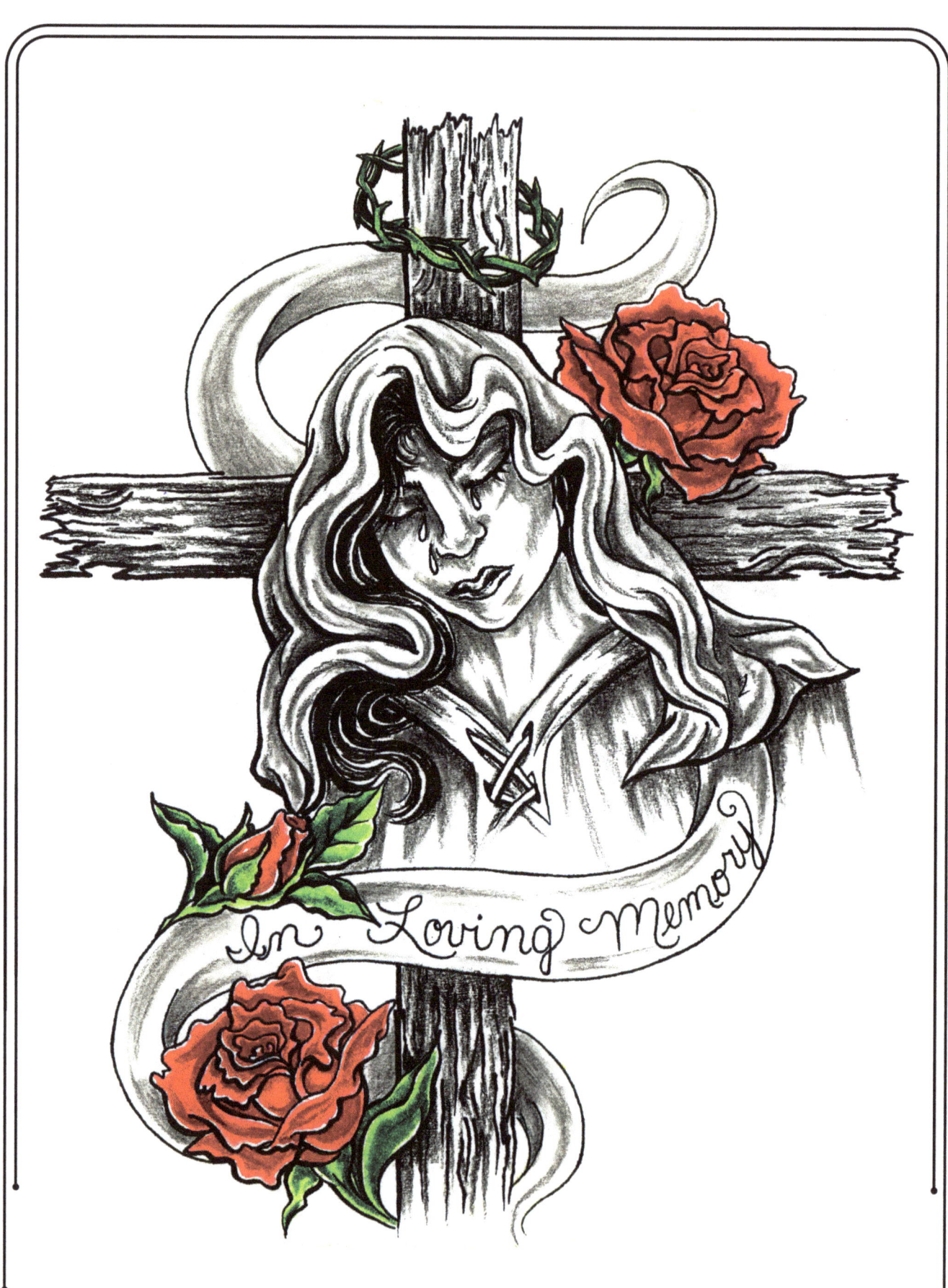

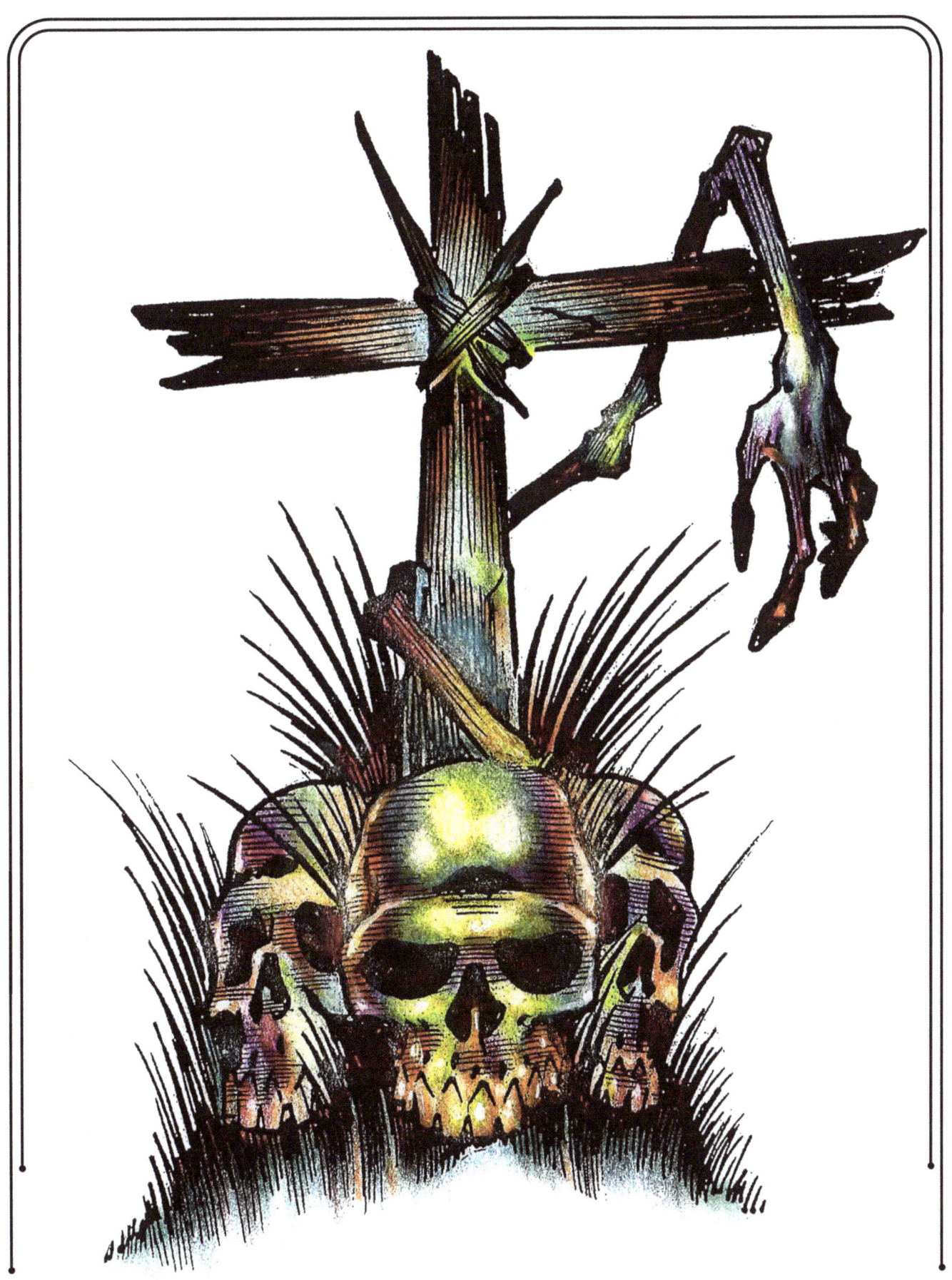

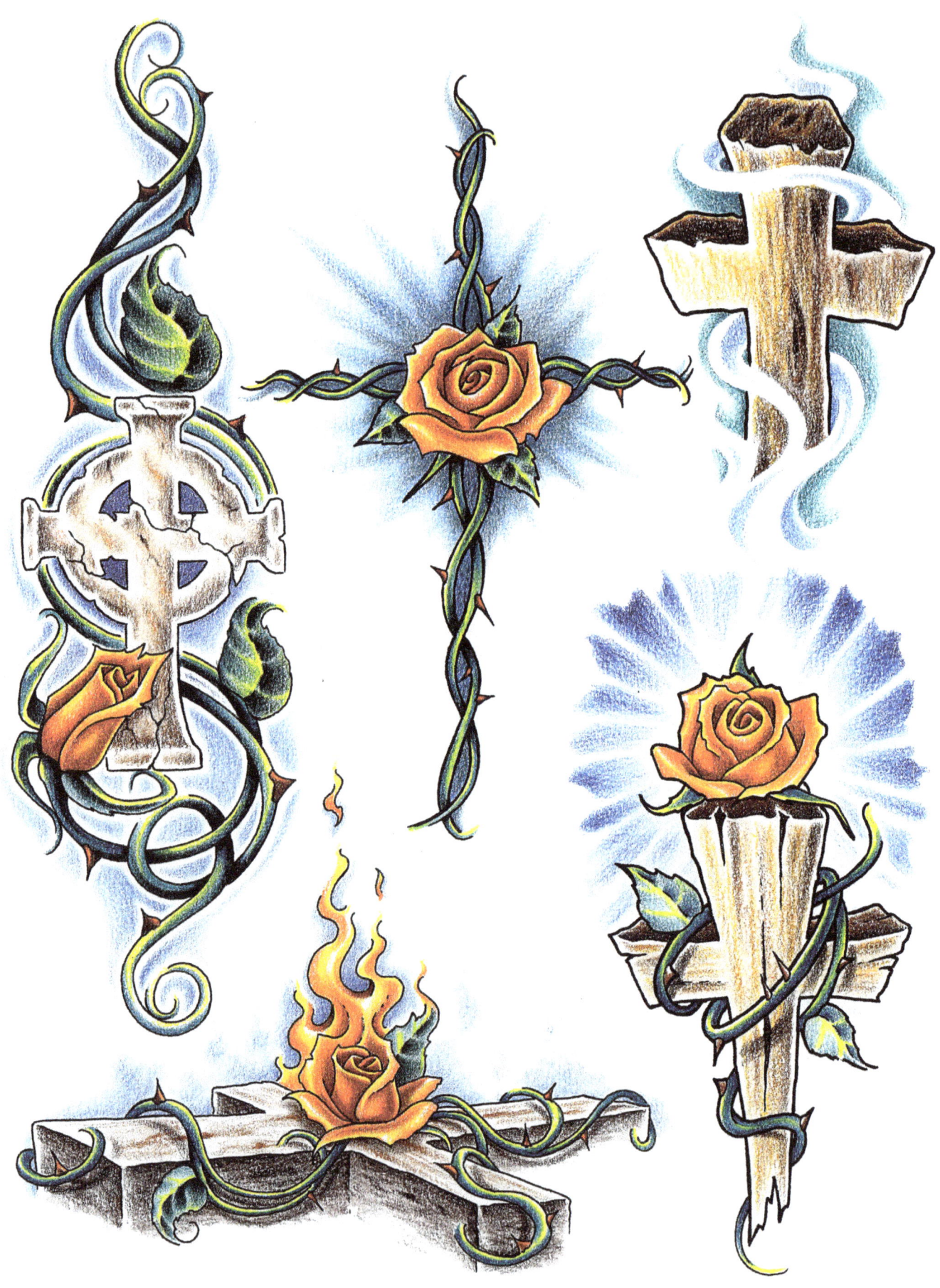

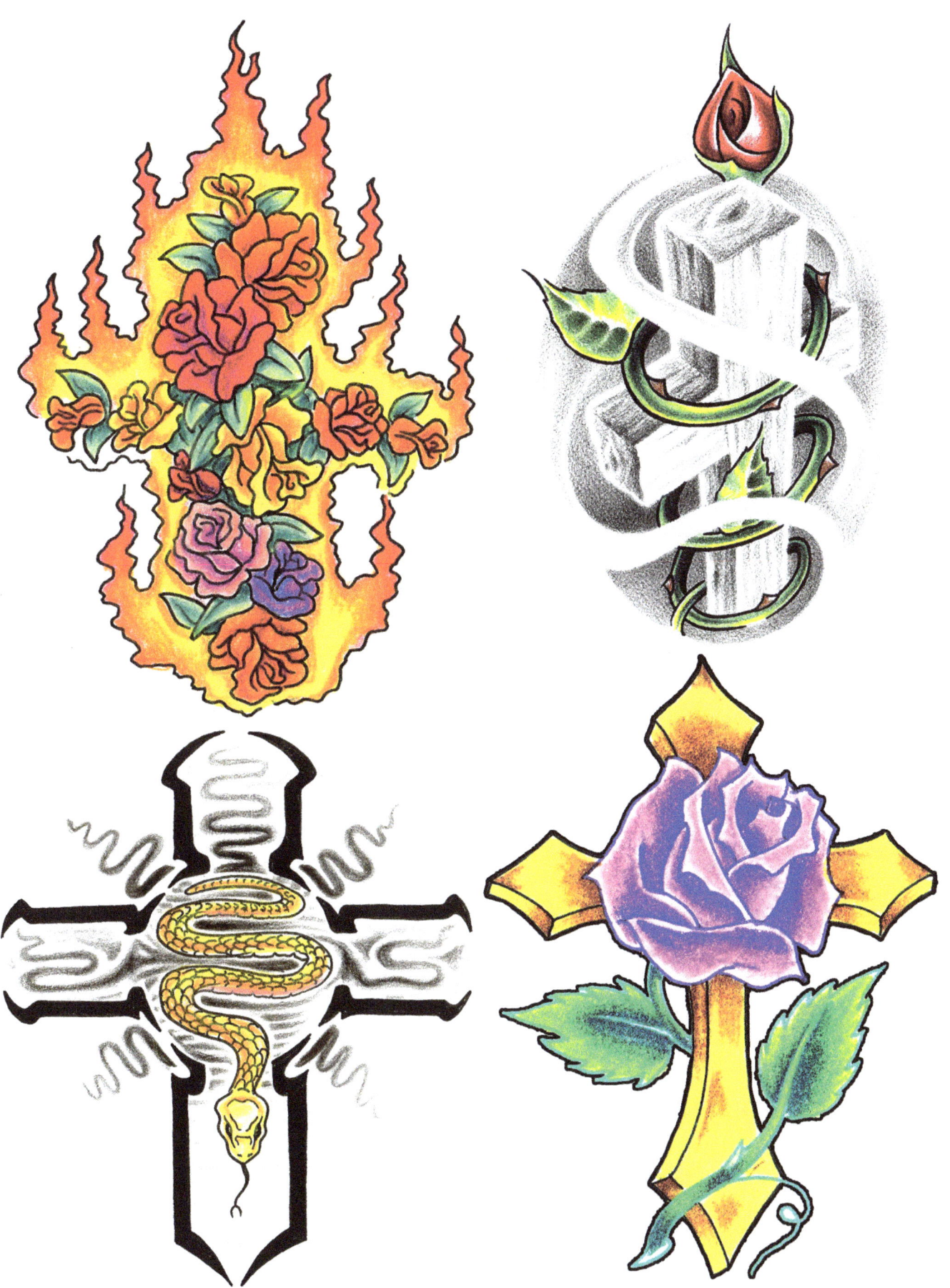

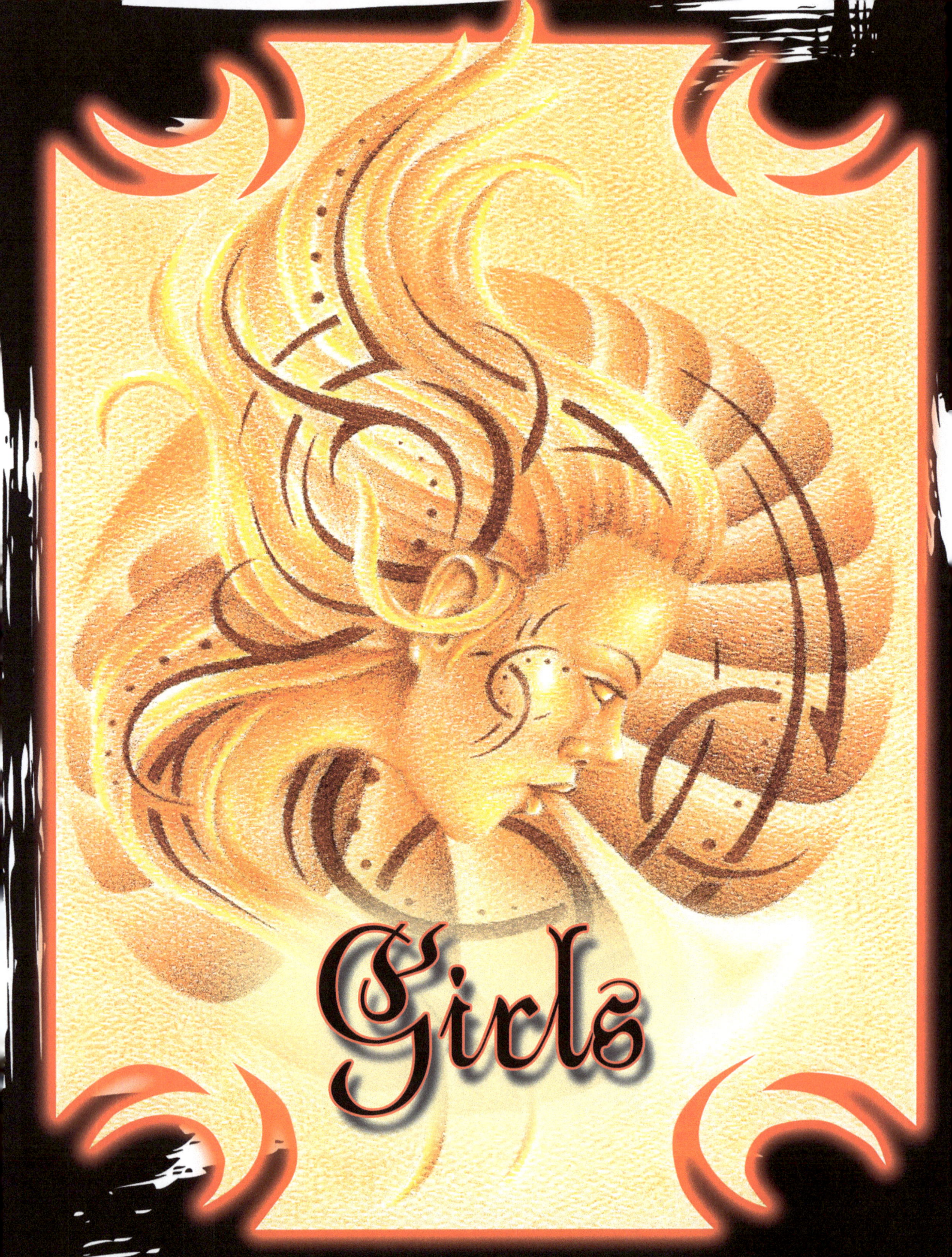

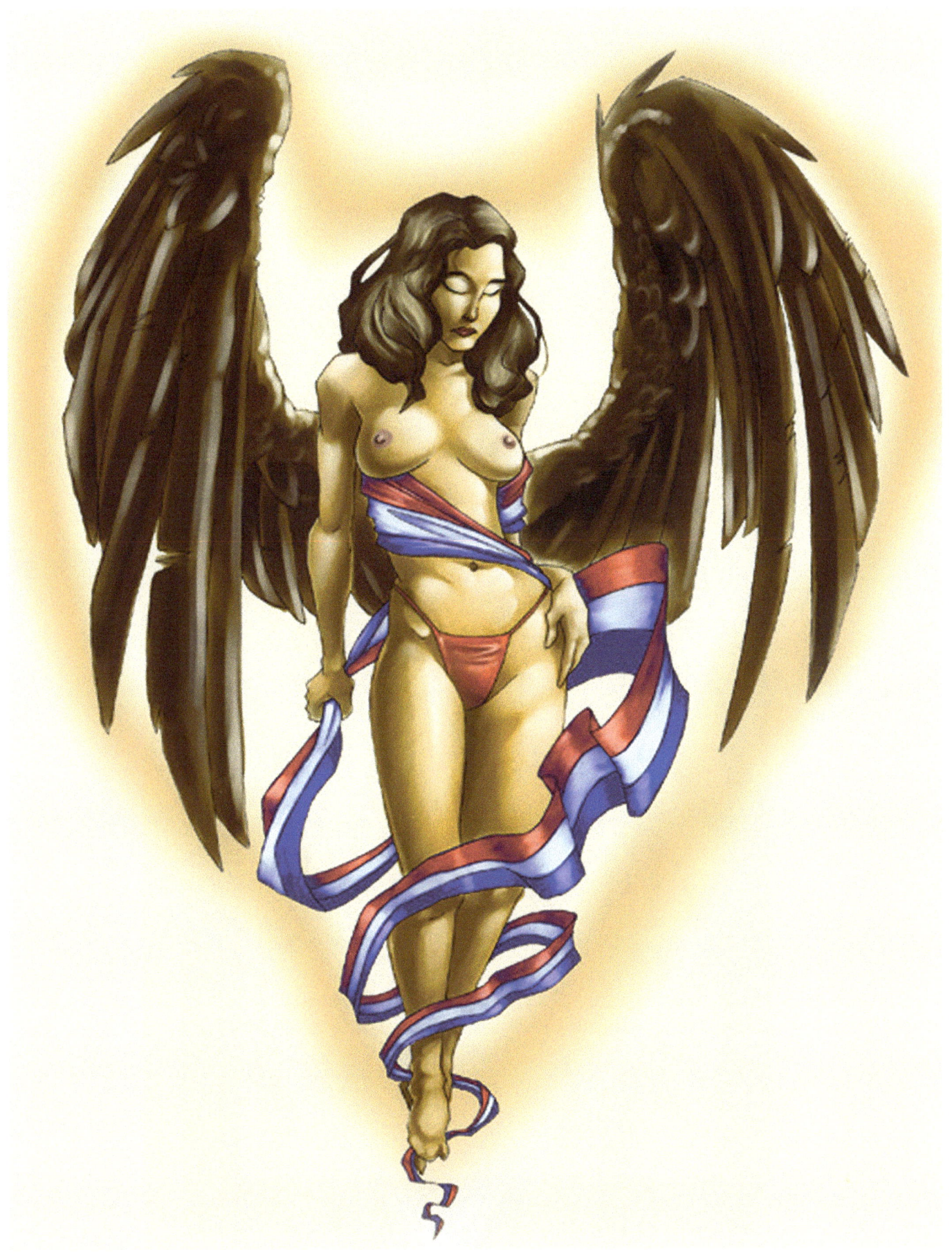

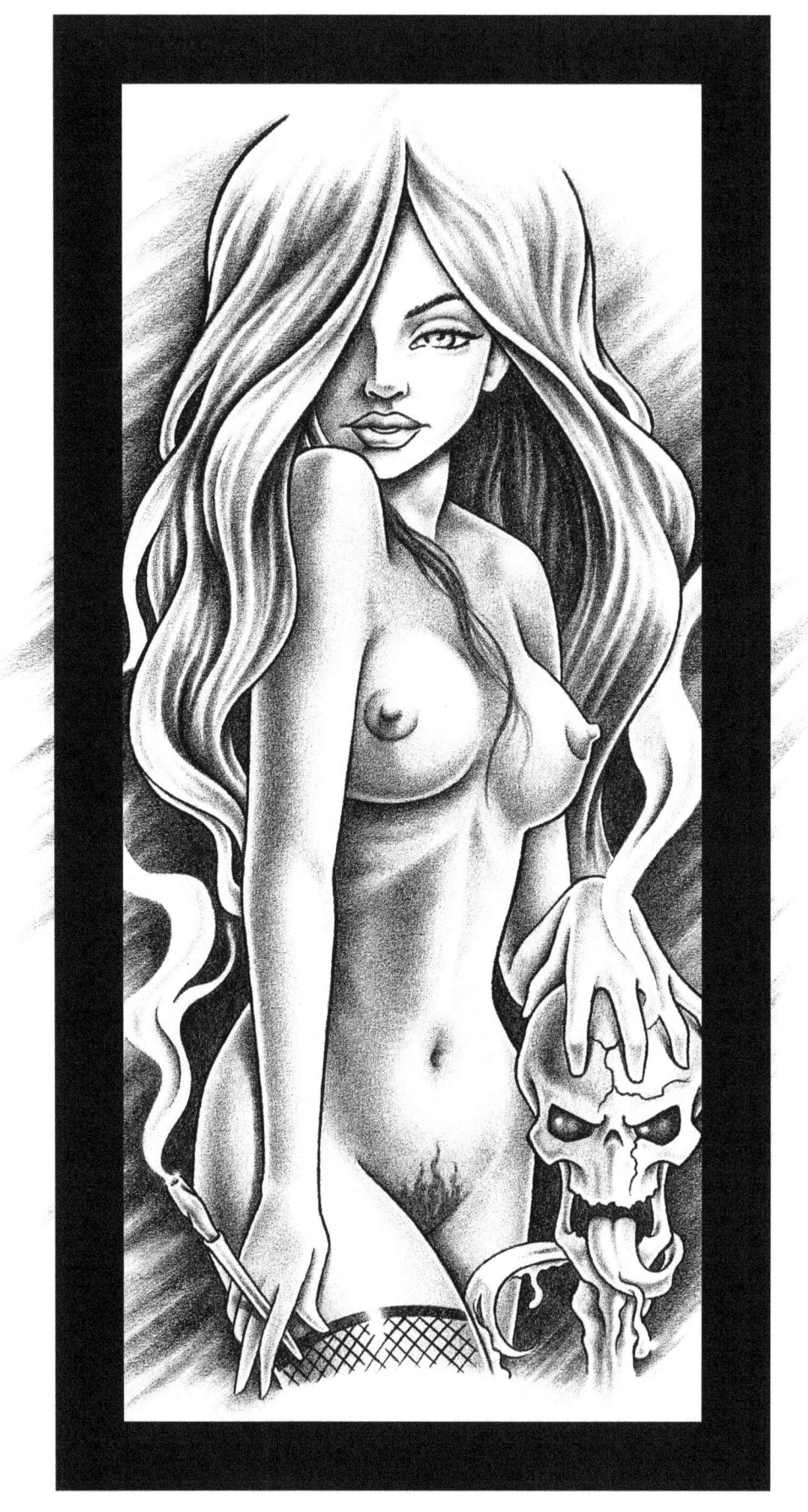

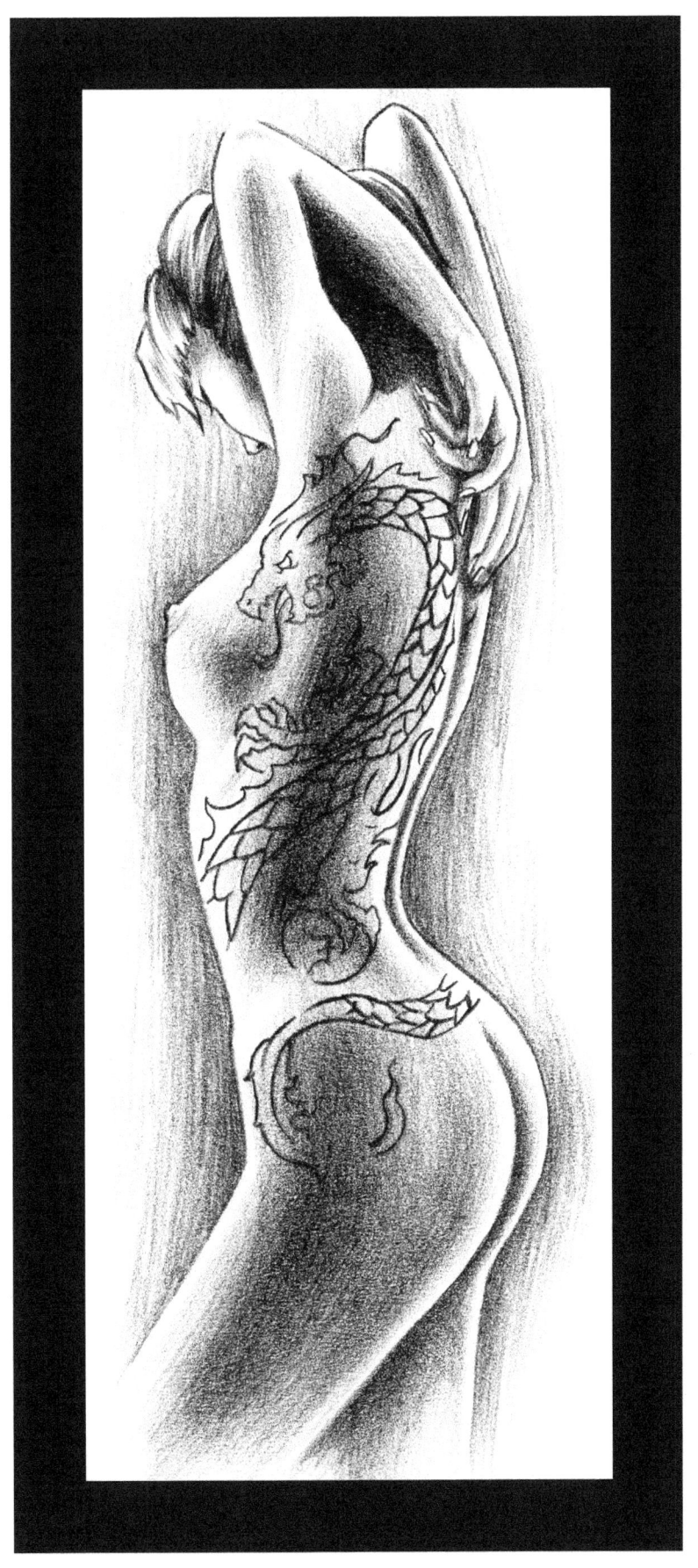

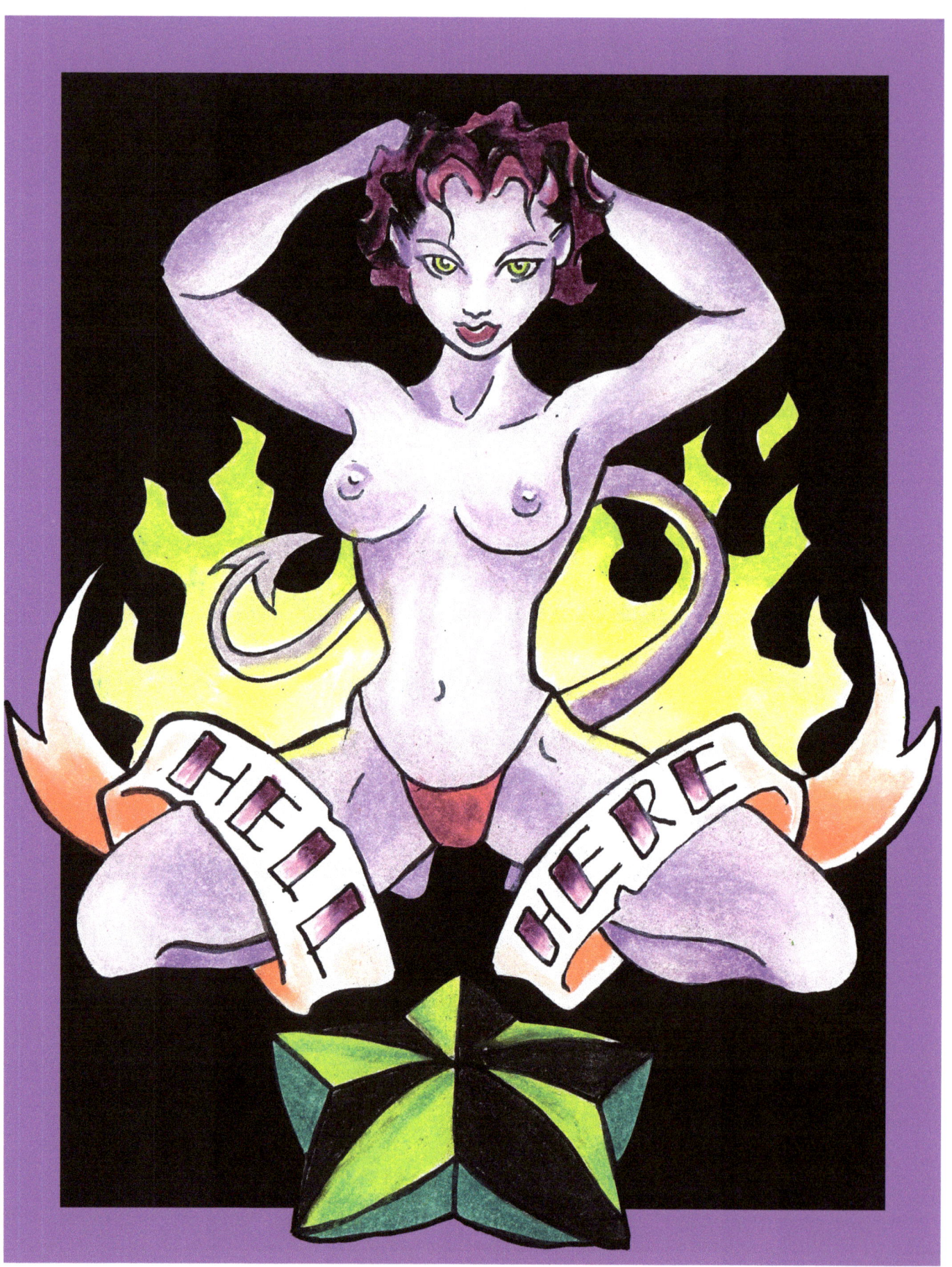

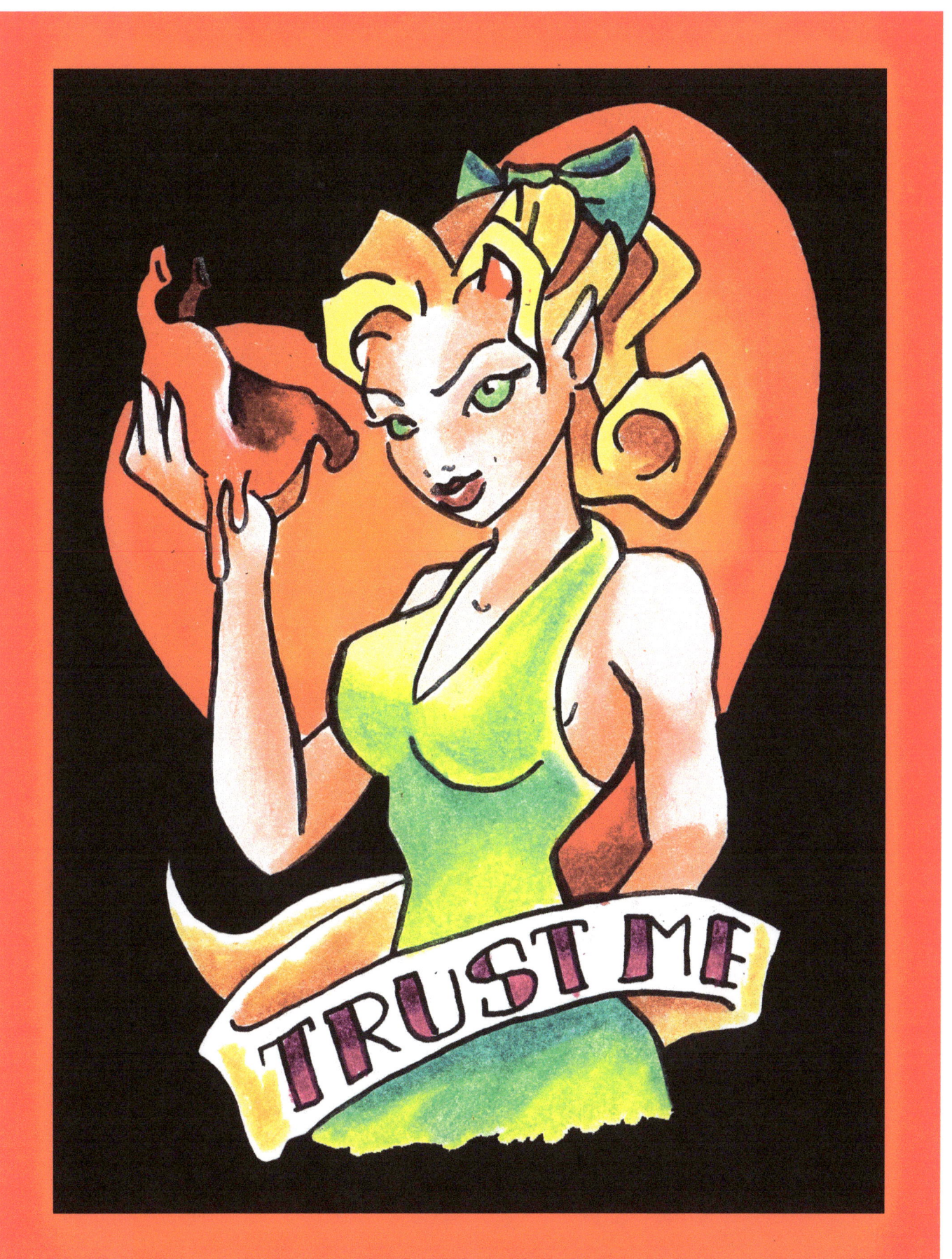

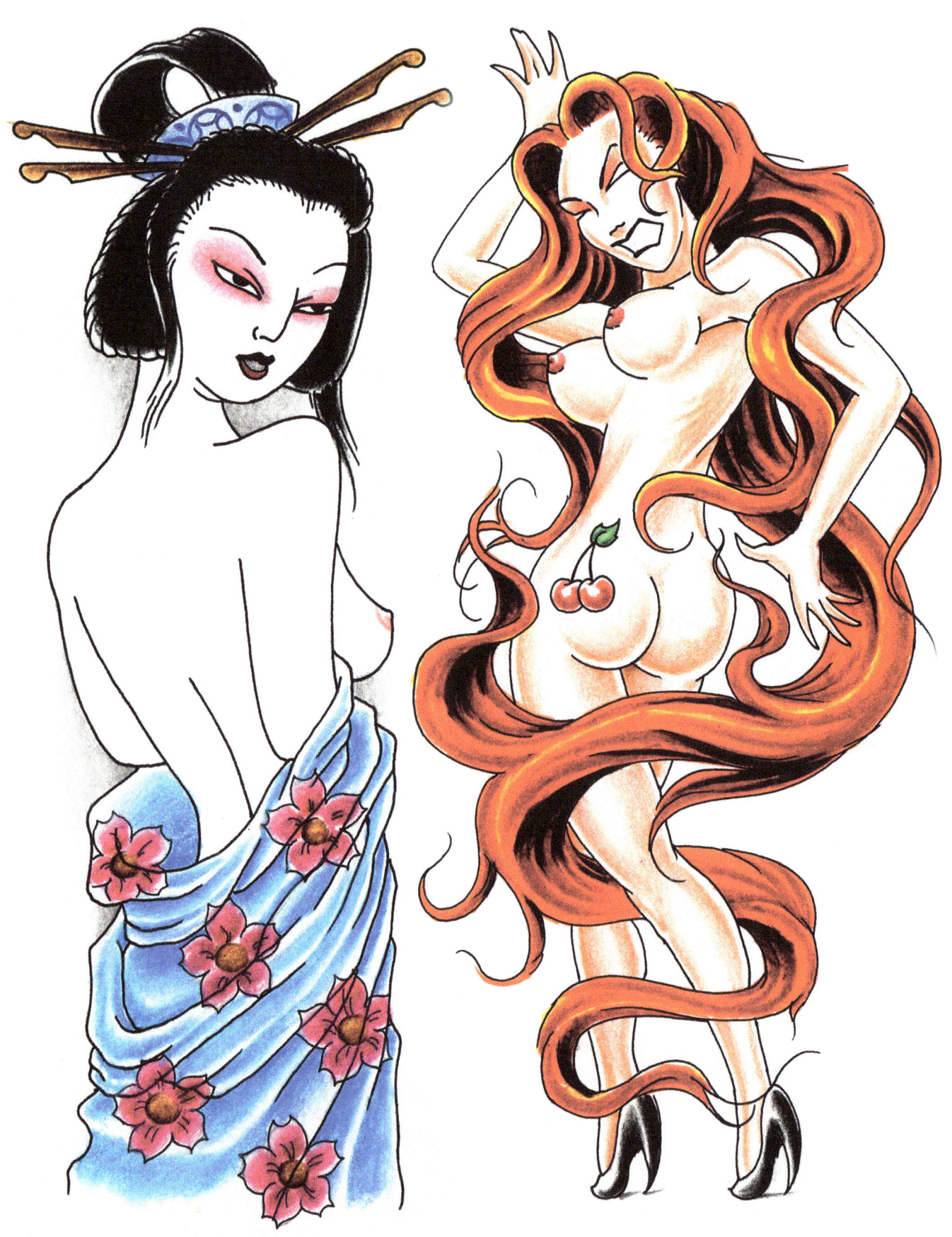

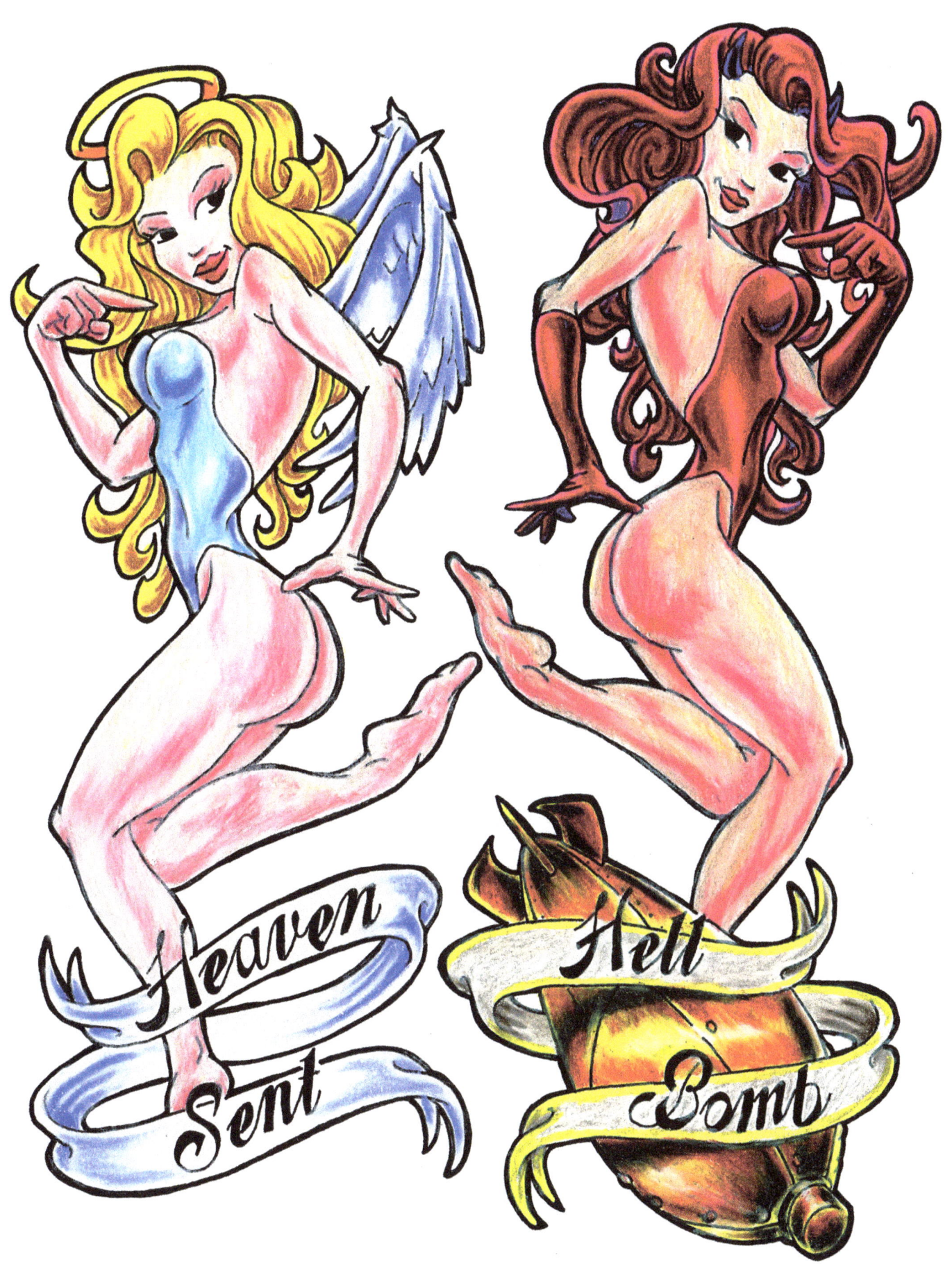

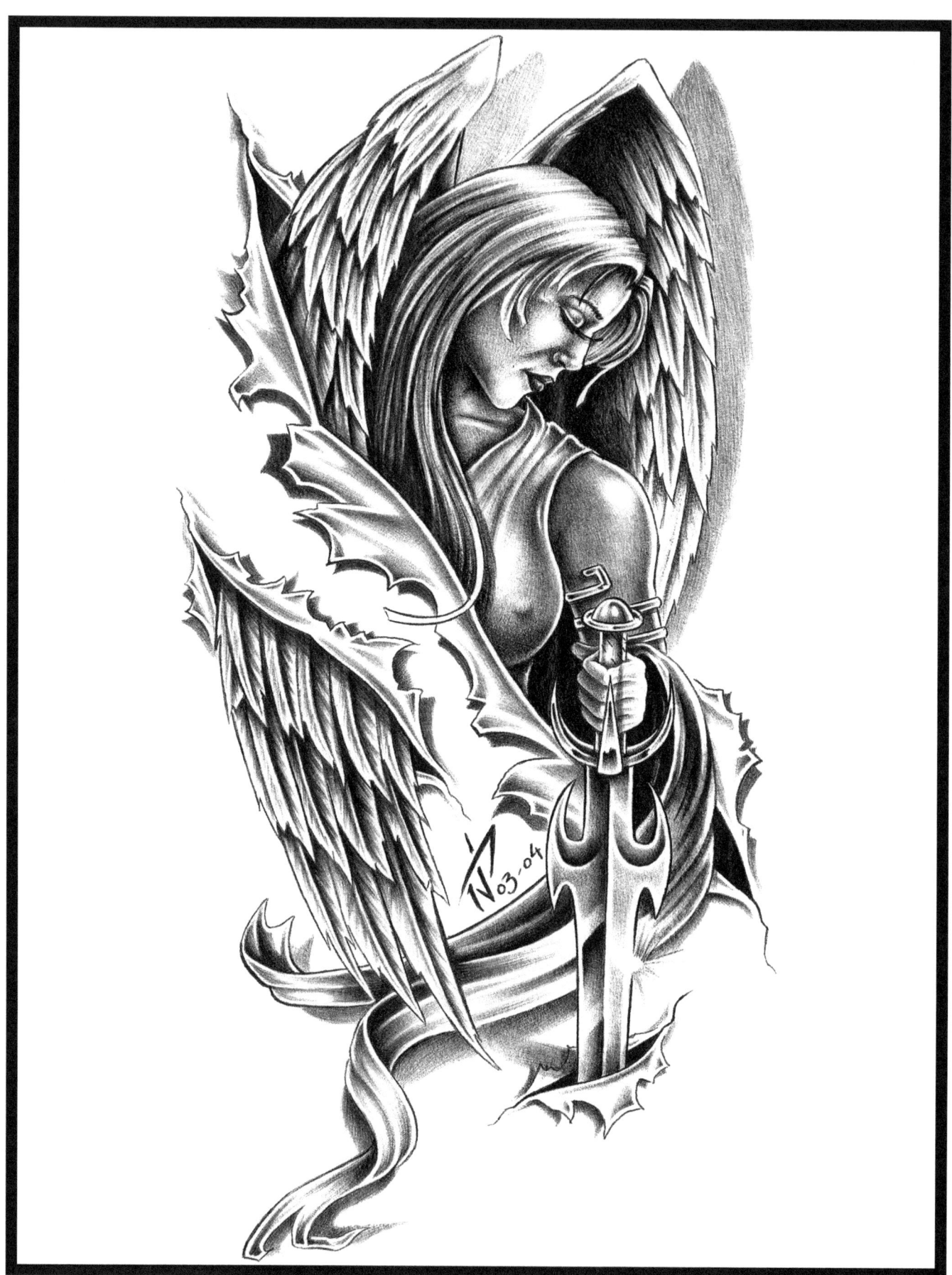

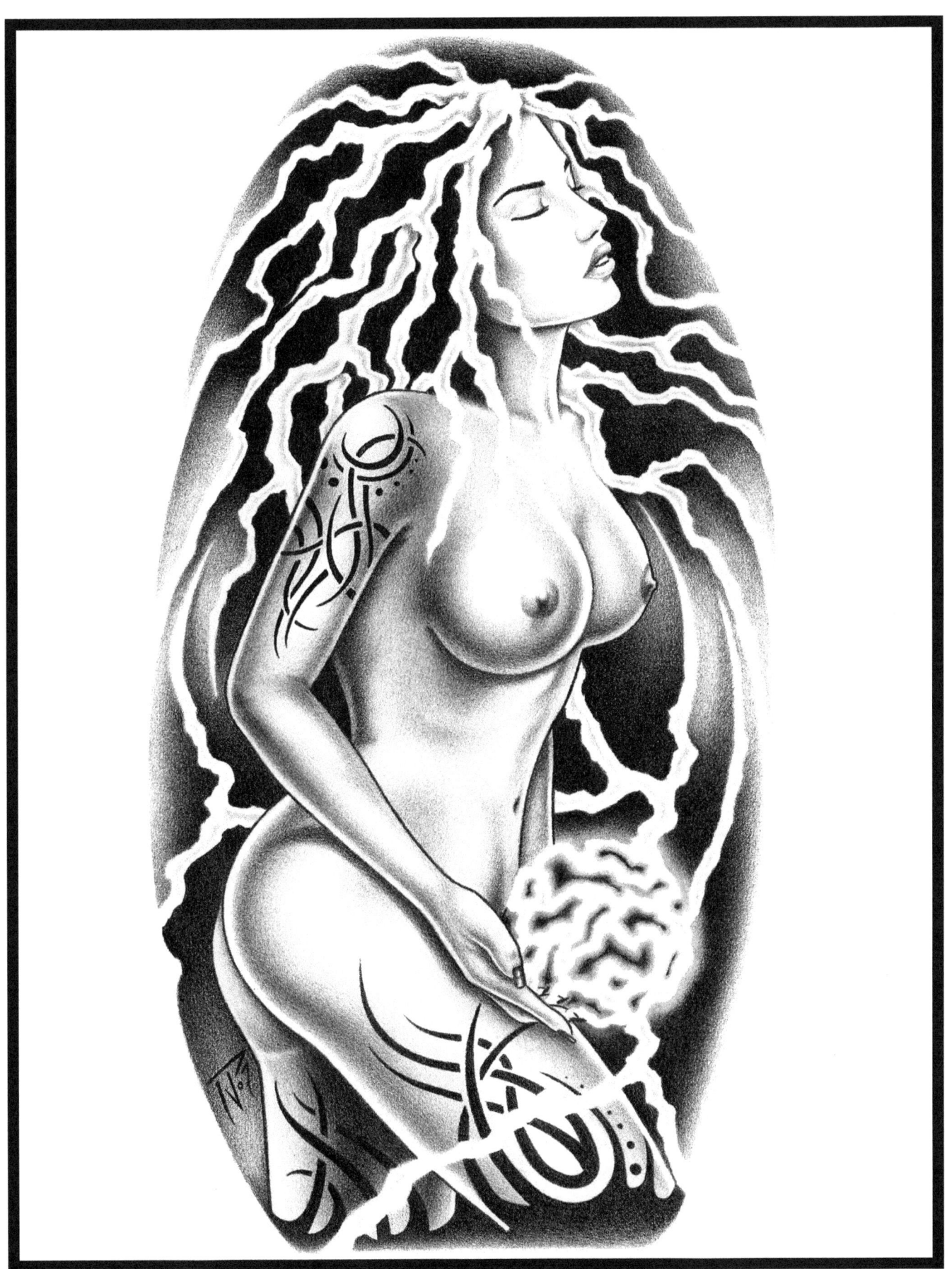

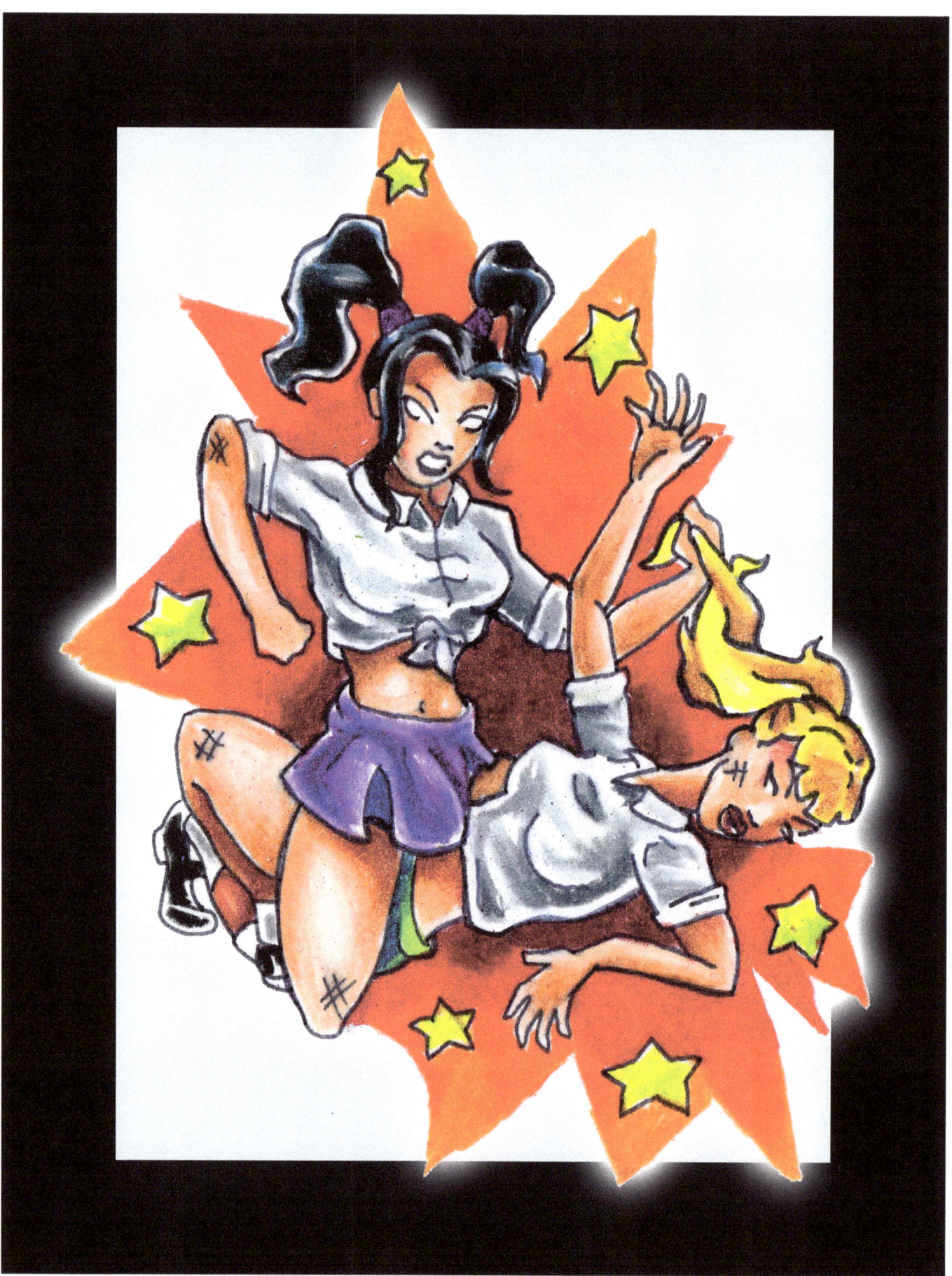

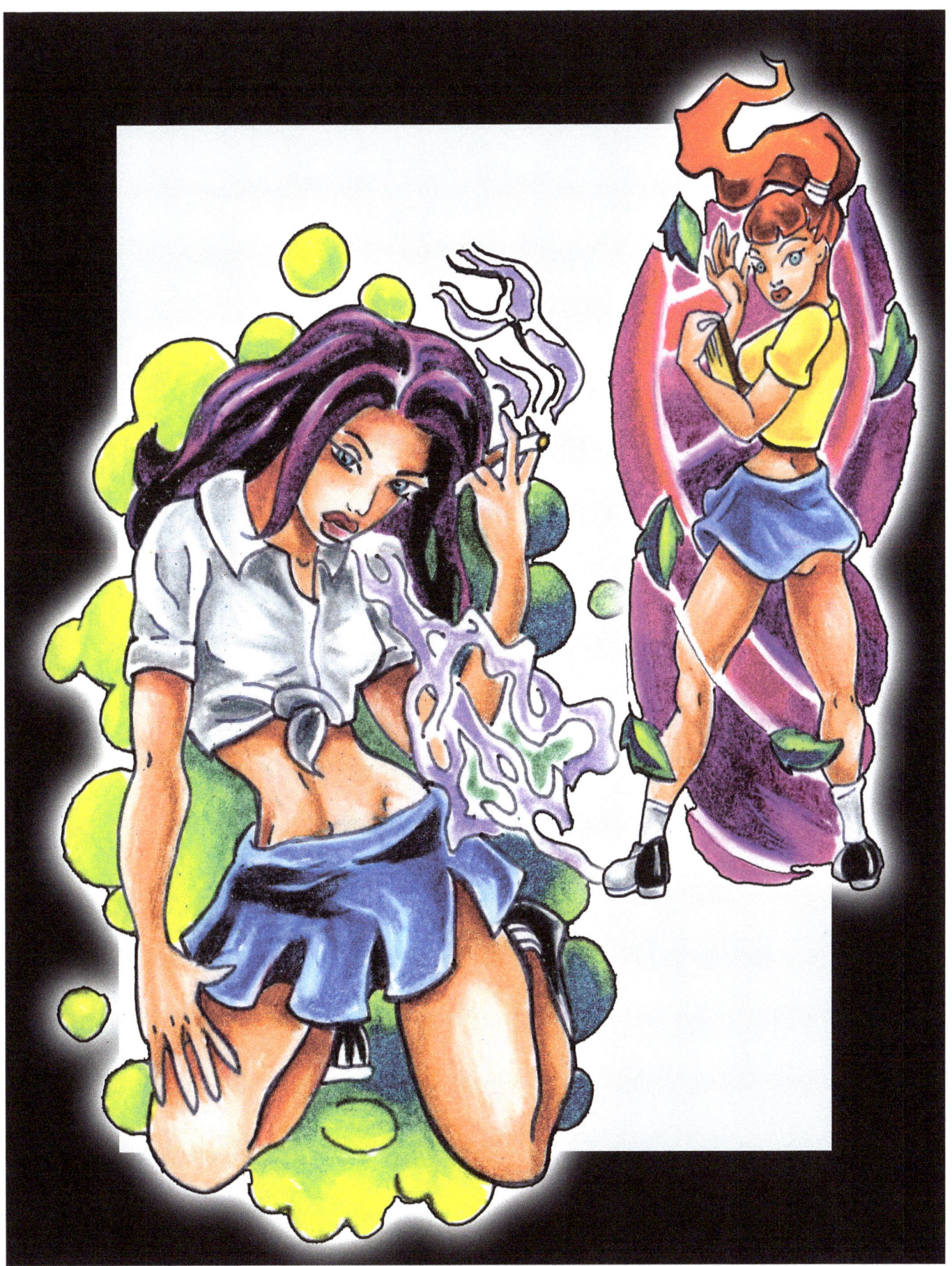

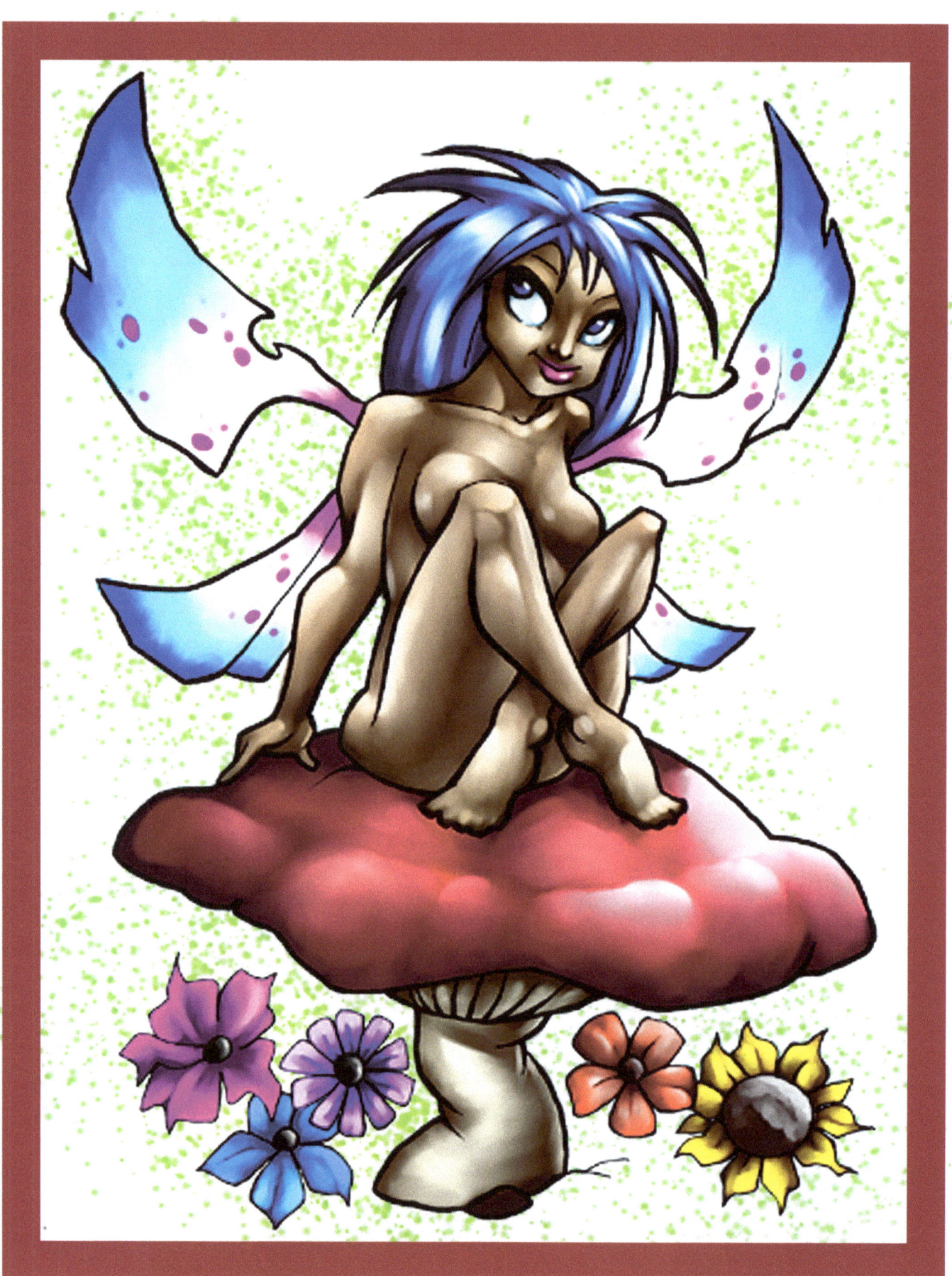

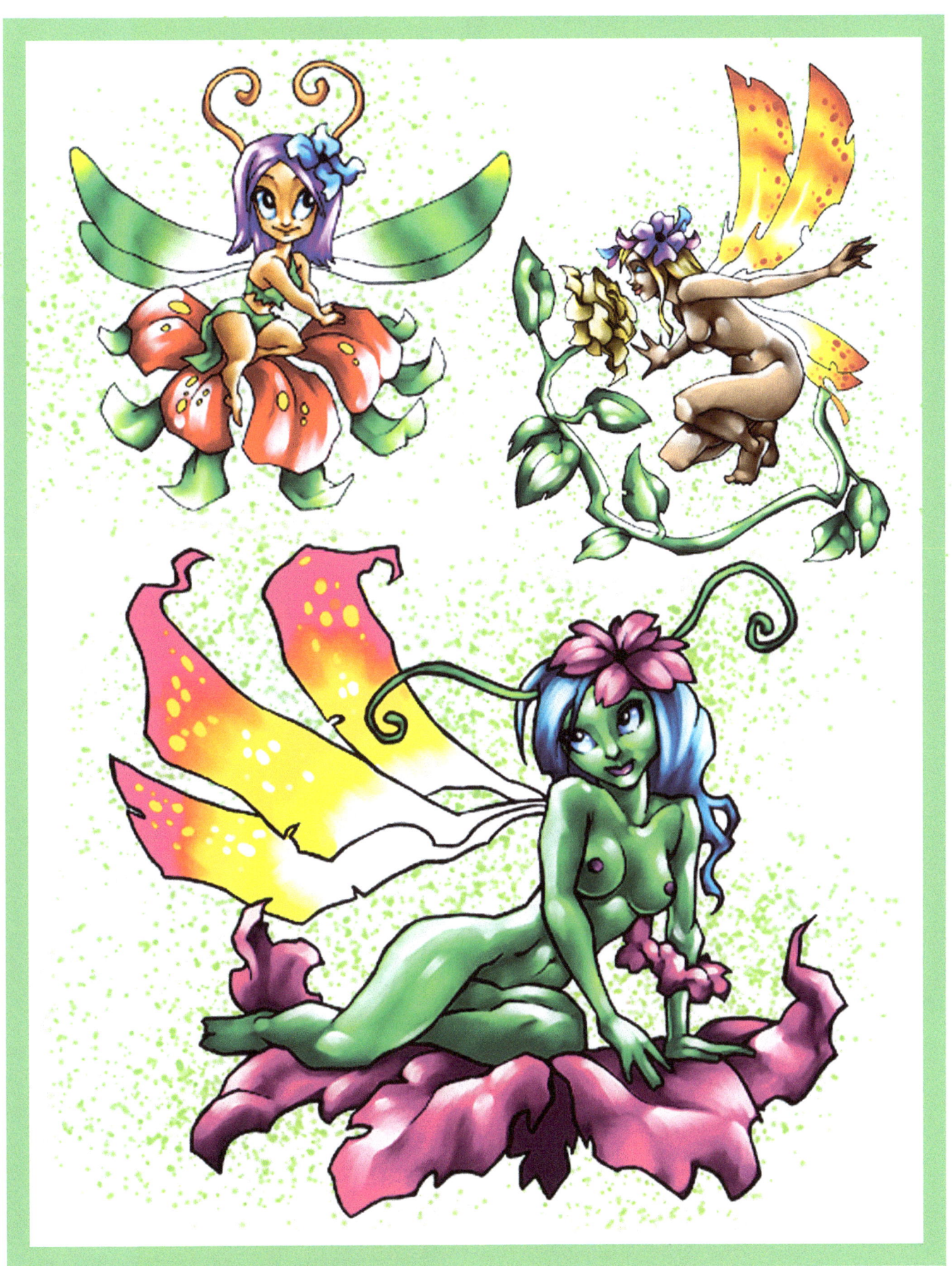

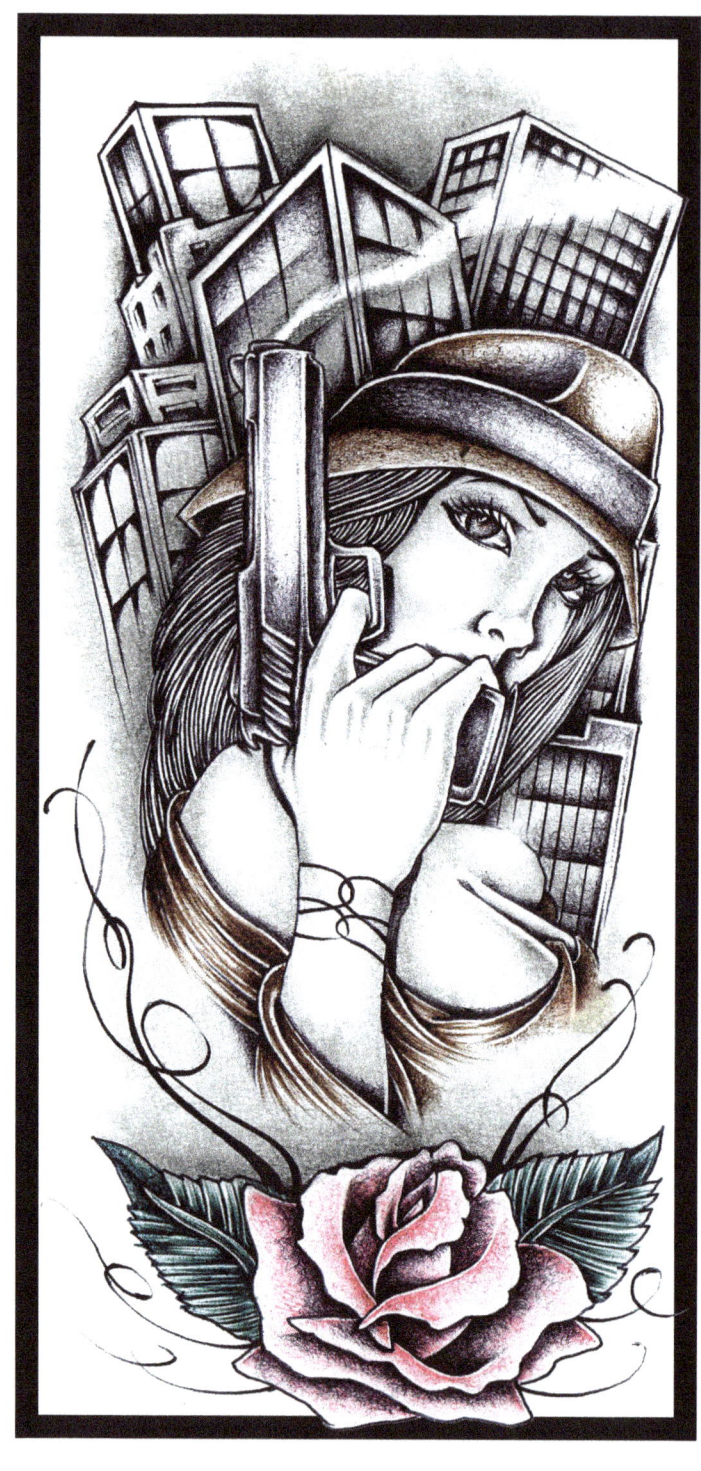
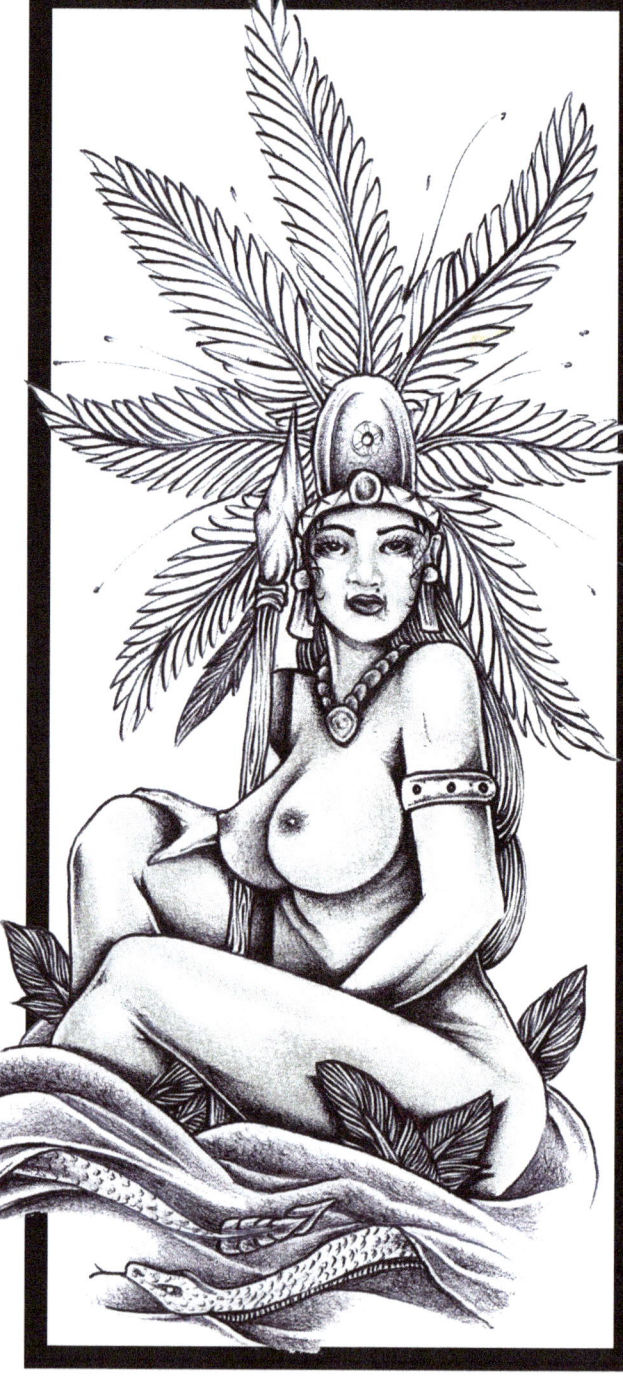

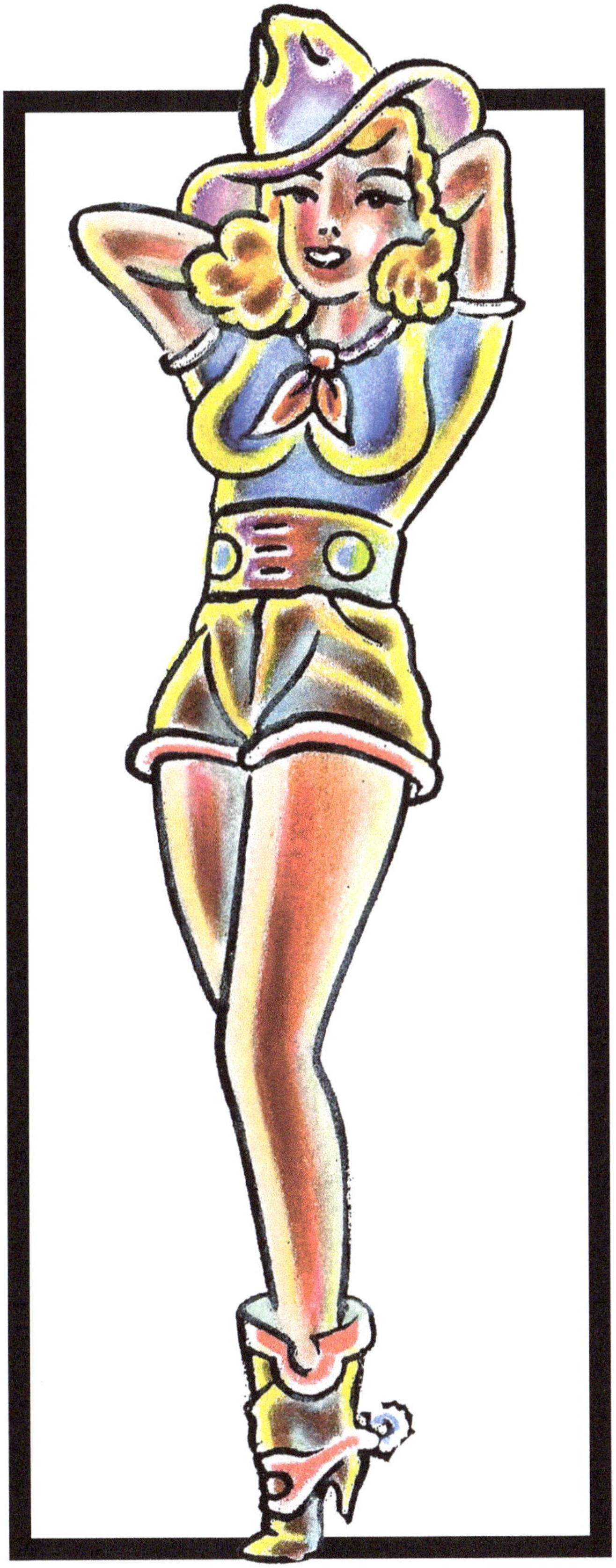

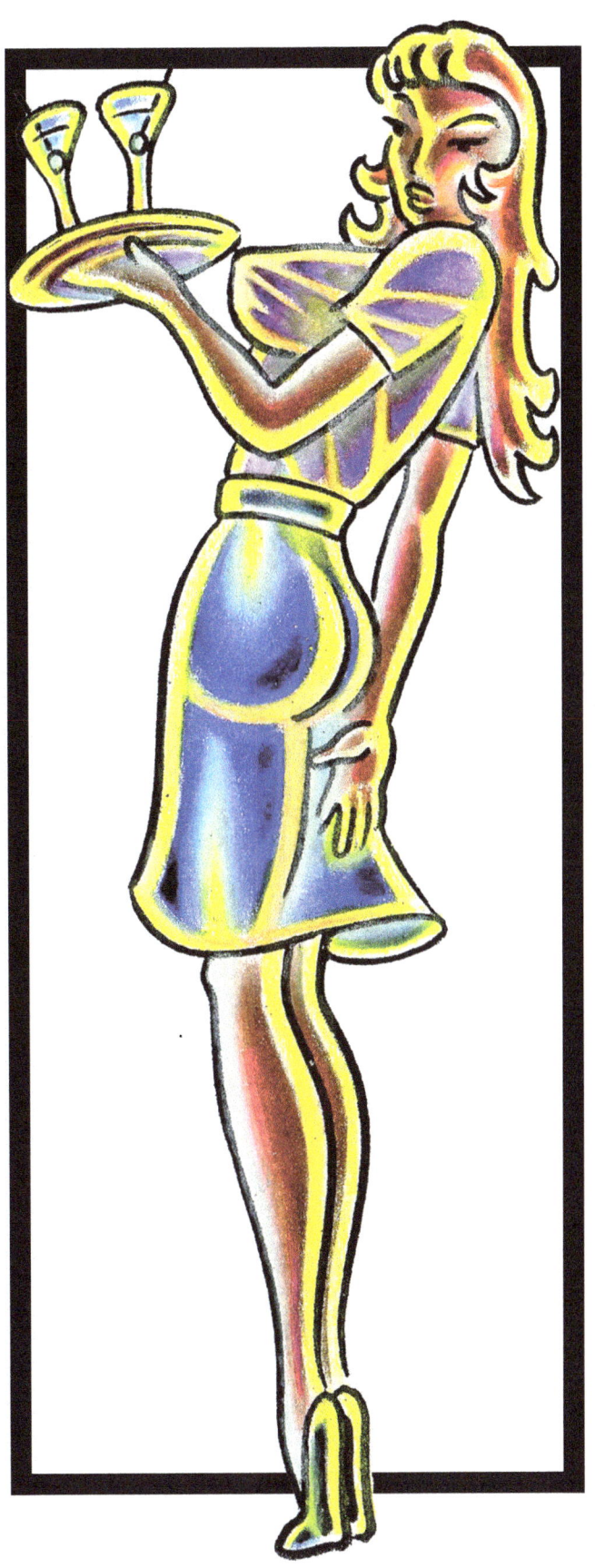

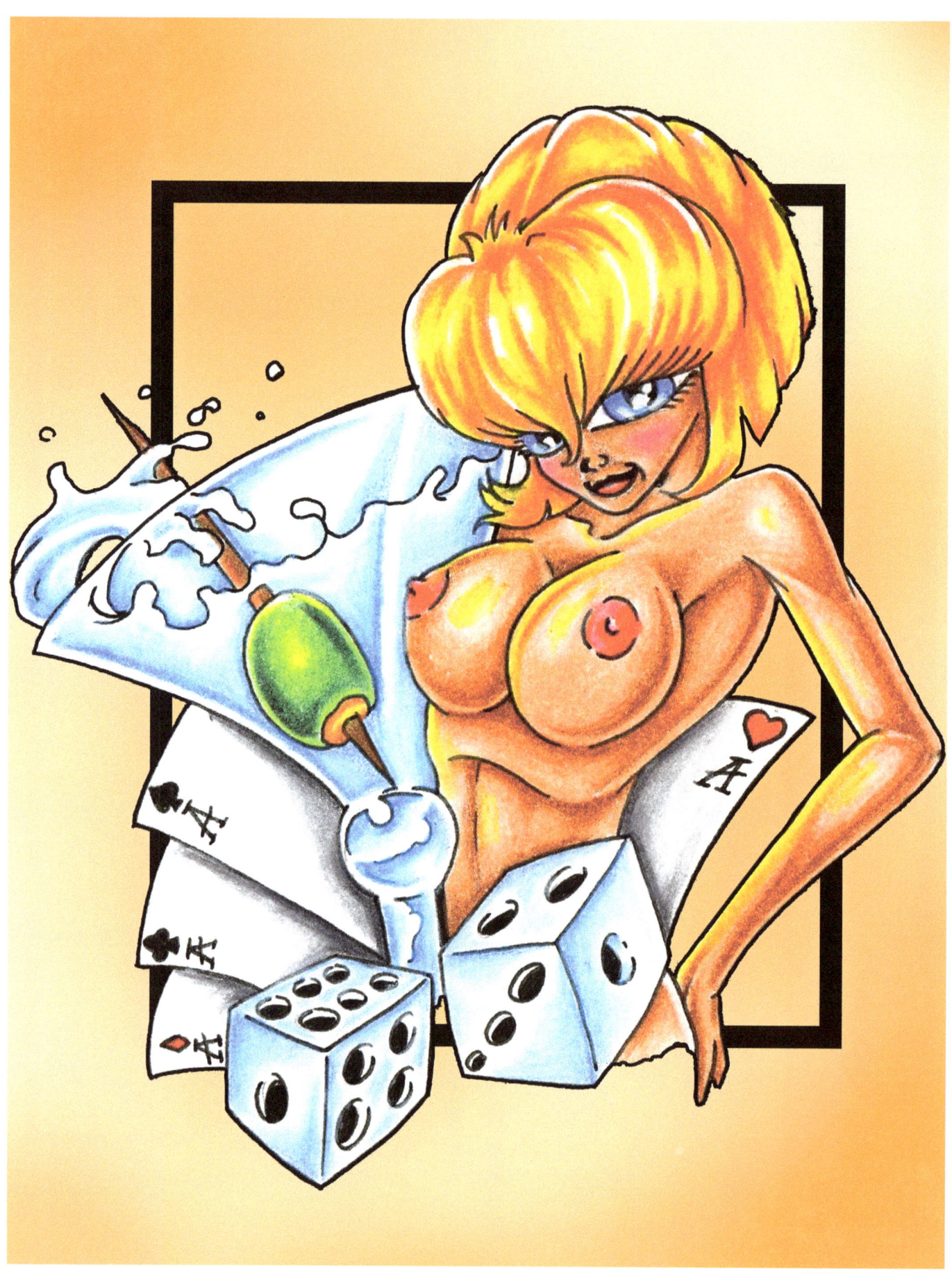

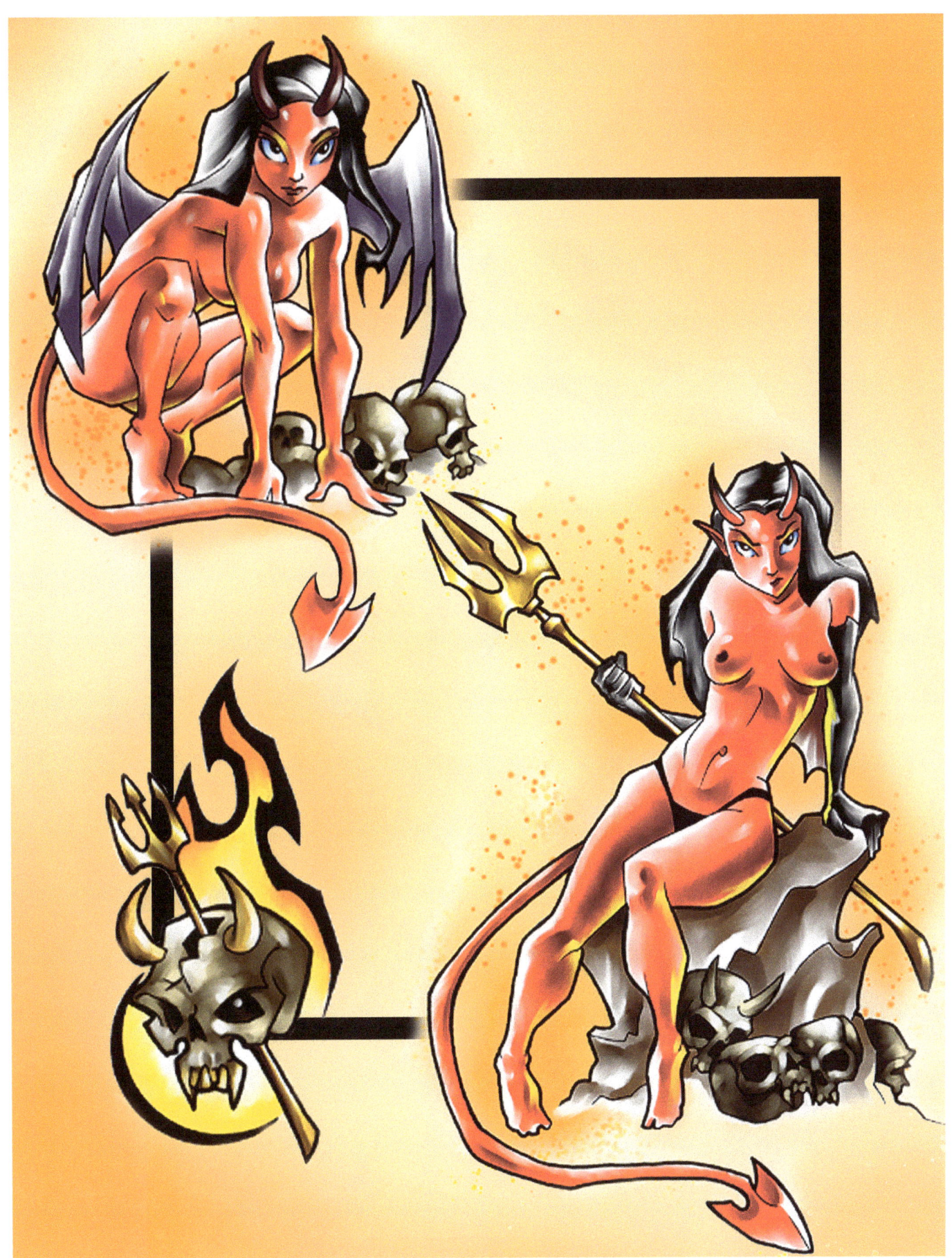

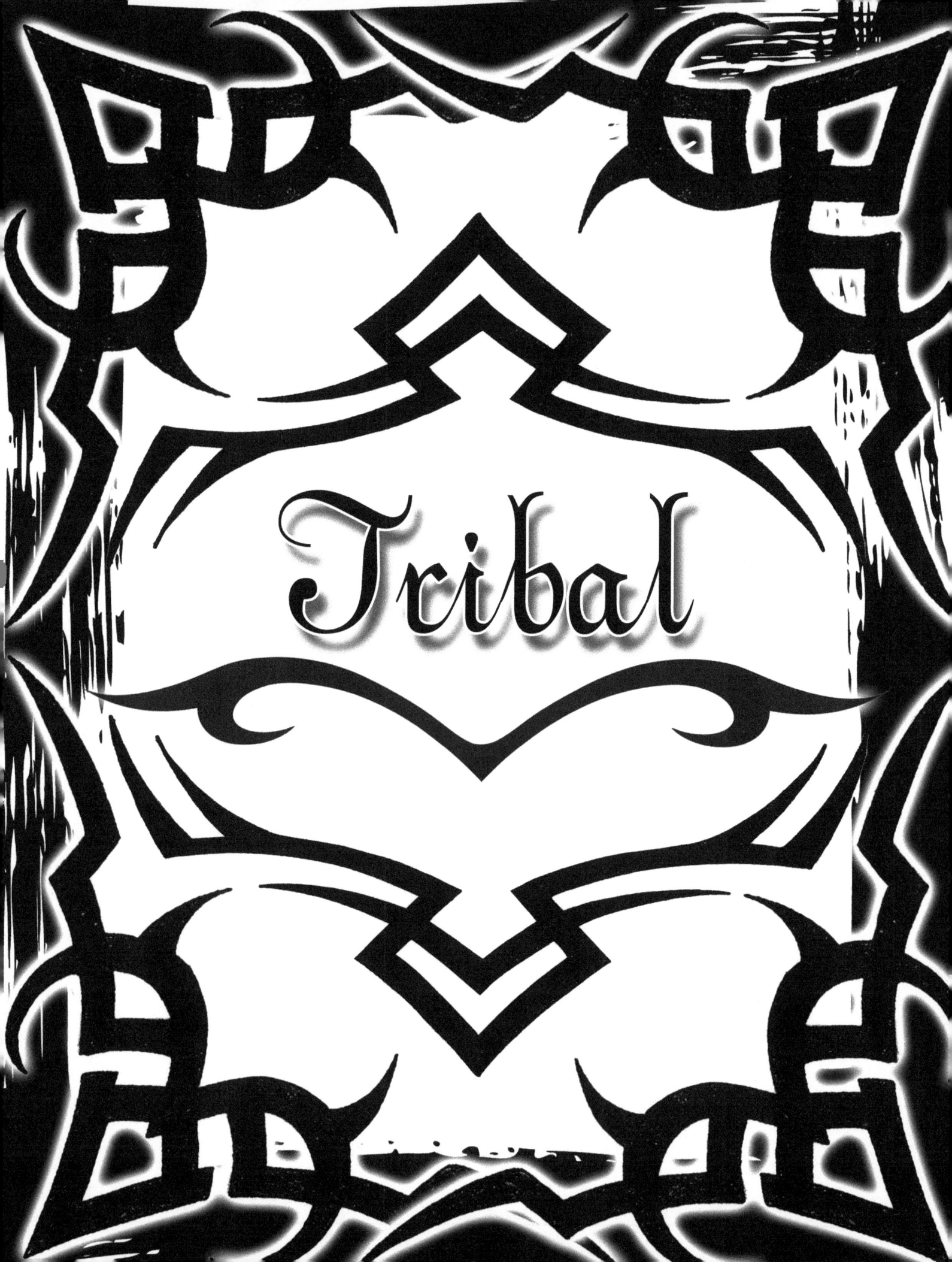

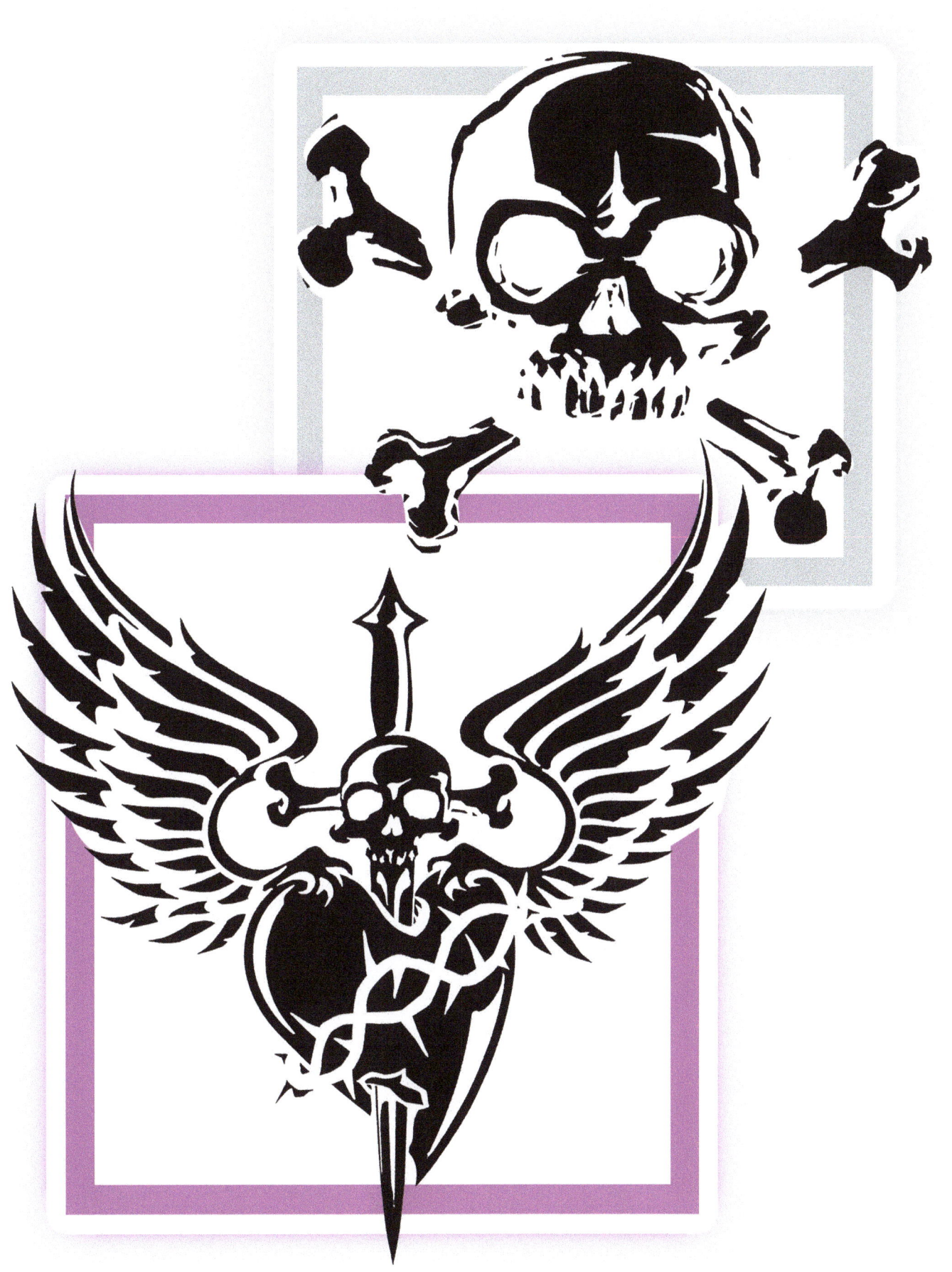

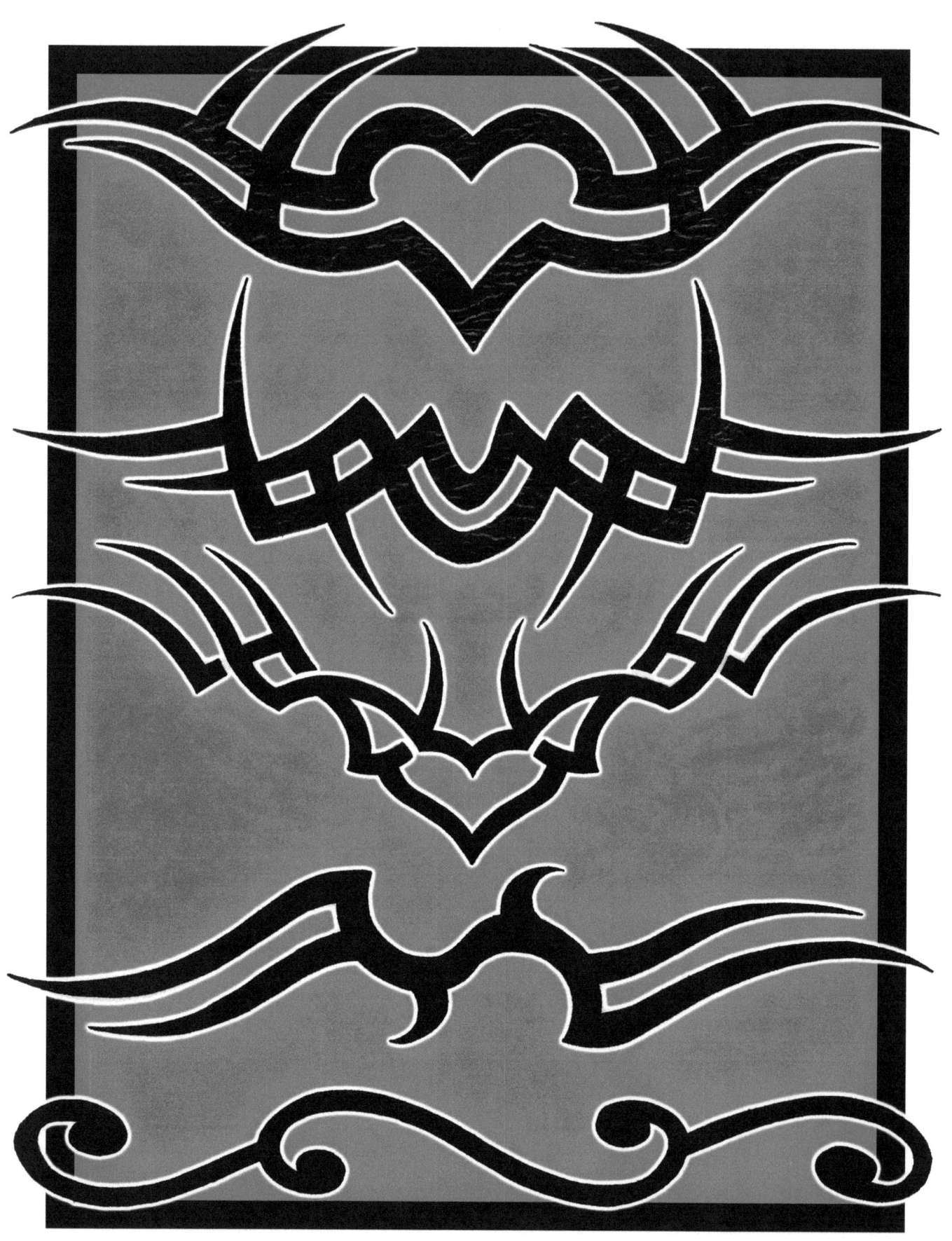

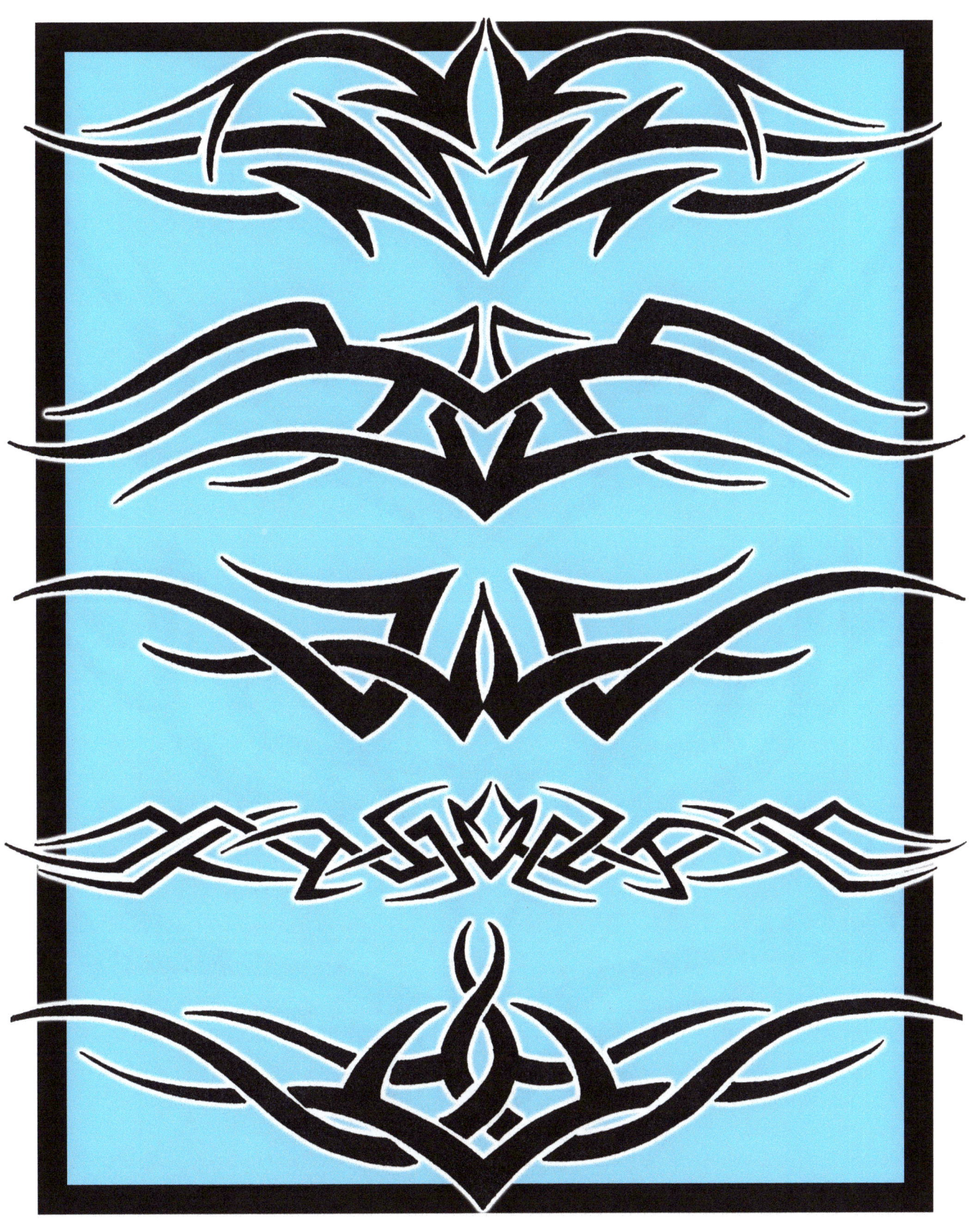

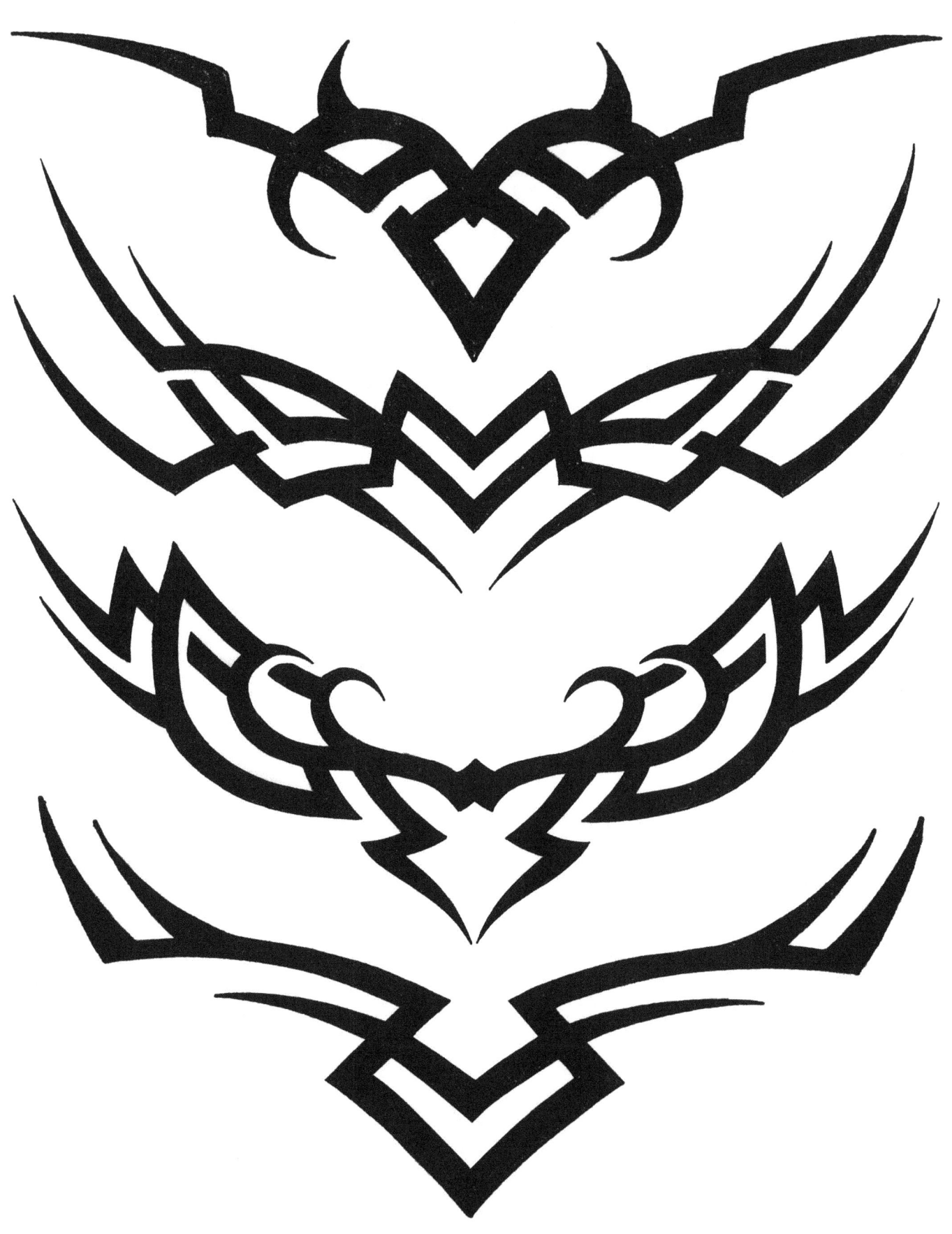

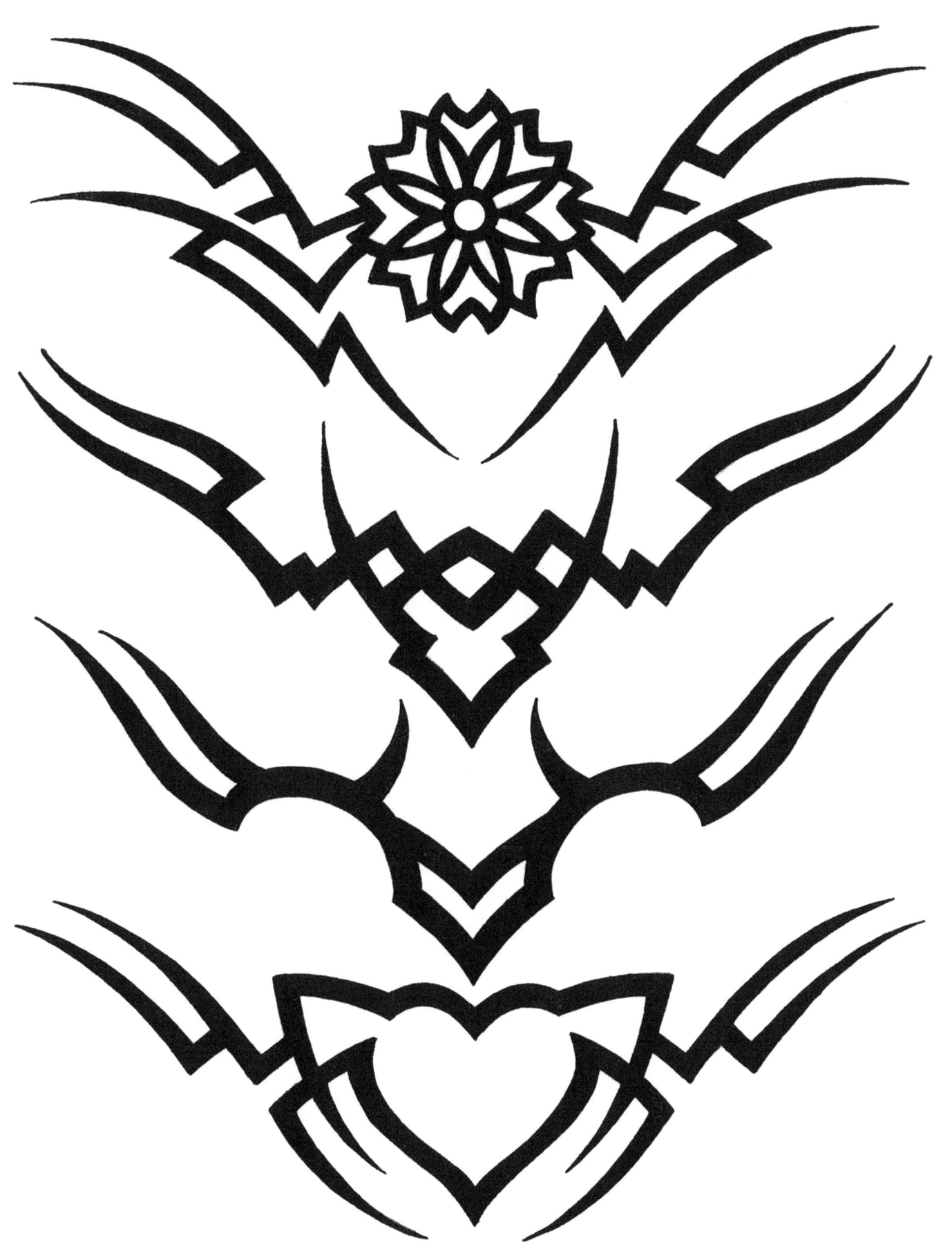

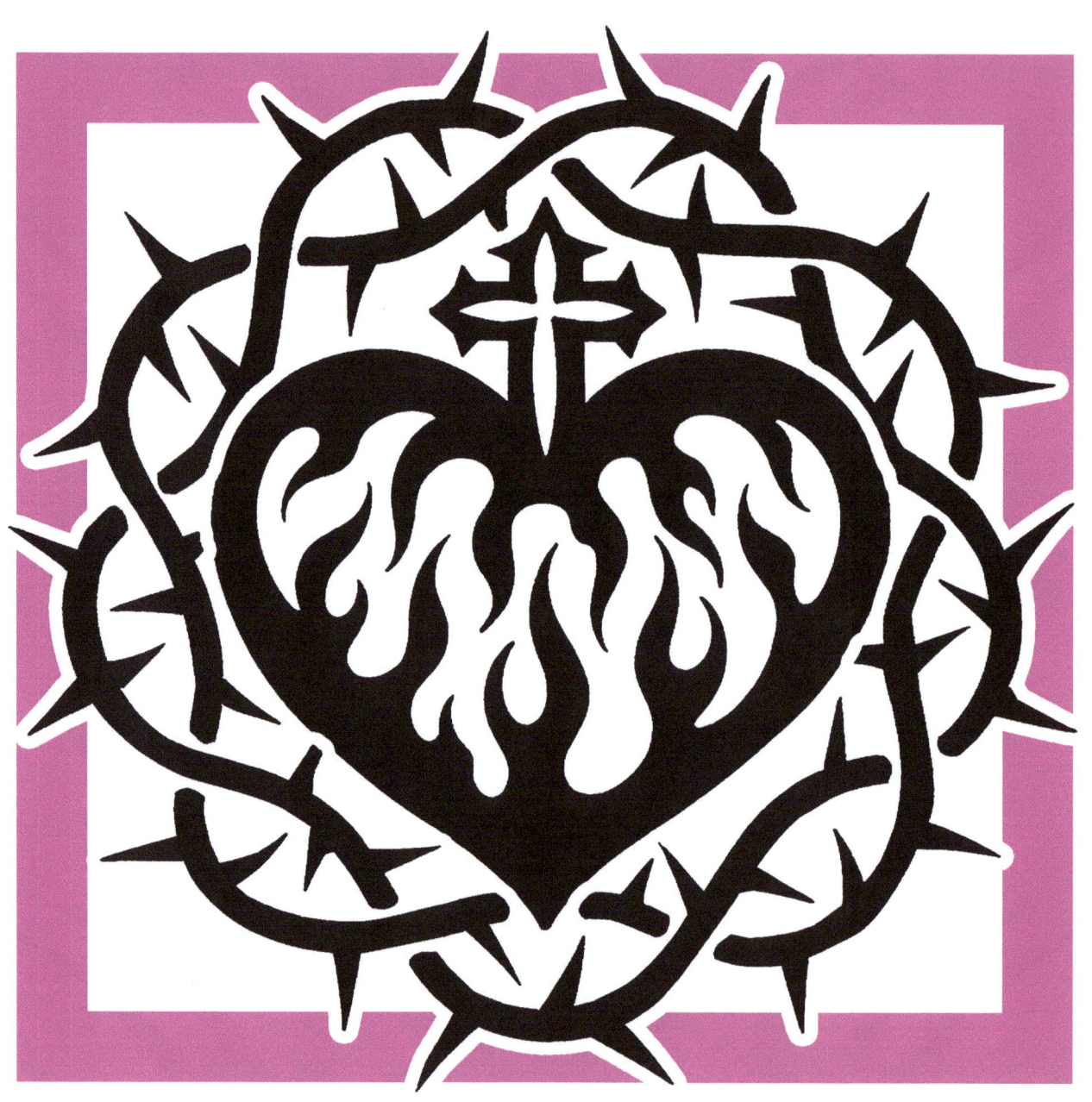

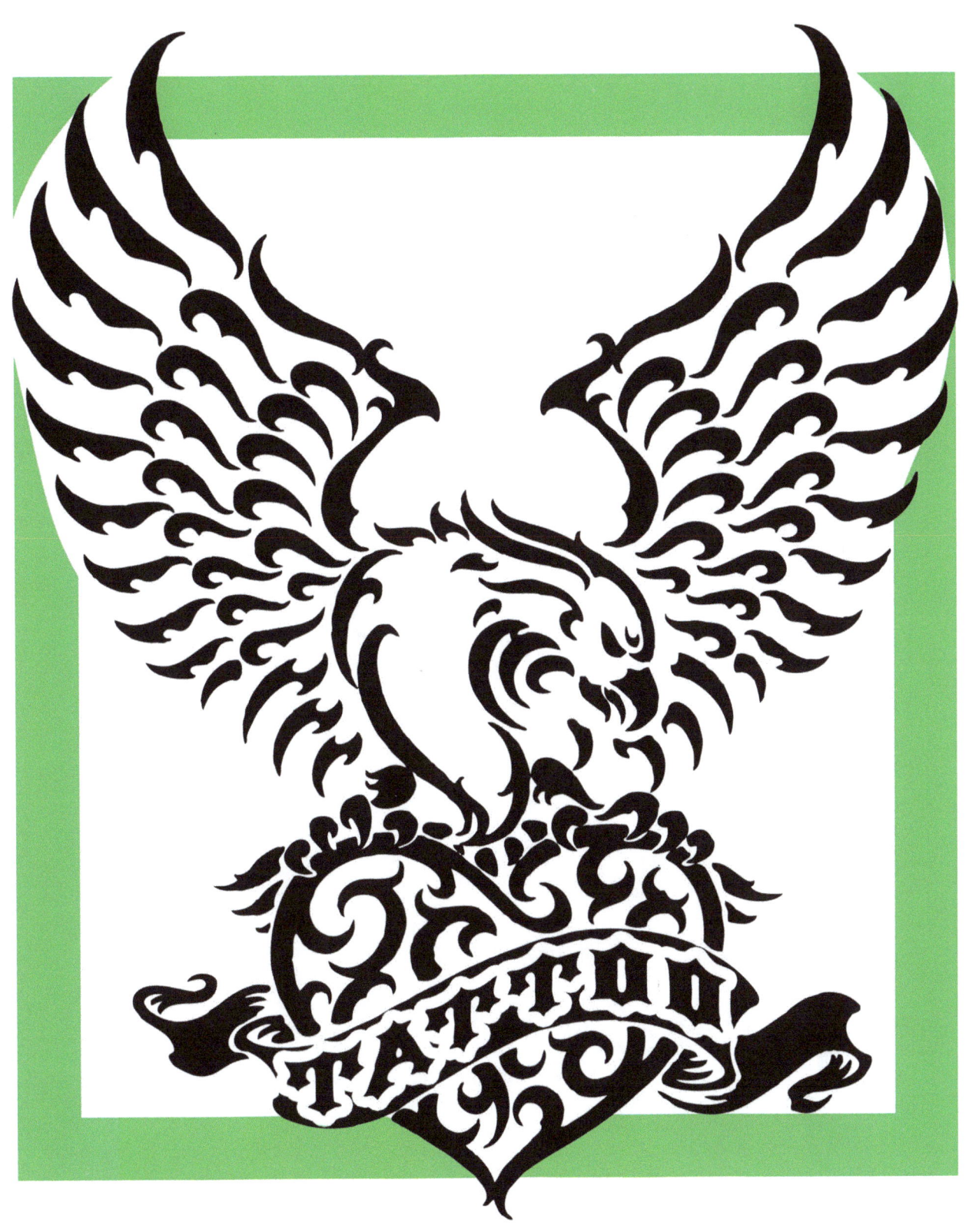

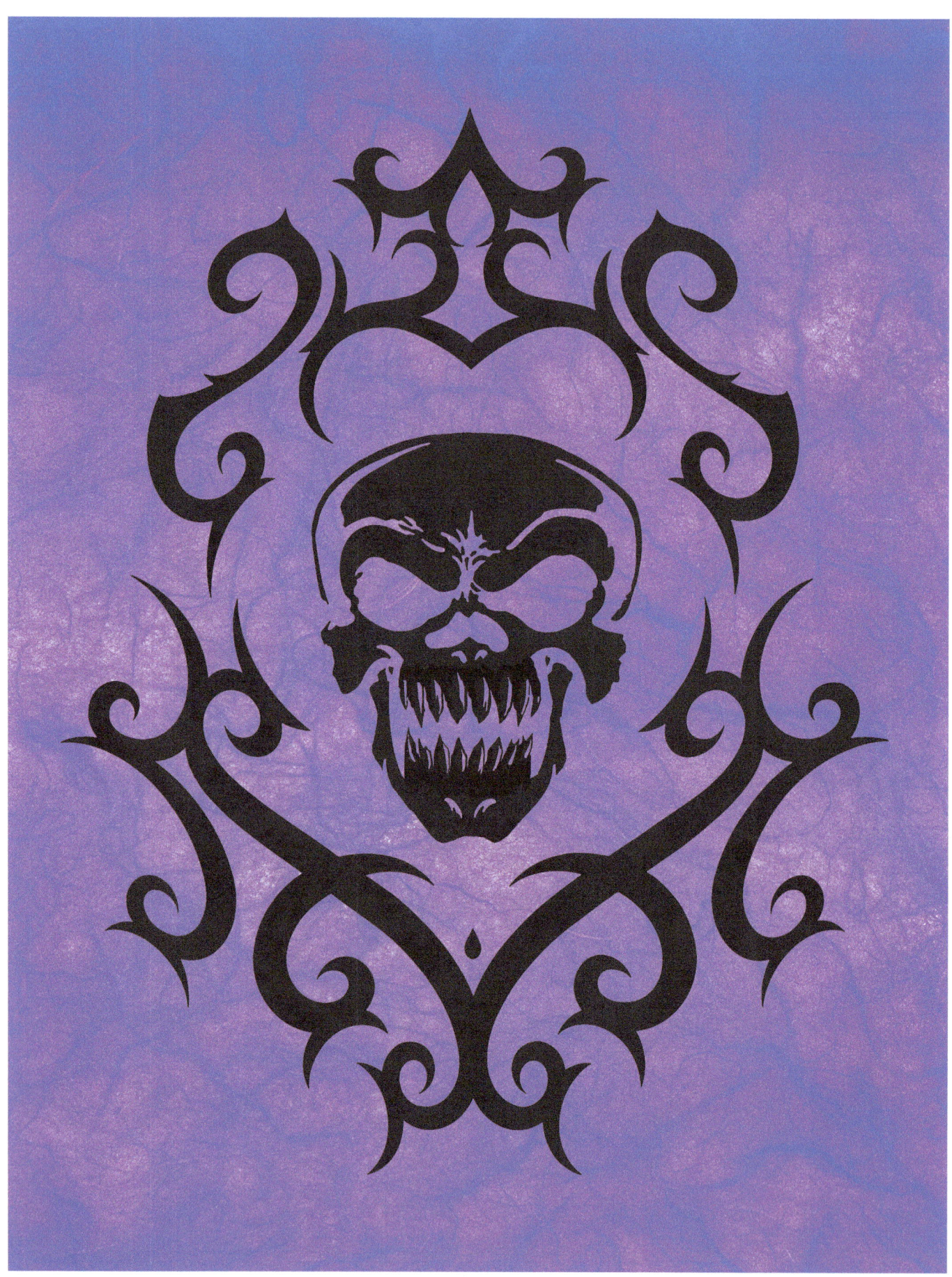

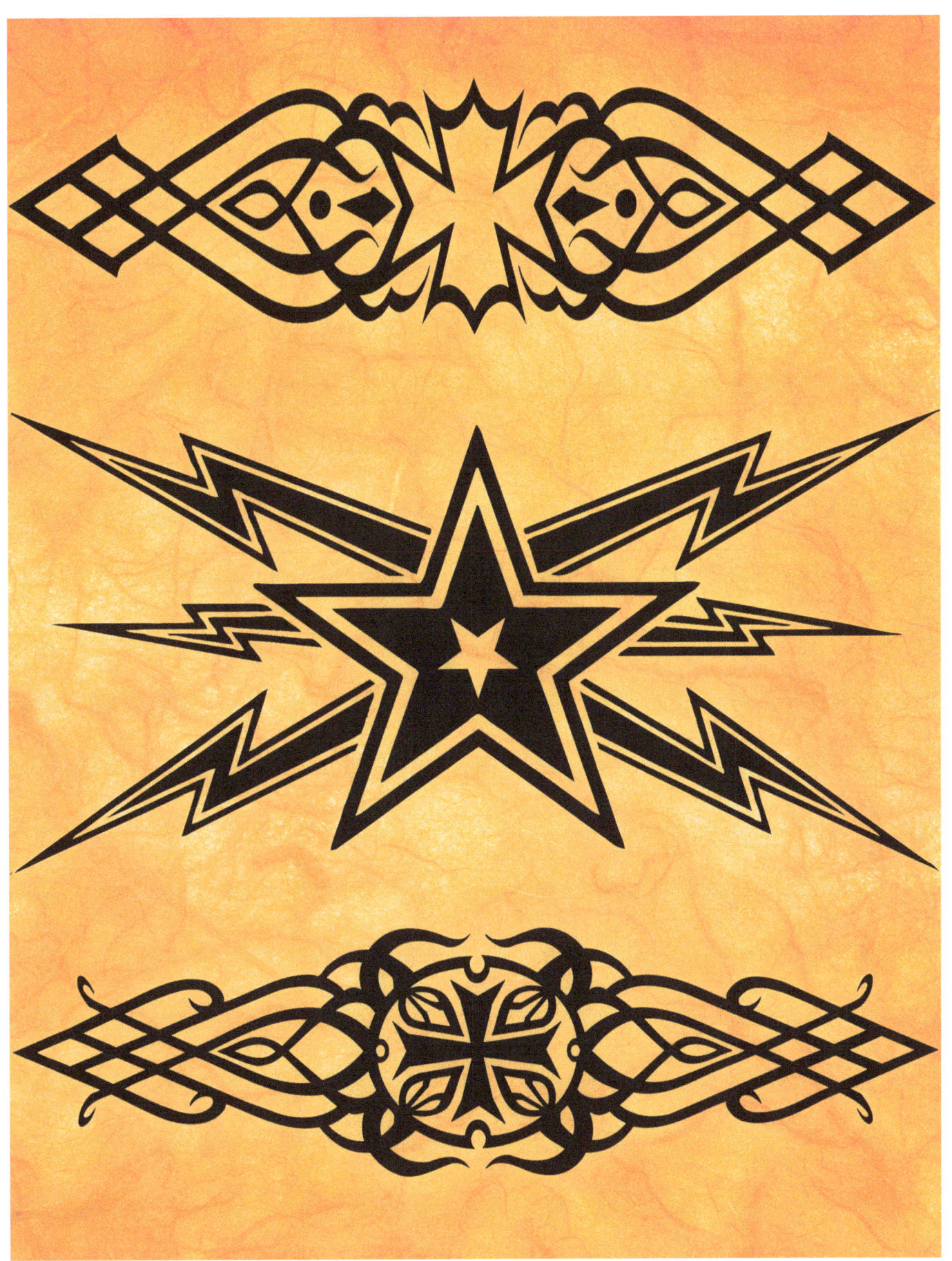

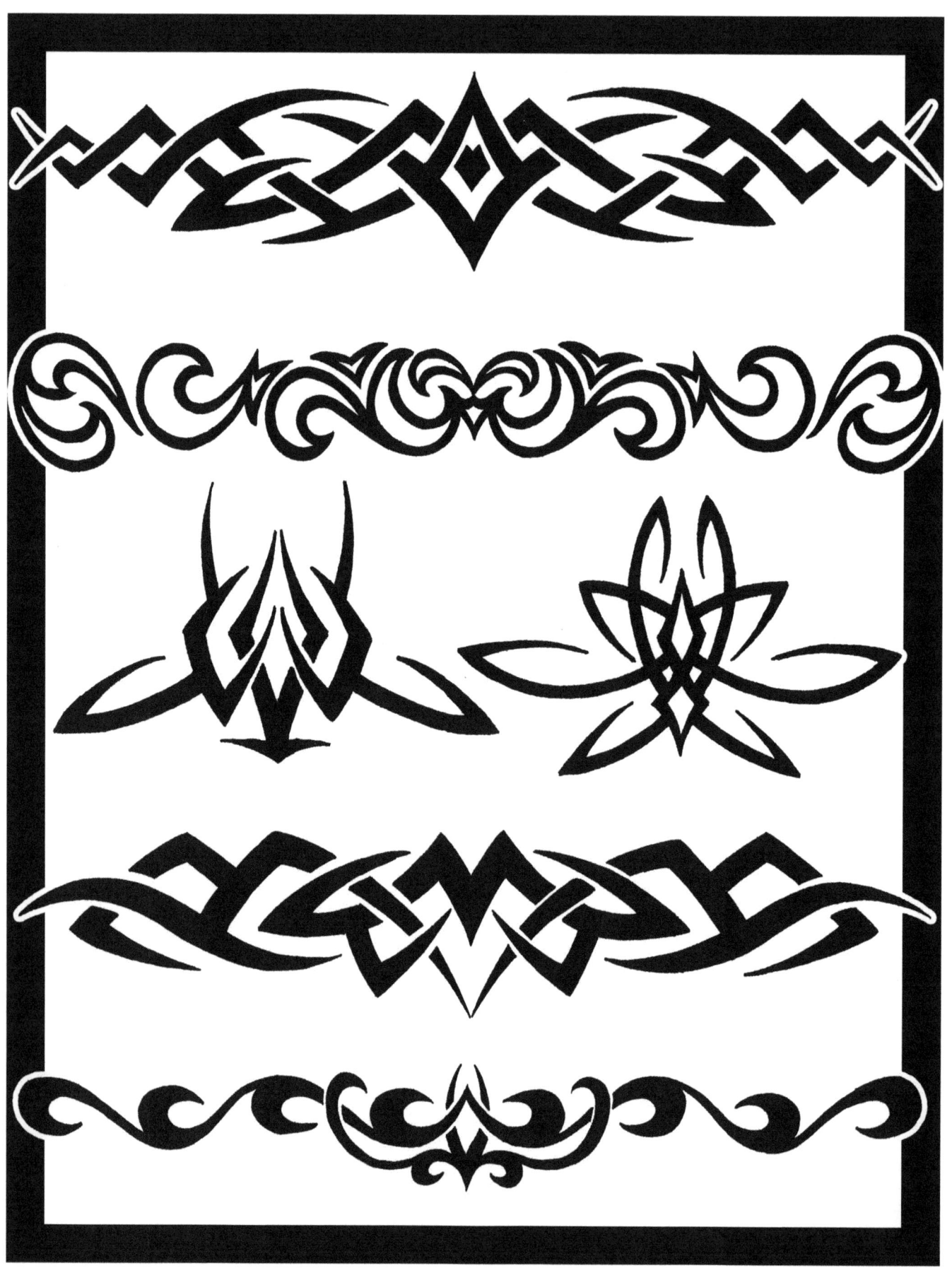

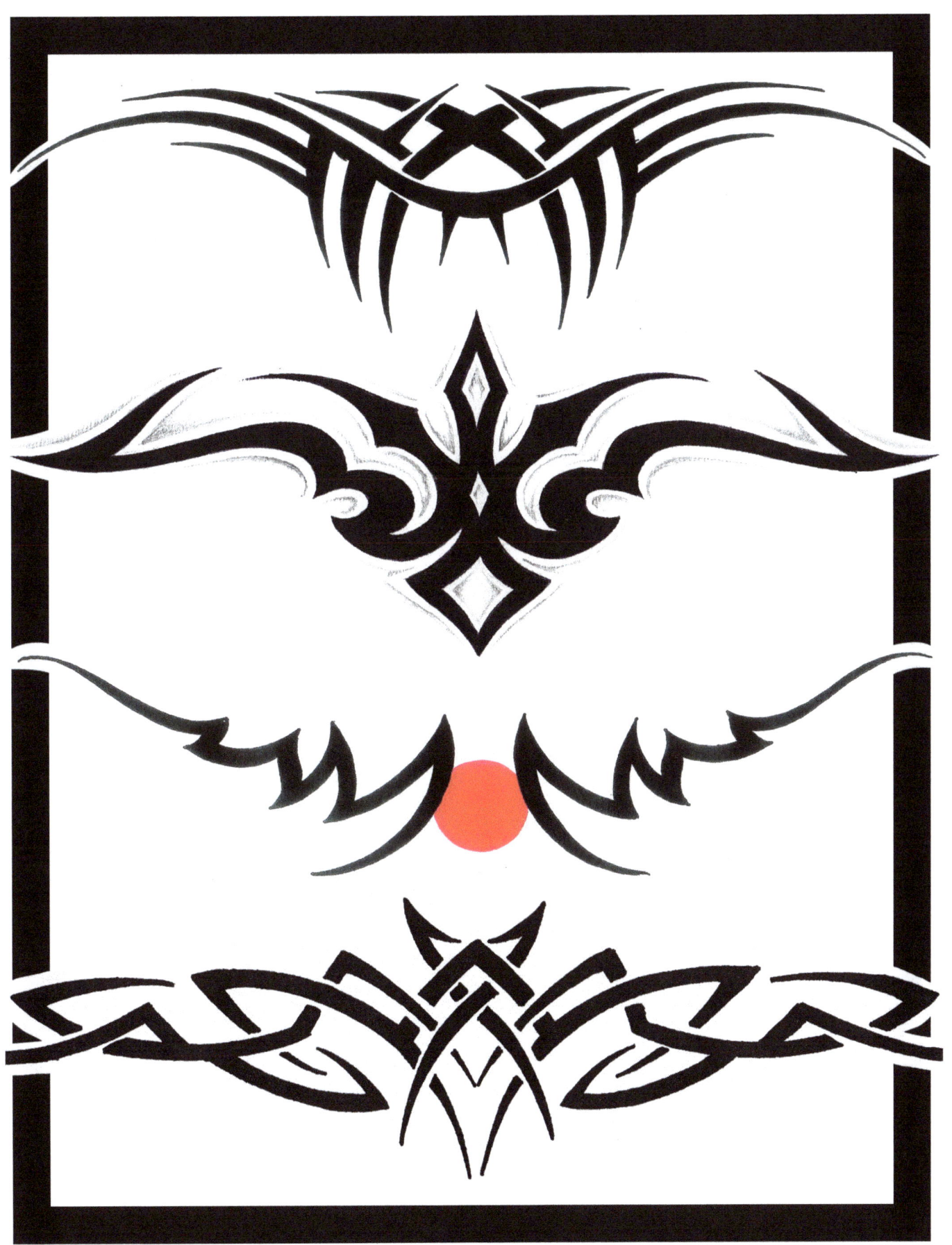

Books from Wolfgang Publications can be found at select book stores and many web sites.

Titles	ISBN	Price	# of pages
Advanced Airbrush Art	9781929133208	$27.95	144 pages
Adv Custom MC Assembly & Fabrication	9781929133239	$27.95	144 pages
Adv Custom MC Wiring - REVISED	9781935828761	$27.95	144 pages
Adv Pinstripe Art	9781929133321	$27.95	144 pages
Adv Sheet Metal Fab	9781929133123	$27.95	144 pages
Airbrush How-To with Mickey Harris	9781929133505	$27.95	144 pages
Body Painting	9781929133666	$27.95	144 pages
Building Hot Rods	9781929133437	$27.95	144 pages
Composite Materials 1	9781929133765	$27.95	144 pages
Composite Materials 2	9781929133932	$27.95	144 pages
Composite Materials 3	9781935828662	$27.95	144 pages
Composite Materials Step-by-Step Projects	9781929133369	$27.95	144 pages
Cultura Tattoo Sketchbook	9781935828839	$32.95	284 pages
Custom Bike Building Basics	9781935828624	$24.95	144 pages
Custom MC Fabrication	9781935828792	$27.95	144 pages
H-D Twin Cam, Hop-Up & Rebuild Manual	9781929133-697	$29.95	144 pages
H-D Sportster Hop-Up & Customizing	9781935828952	$27.95	144 pages
H-D Sportser Buell Engine Hop-Up Guide	9781929133093	$24.95	144 pages
How Airbrushes Work	9781929133710	$24.95	144 pages
Honda MC, Enthusiast Guide	9781935828853	$27.95	144 pages
Honda Mini Trail, Enthusiast Guide	9781941064320	$29.95	144 pages
Hot Rod Chassis	9781929133703	$29.95	144 pages
How-To Airbrush, Pinstripe & Goldleaf	9781935828693	$27.95	144 pages

Books from Wolfgang Publications can be found at select book stores and many web sites.

Titles	ISBN	Price	# of pages
How-To Build Old Skool Bobber - 2nd Edition	9781935828785	$27.95	144 pages
How-To Build a Cheap Chopper	9781929133178	$27.95	144 pages
How-To Build Cafe Racer	9781935828730	$27.95	144 pages
How-To Chop Tops	9781929133499	$24.95	144 pages
How-To Draw Monsters	9781935828914	$27.95	144 pages
How-To Fix American V-Twin	9781929133727	$27.95	144 pages
How-To Paint Tractors & Trucks	9781929133475	$27.95	144 pages
Hot Rod Wiring	9781929133987	$27.95	144 pages
Kosmoski's NEW Kustom Paint Secrets	9781929133833	$27.95	144 pages
Learning the English Wheel	9781935828891	$27.95	144 pages
Pro Pinstripe	9781929133925	$27.95	144 pages
Sheet Metal Bible	9781929133901	$29.95	176 pages
Sheet Metal Fab Basics B&W	9781929133468	$24.95	144 pages
Sheet Metal Fab for Car Builders	9781929133383	$27.95	144 pages
SO-CAL Speed Shop, Hot Rod Chassis	9781935828860	$27.95	144 pages
Tattoo Bible #1	9781929133840	$27.95	144 pages
Tattoo Bible #2	9781929133857	$27.95	144 pages
Tattoo Bible #3	9781935828754	$27.95	144 pages
Tattoo Lettering Bible	9781935828921	$27.95	144 pages
Triumph Restoration - Pre Unit	9781929133635	$29.95	144 pages
Triumph Restoration - Unit 650cc	9781929133420	$29.95	144 pages
Vintage Dirt Bikes - Enthusiast's Guide	9781929133314	$27.95	144 pages
Ultimate Sheet Metal Fab	9780964135895	$24.95	144 pages

Superior Tattoo Biography

Long-time tattoo artist Jim Watson founded Superior Tattoo Equipment in 1991 with help from John Fox. They paired up to create a company that could provide tattoo artists with all the supplies they could ever need. Superior was the first tattoo supply company to seek out new artists and help them obtain the professional equipment and resources they needed to learn the craft of tattooing.

Superior's collection of tattoo flash is unparalleled. From the very beginning Superior set the bar high. Our art, purchased from the best artists in the country, now decorates thousands of happy tattoo customers from shops all over the world.

Lately Superior has seen the industry grow significantly with new TV shows like Miami Ink, Inked and now LA Ink. These shows reflect the growing acceptance of tattoos and tattoo art. We like to think that by supplying quality equipment to the best artists, Superior Tattoo has helped to fuel this growth and acceptance.

According to International Tattoo Art. Superior Tattoo Equipment, Inc. has grown into the Number One tattoo supplier in the world. Our website is the most visited tattoo supplier in the world, receiving over 80,000 unique visitors every month.

Our mission statement has not changed. Superior continues to provide a huge selection of the best equipment at reasonable prices. For nearly eighteen years we have kept the best artists from around the world supplied with their preferred tools and equipment. We look forward to providing quality inks and equipment to both the old masters, and their apprentices.

www.superiortattoo.com

www.ingramcontent.com/pod-product-compliance
Lightning Source LLC
Chambersburg PA
CBHW040542220526
45473CB00016B/2999